The Fou...

The Hospital and Free school

Of King Charles II oxmantown Dublin commonly called the Blue coat school with notices of some of its governors, and of contemporary events in Dublin from the foundation, 1668 to 1840, when its government by the city ceased

Frederick Richard Falkiner

Alpha Editions

This edition published in 2019

ISBN : 9789389169485

Design and Setting By
Alpha Editions
email - alphaedis@gmail.com

This book is a reproduction of an important historical work. Alpha Editions uses the best technology to reproduce historical work in the same manner it was first published to preserve its original nature. Any marks or number seen are left intentionally to preserve its true form.

THE FOUNDATION
OF THE
HOSPITAL AND FREE SCHOOL
OF
KING CHARLES II.,
OXMANTOWN, DUBLIN,

COMMONLY CALLED THE BLUE COAT SCHOOL.

WITH NOTICES OF SOME OF ITS GOVERNORS, AND OF
CONTEMPORARY EVENTS IN DUBLIN FROM THE
FOUNDATION, 1668 TO 1840, WHEN ITS
GOVERNMENT BY THE CITY
CEASED.

BY

THE RIGHT HON. SIR FREDERICK R. FALKINER, K.C.,
SOMETIME RECORDER OF DUBLIN.

DUBLIN:
SEALY, BRYERS AND WALKER,
MIDDLE ABBEY STREET.
1906.

PRINTED BY
SEALY, BRYERS AND WALKER,
MIDDLE ABBEY STREET,
DUBLIN.

PREFACE.

THE duty of a governor of King's Hospital to consult its old records from time to time, led the writer naturally to a perusal of them all, until the task, sufficiently uninviting at first, became the subject of a continually increasing interest. The close connection of the School from its foundation with the City, whose chief magistrate was, for one hundred and seventy years, the standing chairman of the governors, and whose aldermen were always his official colleagues, brought the life of the school into constant communion with the life of the city; whilst the usage, which prevailed during all this period, of co-opting to the Board distinguished persons from outside, brought the governors from time to time into relations with many of the highest personages in church and state, some of them historical and even illustrious, some less known, yet, who once were notables or notorious. Under King Charles's charter, the chief officer of the school, its chaplain and headmaster, was always appointed with the direct sanction of the Archbishops of Dublin, who, in the earlier years, were usually associated as Lords Justices with the government of the kingdom, and as the government of the city very often reflected that of the realm, so both will be found at times to be clearly reflected in the microcosm of the royal school of the city. Thus the old manuscript of our ancient Minute Books, sere and dead to the casual glance, become to the student startlingly revivified, as the names of men long forgotten or half forgotten, rise up, like the dry bones in the valley of the prophet, luminous and animate, as though a breath had entered into them, and the atmosphere of our school, and its place in our mental vision, are then re-peopled with phantoms of the past, figures who were once chief actors on the stage of their day, makers of Dublin in great transitional epochs of her story. No one can be more conscious than the writer of the want of due proportion and of the undue discursiveness in many of the pages that follow. But if the fact that the governors were, throughout, the men charged with the rule of the city, and the conduct of its growth and development, be an inadequate excuse for the pages which have sought to trace the evolution of our Capital since the days of the Restoration, may the writer be permitted at least to hope that he has been enabled to recall some striking incidents of lasting interest, and to present them in lights, which, if not wholly new, exhibit them in relations in which they have not hitherto been familiar. His ambition will be more than satisfied if he has thus made even a slight contribution to the History of our *Nobilissima Civitas*, Dublin.

The sources from which these chapters are drawn have been, for the most part, noted in the text, but a special acknowledgment is due of their constant indebtedness to Sir John Gilbert's great *Calendar of the City Assembly Rolls*, as continued by his talented widow. To the Corporation of Dublin, and their most courteous Town Clerk, Mr. Henry Campbell, and to his friend and brother governor, Mr. F. Elrington Ball, the accomplished author of *The History of Dublin*, the author's thanks are here gratefully tendered.

FREDERICK R. FALKINER.

August, 1906.

ILLUSTRATIONS.

❖

I. THOMAS, EARL OF OSSORY .. *Frontispiece.*
(*From engraving by Vandervane—Sir Peter Lely, Pinx.*)

Facing page

II. EDWARD WETTENHALL, BISHOP OF CORK, 1678, KILMORE, 1699 41
(*From original Portrait by Vander Vaert.*)

III. MAP OF ST. STEPHEN'S GREEN, AS ALLOTTED, 1664 43
(*From Rental Maps in King's Hospital.*)

IV. MAP OF OXMANTOWN GREEN, AS ALLOTTED, 1665 44
(*From Rental Maps in King's Hospital.*)

V. ORIGINAL BLUE COAT SCHOOL, AS COMPLETED, 1675 70
(*From Old Engraving in King's Hospital.*)

VI. CHARLES LUCAS, M.D. 199
(*Photograph of Statue by Edward Smyth in the City Hall, Dublin.*)

VII. FRONT FACADE OF PRESENT KING'S HOSPITAL, AS DESIGNED BY THOMAS IVORY 208
(*From Original Plans in British Museum.*)

VIII. VERY REV. WALTER BLAKE KIRWAN, DEAN OF KILLALA 222
(*From Engraving by Dr. Ward from Painting by Hugh Hamilton.*)

This was painted in 1806, after Kirwan's death, and dedicated in his honour to Lord Hardwick. It idealizes a famous scene when Kirwan, after an outburst, broke down, unable to proceed. Turning towards the orphans below the pulpit, he pointed to them, in the rapt silence, with outstretched hands—the effect was electrical.

IX. KING CHARLES II. 293
(*From Engraving by Vertue of Original Portrait, by Sir Peter Lely.*)

FOUNDATION

OF THE

King's Hospital of King Charles II.

———◆———

CHAPTER I.—INTRODUCTORY.

1.

DUBLIN AT THE TIME OF THE RESTORATION.

THE foundation of the King's Hospital was one of the earliest symbols of the new era of hope and energy, which, notwithstanding the prevalent misery, awoke on the restoration of the Monarchy in 1660, and was destined to transform the mediæval City on the Hill into the modern capital of Ireland. It is thus a significant page in the history of Dublin. For it is safe to say, that the face of the city changed more in the thirty years which followed, than in the three hundred that preceded. To conceive this, needs to have a mental vision of the city at the time of the Restoration, its physical, social, and political conditions. To aid such a conception is the motive of these preliminary pages.

If a citizen of to-day, standing on the central spot of our main thoroughfare, the middle of Carlisle or O'Connell Bridge, could see in vision the prospect eastward as his ancestor saw it in 1660, he could no longer believe he was in his native city. The ancestor could only have viewed from that point if perched on the rigging of an up-river craft, for then the Old Bridge alone crossed the Liffey, joining the Church Street and the Bridge Street on the site of the primæval Ford of Athcliath. Our visionary might rub his eyes and dream he was looking seaward from a railway carriage crossing the salt lake at Malahide, at dunes and sandbanks, the glory of golfers, and level reaches, brown and gray at the ebb, but regained by ocean at high tide ; through these the river wound her channel deviously to the bar and the bay. No quay or sea rampart bound the jagged coasts of the estuary diverging north and south to Clontarf and to Merrion. The north shore trended obliquely behind where the O'Connell statue stands to the further end of Abbey Street, and thus to the causeway, still known as the North Strand, to mark by its name the old sea-line as it passed to Ballybough and the estuary of the Tolka. The tides twice daily overflowed the sites of Eden Quay and the Custom House, the Amiens Street station and all east of it, and the miles of harbour causeway, now known as the North Wall. Landward of this coast were slob grounds slashed with briny pools, behind which rolled green houseless fields upward into the country at Finglas and Artane. So, too, the south-east coast was an unbanked beach. Close to the right of our view-point was a creek covering the sites of Westmoreland, D'Olier and College Streets, and the Theatre Royal. This was the estuary of the riveret Steyne, the mill stream of the old priors of All Hallows, precursors of Trinity College. College Green, so late as 1657, is said to adjoin the seaside. This stream flowed into it opposite the College gates. The space is still traceable underground.[1] More than thirty years ago the writer had part in a bitter battle about the erection of the Provincial Bank in College Street. The contract assumed the foundations would be on ordinary *terra firma*, but the diggers went down down through nineteen feet of sludge, till the cost of the foundations nearly equalled the superstructure, and the fight of bank and builder raged through many Courts for the benefit of the

[1] Gilbert's *Calendar* of Dublin Corporation Records, iv. 121.

law. Charles Haliday tells of a poor servant maid drowned some sixty years ago, when a high tide broke into a basement at foot of Grafton Street. From this creek the coast went eastward under the causeway of Lazars or Lazie Hill in the line of Townsend Street, between which and the University precincts lay cattle-sprinkled pastures. Lazie Hill was so called from a very ancient hospice at the far and isolated end, projected for lepers under vow to embark for the shrine of St. James of Compostello. Near the present S. Mark's Church, the coast swerved to the right by the back of where Merrion Square stands, as famous then for snipe as now for ladies, under the upland of Holles and Lower Mount Street, by the site of Sir Patrick Dun's Hospital to the Beggar's Bush and the Dodder; here it met a ridge of land running back to the bay in a spit, shaped like a hockey staff, the twist of which was the Ringsend. This was corruptly spelled even in 1660, for it means the end, not of the " Ring," but of the " Rinn or point." Thus between S. Marks and Ringsend a great gulf was fixed, flooding all the first mile of the now Wicklow railway, the Lansdowne football ground, the gas works and canal harbour. Here a collier was wrecked on the site of Dun's hospital two hundred years ago. Into this gulf rushed the rapid Dodder, " the brook of Refarnham," without respect of persons in time of floods, for in 1629 it drowned the hope of one of the first families of the city, son of Sir William Usher, who was clerk of the Privy Council and kinsman of the great Primate. The lad was crossing the ford, where Ballsbridge crosses now, on his way to town from the port at Ringsend, whence a car fared to Lazie Hill, carrying passengers at fourpence each, and passing over the sands at low water. Young Usher's fate forced the building of a stone bridge, on Sidney Smith's principle that the sacrifice of a bishop in a railway smash alone would force directors to take requisite precaution. In the very year our Hospital was completed, 1674, our founders, the Corporation, projected the forming in this Dodder gulf the great harbour of Dublin, and imported a famed engineer from London, Andrew Yarranton, whose plans, comprising a royal fort on the site of Merrion Square, are still extant. Behind the Ringsend spit spread the dunes of the south Bull, stretching in flats to Merrion and Booterstown, sweeping over the low-lands of Sydney Parade and to the confines of Old Dunleary—Fort of Leoghaire Arch-King of Erin, when Patrick our first saint came—to be changed to Kingstown, when George, first gentleman in England, came to visit us in 1821. Through these eastern sands the river channels wound, forming four pools—Clontarf Pool and Salmon Pool, north and south of a flounder-shaped sandbank, and further east between the roaring North and South Bulls, the Poolbeg or Little Pool, and the Iron Pool, where the estuary merged in the ocean.[2]

But we are not to think of this eastern Dublin as of a dismal swamp, Dantean Cocytus of slush and sands. Dublin has always had a faculty of being jolly under creditable circumstances, and it is a question whether this scene had not in the Stuart times an animated variety, which for all its increase it lacks to-day. At Ringsend the larger vessels lay stranded at ebb, till lifted by the tide; they transhipped their cargoes into gabbards and barges which sailed up the Estuary to the Wood and Merchant's Quays, which stood as now, to unload at the old Custom House, which then was at the foot of the present Parliament Street. Even sea-going vessels to a draught of six feet could go up on high, spring tides. Maps[3] of the age show the pools at Ringsend crowded with three masted ships, and perhaps there were more of these direct from foreign parts than now, when Dublin imports come chiefly in cross-channel steamers. The wide space on Wood Quay still attests where the wine barrels were trundled straight from Bordeaux and the Tagus to the foot of the old Vicus Tabernorum, Wine-Tavern Street. Viceroys in the eighteenth century landed and left in state at Ringsend. In 1649 iron Oliver in

---

[2] Capt. Grenville Collins' Map, 1686; Haliday's *Scandinavian Kingdom of Dublin*, p. 233.
[3] Yarrantton's Map, 1674; Gill *Cal.*, Vol. V.; Rocque's Map, 1776. Scan. Dub., 113

person disembarked with his 13,000 Ironsides for the terrible campaign, the echoes of which still roll at times through the imperial parliament. In 1657, when his son, Henry, was Lord Deputy, the good frigate of war, Lambay Castle, was launched so far up river as Lazie Hill. There was a thriving herring fishery at Ringsend, salmon were netted in the Salmon Pool, and in the Clontarf Pool was a famous oyster bed, which survived till sanitation and sewer gas poisoned it to death. The Lord Mayor and Recorder had large admiralty jurisdiction under royal charters, and their chronic conflicts with the royal Admiralty at Ringsend, where the jurisdictions joined, gave a lively interest even to Coroner's inquests.

And in 1660 these sands were still written with great memories, for they were then nearly as on that Good Friday, 1014, when King Sitric Silkenbeard and his Queen, the daughter of the Great Brian, watched from the city battlements the fearful drawn battle, surging from Mary's Abbey to Clontarf, watching all day in tremulous tension like the chorus from the towers of Thebes, when the Seven Champions were storming the walls, he to see his Ostmen allies driven to their ships or into the sea, she to learn at night of the three generations of her kinsmen in the battle slain, the grand old Boroimhe himself, his hero son, Murrough, his grandson boy Turlough transfixed and drowned in the Tolka weir at Clonliffe. There on the south bank still stood in 1660, the Pillar Stone of the Steyne by the creek, marked by Sir Philip Crampton's swan fountain now, just as it had been erected eight hundred years before by the invading Vikings, the symbol of their conquest, and the signal for their fleets, where they would land and draw up their war canoes on the beach, like the Argives at Ilium. The Steyne gave its name to all the confines between the sea-shore and road to Baggot's rath, now the Baggot Streets; in the centre lay Trinity College, the old All Saints Juxta Dublin; its Nassau Street boundary was then the depressed causeway of S. Patrick's Well Lane. The pillar of the Steyne was the story of three hundred Scandinavian years written in stone, it still lives only in the parchments of some of our old city leases.

Westward of our point of vision, was more to identify the Dublin of 1660 with that of 1906. Both coasts, indeed, were still pebbly and embanked, and behind the northern slobs were green meadows to the line of Capel Street where S. Mary's Abbey rose. This shore is still commemorated by the Strand Street of to-day, though now severed from the water by the houses and embankment of Ormond Quay, but the shores were now converging towards river shape, and beyond the Abbey rose the tower of S. Michan's Church as now, and opposite to it the tower of Christchurch on the hill of the High Street; and behind these the sunset sky, seen sometimes then as sometimes now, a sky-scape of glory, more pathetic for the luminous city vapours, and which is not to be surpassed in Ireland and therefore in the world. The south shore coursed along Fleet Street, then known as the Strete of the Strand, but close by the old Custom House, where Dollard's paper factory stands now, it turned into a creek piercing up to the Lower Castle Yard, forming the estuary of the Poddle, which flowed in through the low ground below the Castle Creek, most noteworthy in this, that this was of old, the Blackpool or Dhuby Lynn, from which our beloved city is named. At its land end was an ancient mill-pond and dam, which gave name to the Damas gate, chief portal of the city proper close by, and to Damas, now Dame Street, which ran through little more than a narrow lane to the corner of Trinity Street, where was the extreme portal the Blind Gate, opening to Hoggen Green, which adjacent to the new university had already begun to be called College Green. No relic of this pristine Dhubvlin now lingers visibly, save the sluice gate of the Poddle, under the wall of Wellington Quay, familiar only to the seagulls hovering immemorially from the cliffs of Howth and Lambay to dance their airy minuets round the entrance, aiding the tides in their daily task of ablution, and our sanitary authority pending the long promised main drainage.

To the left of our stand point, the sight was pleasant,

where the shore ran along the Fleet or Strand Street, with the bright gardens and villas of a few magnates behind with watergates to the river, their front gates in Hoggen Green and Damas Street. The eastern end, now the site of the Bank of Ireland, had been granted sixty years before to Sir George Carey, to whom Falkland was kin, on the terms of his building a bridewell and Free School. These proved abortive, and Sir Arthur Chichester, first Lord Belfast, was granted the site in fee farm for six and eight pence a year, Sir Arthur telling the city that he might have it as well as any one else; he too was under terms to complete the abortive bridewell into a school, but instead Chichester House was built—" just opposite the College "—This was one of our chief mansions at the Restoration, and here sat the Court of Claims and other public functionaries. Near it was the villa of Sir Arthur Annesley, representative of Dublin in Richard Cromwell's Parliament of 1659. In the city gift it is said to be adjoining the seaside. Annesley was created Earl of Anglesea, and his gardens are commemorated in Anglesea Street. Further west was the mansion of the Lord Chancellor Eustace, given him by the King on the restoration, and still marked by the street of his name, and beyond this, reaching to the Black Pool and Damas Gate, lay the home of Sir John Temple, Master of the Rolls, father of Swift's Sir William, and ancestor of Lord Palmerston; this fronted to Damas Street and its memory is preserved in Temple Bar.

On the further side of these villas spread the Hoggen Green, between the city walls and the University, and back to the south as far as old Stephen Street, and the waste common of St. Stephen's Green. It was pierced on the city side by S. George's Lane, now South Great George's Street. Though sprinkled with some homesteads, it was still the chief pleasance of the town. On the left it merged in the Mynchen Fields that covered the space of Dawson and Kildare Streets to the marshes of Merrion Square, the old lands of the Mynechen's Mantle, or S. Mary del Hoggen, founded for elderly nuns by Dermot MacMurrough, before the Anglo-Norman Invasion. Where St. Andrew's Church now stands was the Bowling Alley, a primæval recreation ground, where the archers shot in Plantagenet times, and behind this another place of sport, called Tib and Tom, where merry makings of the city youth were held before the Restoration and after. But right in front of the Bowling Alley facing Chichester House rose the most striking historic Memorial in the city bounds.—The Danish Mount. Under the enlightened regime of Strafford, the City Assembly passed an Ordinance "that no parcel of the Greenes or Commons of the City, Hoggen Green, S. Stephen Green, and Oxmantown Green shall henceforth be lett, but wholly kept for the use of the citizens to walk and take the air, by reason this citie is at this present very populous," and the Mayor was forbidden even to read any petition to the contrary, under the then dread penalty of £40. Such a law was of course doomed to mutability, even Lord Meath could not have preserved such a policy of open spaces, which the march of time was sure to trample down, but it is a sore pity that it could not preserve one of our most ancient landmarks, which any city in the world might be jealous to uphold. This was the Thinmote or Thing-mount, which gave name to the Green, the Ostman Hogge or hill, which still in 1660 rose seventy feet over the river level.

Here the townspeople gathered in the summer evenings, for the prospect was splendid over land and city and sea. The Ordinance was passed when the city was prosperous, but the necessities of the Restoration times compelled sales of the city lands. In 1661 the Corporation therefore leased the Hill site to the Bishop of Meath, Dr. Jones, who was then contemplating the erection of St. Andrew's Church, as the old parish Church at the Damas Gate was ruinous, and who had also bought the Bowling Green for that purpose, but in the lease of the Hill was a reservation to the city of a passage from the top to the bottom of the Mount—" for their common prospect," and a covenant that no building or other thing should be erected for obstructing of said prospect. But in 1685, alas! the whole was removed by the most flagrant act of Vandalism of that improving age. A fine view might be had elsewhere, but not the Thingmount, thronged with reminiscences that should never have been effaced.

For this was the Hill of Council of our Norse makers of Dublin, their centre of legislature and judicature, of public meeting and moot, their House Things or Hustings, their place of games and of doom. Sanctified, too, by religious awe, for the Vikings, *pro more* raised these "Things" in correlation to their Landing Steynes, erecting near them stone circle temples to Thor and Freya, and we may well think that the Churches of St. Andrew's and St. Mary, both on Hoggen Green in Plantagenet times, and known as St. Andrew Thingmote, and St. Mary del Hogge, replaced these temples here when the North men turned Christian. For the rule of the missionaries, as counselled by Gregory the Great, was not to destroy pagan temples, but to transform them, conciliating their converts by following old forms, and replacing stone circles by rounded Campaniles; and it is scarcely a coincidence that this new St. Andrew's Church was circular in form, and was known as the Round Church, till burned in Queen Victoria's time. The Mount was the scene of a very high comedy in the Strongbow Conquest. His lieutenant Milo de Cogan, about to join battle with Hasculf Mac Torkill, our Ostman King, just relanded at the Steyne with Scandinavian reinforcements, to expel the invaders, feared an attack in the rere from the O'Byrne's clansmen of the Wicklow and Dublin hills. So he made treaty with Gylemeholmoc, then chief, and lord of Glencree and Kilruddery, by which the O'Byrne and his clan were to look on at the battle, and "if God grant us (Norman) to defeat these folk (Ostmen), you are to help us to follow them, but if we prove recreant, you are to join them to slay and torture us." On this pledge Gylemeholmoc "gaily went out, and now is this King truly seated with his people upon the Hoggen over Steyne outside the city in the plain to behold the melee." Here he sat on the top of the Thingmote, impartial as a Nationalist leader at a Ministerial crisis, waiting events, whether he will join Tory or Radical in the lobbies. And next year when Henry II. came in person to win the lordship of Ireland, the wily Plantagenet knowing the Thingmote was the scene of election of the Ostman Kings, and its religious sanctity, chose it rather than the the fortress at the Castle, where to meet the Irish Chiefs, and obtain their homage. Here " he caused a royal palace to be constructed wonderfully by wythes after the manner of the Country, close by the Church of St. Andrew the Apostle outside the city," feasted there the Chieftains, entertained them with military sepctacles and games on the Green, and dismissed them with presents, having held with them the solemn festival of Christmas, 1172.[4] At the Thingmote in later Plantagenet years, was erected under statutes of the Pale,[5] butts for Archery, wheie all men between sixty and sixteen would muster and shoot up and down three times every feast day in summer, which at the Restoration had become the Dublin Bowling Green. The Thingmote was "the fortified hill near the College," the scene of a fierce meeting of Cromwell's soldiers in 1647, which the mutineers seized as a place of vantage, and held it until at midnight they were received to mercy.

The removal of the Thingmount and the Pillar of the Steyne was of a landmark, that had connected Dublin with all the misty romance of the Northmen, with the Tingshogen of Sweden, the Pillar Stones of the Shetlands and Orkney, with Staines and Runnymede, and with La Hogue in Normandy, and thus they tied us to the times when the Ivars, Godfreys, Sitrics, Olafs were kings at once both in Dublin and Northumbria, Lords of the Isles whose war cries were heard often—

> Breaking the silence of the seas,
> Amongst the farthest Hebrides :

in the times when King Olaf sailed from Athcliath to contest the crown of England with Athelstane at Brunnanburgh,

[4] Hoveden, cited in Haliday's *Scand. Dub.*, 183.
[5] 5 Edw. 4.

when contingents from the Liffey joined Rollo up the Seine, when he went to win the Duchy of Normandy, and to breed the iron race of William the Conqueror. The Ostmen who raised this Thingmount we call Goths, but surely they were Vandals who displaced it, and it is sad to record that a distinguished Recorder was the chief Vandal. Sir William Davys' house was opposite the College, where the Provost's house is now, in restoration times, then he took up the Bishop of Meath's lease of the Thingmount, and had a grant of the mount free of the conservative covenants; he became Chief Justice of the King's Bench, and to enlarge his garden carted away our Mons Sacer to make the embankment on S. Patrick's Well Lane to be named Nassau Street, after King William came.[6]

But the life of the town was in the little walled city on the hill, and the few streets raying out thence in starfish wise; little, but packed with varied vitality, quaint mediæval and signally picturesque, its area occupied forty-five acres only. The ancient wall was just a statute mile in its devious girth, pierced by eight towered gates, loop-holed and portcullised, between which rose sixteen other pinnacled turrets bristling along or in front of the curtain. Three of the Gates were in the eastern Wall: the Damas Gate, leading up to the Castle; the Pole Gate, adjoining S. Werburgh's Church, giving access from Bride Street by a bridge over the Poddle. It was through this Milo de Cogan made his decisive charge which broke the Ostmen and secured the English invasion. S. Nicholas Gate, with double towers, one hundred and fifty yards further west, had also a bridge over the Poddle with access to S. Patrick's Street, and S. Nicholas' Church close by within the walls. Between Damas and the Pole gates was the Bermingham Tower, alas, alone and but partially surviving, and Stanihurst's Tower, seventy yards beyond the Castle wall. Between the Pole Gate and S. Nicholas, was Genevel's Tower round, three stories high, with timber lofts

[6] The exact site of the Thingmount is fixed by a comparison of the leases made by the city, which are specified in the 4th and 5th volume of Gilbert's *City Calendars* Messrs. Walpole's warehouses occupy it now.

above. The three ports in the south wall were the New Gate, at the end of Cornmarket, from which the great city prison was called, beyond which S. Thomas Street ran out into the country, Gormond's Gate at the west end of Cooke Street, and the Bridge Gate close near, south of the Old Bridge of Dublin. Between S. Nicholas and the New Gate were three towers—Sarsfield's, Segrave's, and Fagan's. Fitzsimon's tower, between New Gate and Gormond's, and Harbard's tower, between Gormond's and the Bridge. On the northern wall behind the Merchant's and Wood Quays, were the Wine Tavern Gate and S. Audeon's Gate, added to the more ancient defences about the time of Bannockburn, when the city, alarmed by the invasion of Edward Bruce, and not content with the river protection, built them out of the stones of the Dominican Abbey, the site of the present Four Courts, burnt to the ground some years before. Along these two quays, and between wall and river, were Prichett's tower, Fyan's Castle at the end of Fishamble Street, then Casey's, Isoult's, and Buttevant's towers in succession, the last where the south end of Essex Bridge is now, with Bysses' tower, completing the circuit, between this and the Damas Gate.

The graphic aspect of the walls was enhanced by the architectural diversities : neither gates nor towers were of like pattern ; some were square, some round, some demi-round ; some were three storied, some two ; some were nearly level with the ramparts ; some had five loop-holes, some three, some two ; some had wooden attics, rising over the storied walls ; some were only seventy yards distant from the neighbouring tower, the intervals varied, but one hundred and fifty yards was the maximum. The Castle Gate and New Gate were occasionally decorated with the heads of eminent rebels. And the names of the many towers were various as their styles. It was a very old custom for the city to lease them to eminent citizens or guilds, by whose names they were called from time to time, just as government sometimes have dealt with the Martello towers, the lessees being bound to preserve or surrender them if needed for defence. Thus Stanihurst was leased to the old recorder, father of Richard, who wrote the Irish section for Holinshed's chronicles; Buttevant was known as Newman's in the Stuart period, from Jacob Newman, the father of Sir James Ware's wife. Fyan's Castle became Proudfoot's after the Restoration. Bysse's was leased in Strafford's time to the father of Sir John Bysse, Chief Baron at the Restoration, to whom the city renewed in respect of his eminent services as recorder, adding the tower over Damas Gate, all for ninety-nine years, at six and eight-pence yearly. Then Gormond's Gate, legendarily referred to Gormo the Ostman, was corrupted into "Ormond's" in the great Duke's day, and then, again to Wormwood Gate, the name which still abides to mark the site of our vanished bulwark.[7]

But the name which charms most is Isoult's Towers, Stanihurst says it took the name from " La Belle Isoult, daughter to Angus, King of Ireland." How came this Irish beauty into the Arthurian legend ? There was an Angus, King of Munster, about the time of Patrick, and the shadowy Arthur's, and the best opinion now bases the Table Round on the traditions of the Celtic bards, Welsh, Irish, or of North Britain, indubitably then connected with Armorica and Brittany, where the romance expanded under the harps and the lutes of the troubadours of France. Scarlet Lane threaded up west of the present Parliament Street from Isoult's Tower to the Castle. Outside the Walls were at least six other gates at furthest end of the radiating streets. S. James' still marked by the name of the great brewery, S. Thomas guarding the precincts of S. Thomas and Donore, S. Patrick's close by the great Cathedral, S. Kevin's near hand, guarding the Archbishop's Palace of S. Sepulchre. The Hogs, closing the entrance to the White Friars by S. Stephen's Street, and the Blind Gate at the further end of Damas Street leading into the Hoggen or College Green.

[7] When the above was written, the writer had not seen Mr. Leonard Strangways admirable map of the old walls, prefixed to C. Litton Falkiner's *Illustrations of Irish History*. Our nomenclatures do not all coincide, for many gates and towers were differently known at different periods.

The main artery of old Dublin pierced the walled city from Damas to New Gate, through dense congestion. Passing the Castle to the top of the Fish Shambles Street, it contracted into the streetlet, Skinner's Row, running in the present line of Christ Church Place to the High Street, narrow as the Ghetto of a Continental town, only seventeen feet from house to house, which, with basement, cellars below and projections above, gave only twelve feet for the carriages, which could scarcely pass each other. Yet this was the very heart of Mid-Dublin, for on the right between it and the Cathedral were the Four Courts, for which James I. took lease of the old house of the Priors of Holy Trinity and Deans of Christ Church, whilst on the left corner next High Street was our Guildhall or City Tholsel, where the Mayors were chosen, and the Corporation met, where the Recorder's Court held unlimited jurisdiction—Civil and Criminal—within the City, often, too, used by the King's Courts and at times by the Parliament. Here, too, was the home of the Publishers; their trade fared ill in the Civil Wars, but after the Restoration they swarmed, so that the narrow streets were busy like Paternoster Row and Ava Maria Lanes, and there were far more Publishers within the limits of the old walls than in all broad Dublin to-day.

In the open between Skinner's Row and High Street, where Nicholas Street intersects, was "the chief and ancientest monument of this city"; repaired as such some forty years before, for our memorials were held in honour of old. This was the High Cross, the very core of the city, where the public proclamations were read and the public penitents would stand, clothed in white sheets, white wands in their hands, white paper caps on their heads inscribed with their sins. The atonement of Constance Kynge and her paramour here in Elizabeth's time reads dour and quaint as a chapter of Hawthorne's *Scarlet Letter*. One of the latest ordeals here was that of Eliza Jones, her forehead inscribed: "For harbouring a Collegian," contrary to an Act of State of Strafford forbidding any *Fellow*, student, or scholar, to enter an Ale-house without permission under the Provost's hands. How many such licences the Provost issued we are not informed.

The area round the High Cross was the central market. The Cross had steps about it like Nelson's Pillar, and a vivid scene was here. So as "not to pester the market," the flour sellers were to stand on those steps, the butter sellers with firkins in front must stand out in the street in lines of six each to allow passage between the intervals; the bacon-sellers in like lines on stools in front of them; the bakers were to stand along the wall of S. Michael's, whilst larger wares were relegated outside the walls. At the Castle Street end of the strait Skinner's Row was the great lantern-shaped Pillory.

Thus this centre was like the Forum at Rome, the focus of intellectual, commercial and civic life.

It was the centre of other things, notably strong drink, wherein Dublin has ever held high place.[8] Here was "Hell" in a sunk passage between the Four Courts and Cathedral, far below the aisles, further from God by reason of the propinquity. Some thought it was so called in compliment to the law, but it certainly reeked of the drink-demon. Famous or infamous, it caught the fancy of Burns to immortalize it in his satire on the Doctors, Death and Dr. Hornbook, saying his tale "is just as true 's the Deils in Hell or Dublin City." The place was soaked with cellar taverns in the basements of the Cathedral, with whose rulers rested the original blame. In early Tudor times they leased them for wine taverns, and a century after there were seven of these paying rent to the Chapter. The Dragon, Red Lion, Red Stag, Star, Ship, Half Moon, and Hell. These things vexed the great soul of Strafford, who did his own "thorough" best to suppress them; his denunciatory letter to Archbishop Laud is like the scourge of small cords that purified the Temple. But even Strafford's strength could not prevail against the gates of hell. In the days of the Restoration there were 1,180 public houses and 91 public breweries in the little city, and in a Celtic letter from an Irish priest in

[8] Gilbert's *History of Dublin*, i., 33.

Rome, in 1667, it is called the city of the Wine Flasks. Wine was the old staple, it is fluent even in the Charters of King John, and for the Scottish War of his son, Henry III., fifty-four hogsheads of red wine were actually exported from Dublin to his army. In Mary Tudor's reign, Patrick Sarsfield, ancestor of the hero of Limerick, most hospitable Mayor of Dublin, spent twenty tuns of claret in his year, 1554, over and above white wine, sack, malvoisie and muscatel. In the next reign, Blount, Lord Mountjoy, sold the wines of France and Spain by pints and quarts in his own cellars. The very drovers would not return from the fairs till they had drunk the price of cow or horse in the "King of Spain's daughter," as sherry was called. She was also known as Usquebaugh, for the time of whiskey was not yet fully come. But that of ale was with a vengeance. *Tempore* James I. we read "it had sale every day in the week, every hour in the day, and every minute in the hour, for every woman is free to brew, and as many householders in Dublin so many brewers. The better sort are the aldermen's wives, and their husbands wink at it." This was probably because they thus earned their own pinmoney. Barnaby Rych, who writes this, concludes that the whole profit of the town rests on ale houses. If alive to-day he could say little else. At the Restoration the drink river ran in rival currents like the Rhone and Arve. When the Duke of Ormonde entered as Lord Lieutenant in 1665, a conduit was set up in the Corn Market, from which wine flowed free for the citizens at large.

If churches could have checked it there were plenty of these, for this was church centre too. Five clustering round the Mother Cathedral :—S. John's, separated by a lanelet only, on the river side; St. Michael's close by at the corner of High Street on the site of our Synod Hall; S. Audeon's, or Owen's, further down the street. On the opposite of the main artery S. Werburgh's as now, but near and within the Pole Gate; and S. Nicholas, similarly within the gate of that name, all parishes at the Restoration as they had been for ages. The Cathedral, S. Michael's, S. Nicholas', founded by the Ostmen,

S. Audeon's by the Strongbow conquerors, for the paladins De Courcy and Armoric de S. Lawrence had taken their oaths of chivalry at S. Ouen in Rouen, where the bones of Cœur de Lion not long after lay, and so S. Ouen's was founded here to connect Dublin ever after with one of the fairest Gothic Churches in Christendom.

Outside the Damas Gate was old S. Andrew's; S. Bride's outside the Pole Gate, with S. Patrick's Cathedral at the foot of the long street; S. Peter's and S. Stephen's not far eastward; S. Catherine's in James' Street. Thus the old city had some claim to be Capital of the Island of Saints.

And the little city was merry with music. For a century before the Restoration the city maintained a band, not merely official trumpeters and drummers, but "a full concert of good musicians," clothed in light blue livery of broad cloth, which was voted them yearly with ninepence quarterly each by rents of the twenty-four aldermen, sixpence from each of the forty-eight of the Upper and fourpence from each of the Lower houses of the Council. For this they must work hard, every Sunday, Tuesday and Thursday in the year, and at all civic functions beside. But then they had a monopoly, being authorised to arrest all stranger musicianers. The band sank low in the Civil War, but the city music reappeared at the Restoration on the entry of the Duke of Ormonde. A restoration of the custom might settle something now such as the nuisance of the Greman bands and the organs.

Nearly everyone lived in town from the Viceroy down until the renaissance of the Restoration. How they were packed is hard to say, unless they slung hammocks in the bedrooms, like berths in steamers. So through the narrow ways, ports and passages, sauntered or pressed the motley crowds, perriwigged courtiers, ermined judges, civic magnates, fur robed in scarlet and violet, gowned churchmen, wigged lawyers, doctors alert or grave, hurrying merchants obstructed anon by the "idle women and maydens," the apple women and orange girls wherever they could plant a stool, and who survived to our day round the College Gate and Carlisle Bridge. And with these the "idle boys without any lawful calling," precursors of the corner boys who are still with us. For all these casuals a law was made only the year before the Restoration, unfortunately obsolete now, by which beadledom was to arrest and set them in a cage in the Cornmarket built at the city charge, for as yet we had no Zoological Gardens, where the happy family would well repay a visit. Soldiers' uniforms brightened the scene, for there were two city regiments, of which the Mayor and one of the Sheriffs were respective colonels; Kiliarch's both, for there were a thousand men in each, and soon came Ormonde's Royal Guards. And all were in perpetual peril of the carmen furiously driving through streets and unpaved strands. In the previous reign "their speediness" was repressed by law, but at the Restoration they were badged and reduced, first to thirty, then fifty, of whom the majority were to hazard outside the Walls, only a few being admitted to stand within the city. But this asphyxia could not hold out in the face of modern ideas. The open spaces laws were repealed spite of the shrieks of the vested interests within the city, where the house rents were enhanced by the want of room. Already the tide had set suburbwards, then it came with a rush. One by one the old gates vanished like cloud castles in the air. Verily the thoroughfares that have replaced them, now chiefly slums, are but sorry equivalents. Mediæval Dublin died with the dismantling of her towers.

II.

OXMANTOWN.

THE Blue Coat School still bears this name which once comprised the whole of Dublin north of the Liffey.

Place names are the hieroglyphics of history. Osmantown, the villa Ostmanorum, is the sole word-record here of the race that founded Dublin and ruled it three hundred years with an influence upon our history more potent than is often recognized. For the maritime Ostmen having made Dublin their chief place, the maritime English, by its capture, were able to make it the fulcrum of their power. It was the genius of the Norse colonies to merge with the natives when they were allowed to do so, as they did in Normandy, in England, and in Italy, but which the Irish were slow to allow, though the merging was beginning when the English came; but coalescing with the vanquished, the victors made Dublin their capital, and seat of their empire through all the ages since.

The victors did not purport to conquer Ireland. Henry II. was content with the homage of the Irish Chiefs, whom he banqueted on College, then Hoggen, Green, under the Ostman Thingmount; he even confirmed O'Connor as Arch King of Ireland. Leinster, indeed, he left to Strongbow, not as conquered, but by right of his wife, Eva, the daughter of MacMorrough, the Leinster King, but the Ostman dominion he appropriated, probably to the joy of their Irish enemies. This reached over the lowlands of Wicklow and Dublin, from Arklow south to Skerries and Gormanston north, and east to west from Howth to Leixlip, all Ostman names, amongst, perhaps, not fifty which still abide in Ireland. Their realm is still marked by the See of Dublin, whose limits are the same ever since Gregory, the Ostman, became Archbishop of Dublin in 1152; it was also marked for ages by the admiralty jurisdiction of the Mayor and Recorder along the coast-line from Wicklow to Meath. The Liffey plain to the Meath borders was Fingal, the *fine* or district of the stranger, or perhaps, simply the finn, or white stranger, many of the people of which still in their light hair and impassive mien bear the traces of their Ostman lineage. It was largely owned by the Thorkills, of the family of the King Hasculph Mac Thorkill, whom Strongbow conquered—Thor Gille, Votary of the God of Thunder. The city and its suburbs by the sea from Blackrock to Clontarf, Henry gave to his men of Bristol, and afterwards to his citizens of Dublin, as defined by the charter of Prince John, his son, in 1192, and as perambulated for centuries by the Corporation triennially in festive cavalcade.

The Ostmen were not driven from the city, but the walled fortress on the Castle Hill was held and colonized by the victors. As a community, the Ostmen were confined to the north bank of the Liffey, where they had long since formed a suburb round the church built by Michan, their saint, in 1095, and S. Mary's Abbey founded by them probably about the same time, and where, just outside the north boundary, they had granted lands to their foundation of the Holy Trinity, Christ Church. Here they were hemmed in; for the victors not only confirmed S. Mary's and Christ Church and enhanced them, but they founded Kilmainham in the west, All Hallowes on the south-east bank, S. Thomas and Donore, and S. Sepulchre to the south of the city. Ruth for their rapine may have been their motive, but if there was religion there certainly was policy, for they thus girdled the Ostmen with a cordon of holy ground, bulwarks against Ostmen within and Irish without, who had both now come to regard these with more awe than fortress or stone walls. Thus the rule and the tongue of the Northmen went into oblivion within a generation, for they kept no chronicles, which the Irish surely did.

They were not named Ostmen here merely because their old home is east of Ireland. The Irish called them Galls, Strangers, Black Strangers, White Strangers, Danes. There were tribes in Livonia, whom the Greeks called Ostiones and the Latins Aestii, perhaps, because they lived by the Eastern Baltic, perhaps from the cradle of the Goths in farthest Orient. Ware's high authority attributes the name to these. At any rate the Norse were called Easterlings in England from very olden time.

So Ostmantown was founded. The name in its larger sense covers all the north bank from Kilmainham bridge to the sea within the chartered city bounds, for the Abbey in the centre is that of St. Mary of Osmanbury, or town of the Ostmans, and the city records apply the name to all the north-east space behind and around the Abbey and its meadows to the east where the Abbey streets now run, and the whole north bank was the single parish of St. Michan's, but we may generally confine the term to what lies between the Park and the line of Capel and Bolton Streets. At the restoration it had but one street from the old bridge known as St. Michan's or Ostmantown Street running north to the Broadstone, each side of this was chiefly waste, though dotted with homesteads and some villas of notables. After the Abbey was dissolved by Henry VIII., it passed to Matthew King, Clerk of the Cheques of the Armies of Ireland, in 1561, from whose family the lordship was bought by Garret, first Viscount Moore of Drogheda, and the abbot's house became the home of the Drogheda family. At the restoration, Henry, first Earl, built a new mansion near where St. Mary's Church now stands hard by the Abbey, and its Little Green, still marked by Little Green Street, and the Recorder's Court, brought thither in 1796, and thence eastward the Drogheda estate spread to form, under Henry, the third Earl, Henry Street, Moore Street, Drogheda Street (changed to Sackville Street, when Duke of Dorset was Lord Lieutenant), and Earl Street away to the north Strand. Archbishop Bramhall had a mansion in Oxmantown at the restoration, even before the Cromwellian magnates were building villas here—Sir Theophilus Jones, brother of the Bishop of Meath, Charles Coote, afterwards Lord Mountrath; and Clotworthy, Lord Massareene, Cromwellians ennobled by Charles: and there were parks, enclosures, Phipoes Park, Ancaster Park, ancient spaces but only half built on. In the far west of the Ostman bounds was a triangular meadow in the valley of the Liffey, its apex near the Island Bridge of Kilmainham, with the river for its south side, the other trending north-east along the slopes of the plateau, where now rises the Wellington Column. Passing at the meadow corner the Fountain of La Belle Isoult, our shadowy heroine of Arthurian romance, fossilized in Chapelizod, the boundary mounted the highland and crossed an angle of the present Phœnix Park, into the ravine by the Military Hospital, called of old the Gybbett's Slade from an ancient gallows on Arbour Hill. Leaving this on the right it passed on through the orchards and barns of Grangegorman, of Christ Church, and thence north, and then east to the Tolka and the sea, whence it turned back along strand and river to the Church of Our Lady of Ostmaneby and the strete of Ostmantown, thus completely circling the Abbey. These borders were a little fluctuous, for there were no maps; they were preserved by the city magnates in triennial jollification for centuries known as "Ryding the Franchises." The Mayor and Recorder took horse with the Aldermen and Sheriffs and the Swordbearer, and the Clerk armed with the Plantaganet Charter, by which with a bush here and a stone there they felt their way, halting now to take counsel and then for a banquet, but at times for a dispute with the powers of Kilmainham, or the Priors of Christ Church or S. Mary's. The western triangle was Ellen Hore's meadow, so named in the "Rydings" of 1448 and 1603. Afterwards it was owned by Sir William Parsons, who succeeded Strafford, when sent to his doom, and who held many city acres through Alderman Lang, the father of his wife. In his hands it is said to be adjoining Ostmantown, and when, after the Restoration, the Park was in formation, the Lord Lieutenant Essex writes to the King, who was much interested in the scheme, that a part of the new lands proposed to be enclosed belongs to Sir Richard Parsons, the Lord Deputy's great grandson, and cannot be purchased during his minority. This minor became the first Baron Oxmantown and Viscount Rosse, and when on failure of the line of the old Deputy, the honours were renewed in that of his brother Lawrence, both titles were conferred, and the present Earl of Rosse in his second title of Lord Oxmantown alone represents to-day the ancient Villa Osmanorum."

The highest ground east of the Gybbett Slade over Arbour Hill is called in John's charter Knocknaganhoc, the site of a tale by Richard Stanihurst in his Irish contribution to Holinshed's Chronicle in 1577, and told with a humour too quaint to abbreviate :—" In the the further end of the Ostmantowne Greene is there a hole, commonly called Scaldbrother's Hole, a labyrinth reaching two large miles under the earth. This was in old tyme frequented by a notorious thief named Scaldbrother, wherein he would hide all the bag and baggage that he could pilfer. The varlet was so swift on foot, as he has eftsoon outrun the swiftest and lustiest young men in all Ostmantown maugre their heads bearing a pot or pan of their's on his shoulders to his den. And now and then in derision of such as pursued him, he would take his course under the gallows which standeth very nigh his cave, a fit sign for such an inne, and so being shrouded within his lodge he reckoned himself cocksure, none being found at that tyme so hardie as would venture to entangle himself in so intricate a maze. But as the pitcher that goeth often to the water cometh at length home broken, so this lustie youth would not surcease from open catching, forcible snatching, and privie prolling, till time he was by certain gaping groomes that lay in wait for him intercepted fleeing towards his couch, having on his apprehension no more wrong doone him than that he was not sooner hanged on that gallows, through which in his youth and jollitie he was wont to run." In a little book[10] published anonymously in 1845, it is said that even then when digging

---

[9] After some research I have been unable to find any other trace of the Parsons in Oxmantown. I have tracked these boundaries on foot and by comparison of the Charter of Prince John, 1192, the very quaint Ridings of the Franchises, 1488 and 1603, in Gilbert's *Calendar*, Vol. I., pp. 3, 190, 492, also the Inquisition of Richard II., and the modern Perambulation, continued nearly to the passing of the Municipal Corporations Act, 1840, described in Warburton and Whitelaw's *Hist. of Dublin*, Vol. I., p. 103. Lord Essex' Letter to Charles II., is amongst the Essex papers printed for Camden Society, 1890.

[10] NOTE.—*Oxmantown and its Environs*, Dublin, 1843. It is by the Rev. Nicholas Burton.

the foundation for houses in Oxmantown, they often came upon Scaldbrother's Hole, that in Smithfield it is sometimes made use of as vats by the brewers, and in Queen Street some vaults of the houses are formed from it, and boys playing on the hill have been known to fall up to their necks in it where the ground is thin. The tradition still lives with the usual variations, and the Blue Coat boys still have a legend that caverns underlie their schoolroom.

From Arbour Hill the Ostman bounds crossed Stonybatter. This, centuries before the Ostman came, had been part of one of the five main roads—Slighs—of Erin, that which reached from royal Tara to saintly Glendalough; it crossed the old Ford of Ath Cliath, passing into Fercullen and the Dublin and Wicklow hills. It entered Dublin by Cabra, and thus Boher-na-cloghan—the stony road—Stonybatter, is one of the oldest streets of Europe. From Stonybatter the boundary went on to the granaries of Gormo, called in Prince John's charter, the Barnes of the Holy Trinity. They were large and long lived, and seem to have trespassed over the line; for riding the bounds in Henry VII.'s time, the Mayor and his brothers met the Prior of Christ Church, who was fain to admit the macebearer by a ladder and a window into the barn, where was found on the floor a stone which was the landmark between town and prior, whence they went on east through the orchard and so into Ostmantown Green. And when in the first of James I. the function recurred, Sir Henry Harrington, who had been one of Elizabeth's magnates, was owner of the barns and the manor house hard by, the calvacade went straight for the stone in the "ould barne," and then to another, when the Mayor ordered the swordbearer to thrust the King's sword through a window, telling Sir Henry that but they had made him lately free of the city, they had broken a greater passadge. Sir Henry, however, was a statesman, he made a banquet to the Mayor in the Manor Hall, yet, when they had dined, the persistent guests passed the sword through a hole in the south wall and then went on through the orchard into the green. The manor came after to the family of John Stanley, sheriff in 1632, they held it for two hundred years, and in one of the more modern ridings some hundred and thirty years ago, the Lord Mayor and suite passed, like their predecessors, through Colonel Stanley's house. The name is preserved in the little Stanley Street not far from the broadway of Manor Street, but an heiress of the Stanley's, in 1663, became the wife of Henry Monck, whose family ever since have been Stanley Moncks, and the present amiable Viscount is lord of one half of the ancient Grangegorman.

The manor house, however, came in time to the Sisters of Charity. The site is now a Girl's Training School, managed by the nuns, surrounded by high walls, but the writer, tracking the old bounds lately, was most kindly shewn over the precincts by the Lady Superioress. Old things have passed away, but a beautiful new chapel, designed by Mr. Ashlin, has recently been built, a truly architectual gem, like a pearl in the shell, secluded from the world, where the barns of Christ Church so long stood. But the orchard eastward, where the city rulers rode through the ages, now a procession of Banquo's ghosts, has a special grace for us, for it was one of the early gifts to our King's Hospital, devised by a Mrs. Taylor, in 1686. Our rental still calls it the Dean's Orchard, but that also is a *lucus a non lucendo*. It bears the fine name of Fitzwilliam Place, a *cul de sac* to the west of the wall of the Richmond Asylum.

Behind the manor stretched the sylvan land of Gormo, known in middle ages as Grangegorman in *Sylvis*, and the Wood of Salcuit, reaching from Ostmantown Green to the hamlet of Phibsborough, called from the Anglo-Norman Faipoes or Phipoes, vast grabbers of Ostman lands. There is a fine tradition of these woods, which, for the honour of our Hospital, so near, we fain were proveable, that from these came the oak of the glorious roof of Westminster Hall, invincible by time or worm, or as Hanmer says :—" No English spider webbeth or breedeth to this day." [11]

[11] Dalton's *History of Co. Dub.*, 517.

There are legends all round. Gormo himself looms in romantic chronicles, a mythical hero, an African prince, who came from Spain and conquered Ireland, and then with an Irish host, joining Hengist and Horsa, conquered England. The myth is a manifest travestie of the Viking invasions of both countries, the Paynim Moors taking the place of the Paynim Northmen, and yet it was seriously used by Queen Elizabeth's cunning lawyers as a support of her claims as Queen of both islands in the rebellions of O'Neill as successor of our Ostman of Grangegorman.

Another myth[12] less traceable, connects us with Sherwood Forest, telling how when Robin Hood's merry archers were broken up, Little John, his First Lieutenant, drifted to Dublin. Prayed by the natives to show his prowess, to their joy he shot a shaft from the Bridge of Dublin to Arbour Hill, the fame of which has been flying through the ages since. In Elizabeth's time was still shown where " standeth in Ostmantown Green, an hillock named Little John his Shot." The legend says that being pursued by the English to eschew dangers of the laws, he fled into Scotland. This is indeed mythical : to avoid English law surely Ireland was his sanctuary. More likely is the other legend that makes his ending on the gallows by Gibbet Slade. But traces surer than legend have lasted nearly till to-day, though doomed to perish to-morrow. Very old records speak of the orchards of Grangegorman; between the Royal Barracks and North Circular Road, was an open space known to very few, for it was built all round, yet, four years ago it contained more than twenty acres, which in the spring were rosy and radiant with apple-blossoms, a paradise in this obsure corner of the city. It has belonged to the Palmerston Temples and has been now sold to the Artisan's Dwellings Company, and already the golden groves have been sawn down to the earth level; but the circles of dark wood wreathed with shoots of apple leaves could still be measured, and many were two feet in diameter denoting for fruit trees, a growth of many

---

[12] Gilbert's *History of Dub.*, 1, 341.

centuries. The folk-lore of the neighbourhood holds them to have been planted by the Danes. The workmen's homes will prove a blessing, but it is a pity the red brick or gray monotony should not be relieved by a few of these old Ostmen, who renewed their youth each recurrent spring, and kept venerable memories green. We were fortunate in finding these reliquiae Danaum (forgive the word) before they were doomed to oblivion.

The old Ostmantown street ran to the hamlet of Glasmenogue and the Broadstone. Beyond the church, and west of the strete, rises in the old records a tower, Young's Castle, like a lighthouse over a vague sea, perhaps named from Younge, Abbot of S. Mary's in 1467. East, west, and north of this urban wedge, spread, as we have said, fields and meadows, pastures and orchards.

North of S. Michan's, and west of the street, was an immemorial swamp, Loughboy, the Yellow Lake. It was caused by the riveret Bradogue, which entering the suburbs, as now where Grangegorman Lane joins the North Circular Road, it coursed by the lane and under the site of the future prison, thence to the Broadstone, where it probably accounts for the glas, or watery ground, of Glasmenogue. Thence it spread deviously down the slopes toward the river, forming a marsh, which drained into the Pile, a narrow estuary, long marked by Pill Lane, now Chancery Street, filled in when the Ormond Quay and Market were formed by the Duke. So late as 1681 the city Militia could not march to their parade on Ostmantown Green by reason of the swamp. Then the Bradogue was forced into regular channels running to the river, the main stream by Bolton, Halston and Arran Streets ; another by Brunswick Street, then and thence called Channel Lane. At the Restoration, when the Cromwellian royalists were in the ascendant, Clotworthy, first Lord Massereene, had a grant of Loughboy from the city confirmed in fee farm to his widow, from whom it passed to a great great great grandfather of the writer, whose relatives now possess a part.

But the pride of the place was Ostmantown Green, the

great lung of the old city within the walls, all to it that the Phœnix Park is to Dublin of to-day, and more; its Champ de Mars, the musterground of the civic and royal regiments for parade, for pageant, or for war, in it Charles' Coronation was proclaimed in 1660, and here was the great cattle fair, its common of pasture, the rendezvous of civic festivities, public and private. A lane passed through it by the river from St. Michan's to the Gallows by the Slade, known in the Middle Ages as Honkeman's, Hongman's, Hangman's Lane, still cryptogrammed in Hamon's Lane to-day. In Henry VIII.'s time a law is passed that the market of all quycke cattle shall be only in the green; this meant live bovines, for sheep and poultry were sold in the city market, and pigs were ever favourites in Dublin streets. When after the Restoration the Green was enclosed, the old usage was maintained, and Smithfield and the Haymarket, ever since kept open, are now the sole remnants of the olden Green. In Elizabeth's days there were angry complaints to the Corporation that the cattle of foreigners were trespassing on the Commons; foreigners meant people not free of the city, as the rest of the world were as Barbarians to the Greeks, and orders were given to John Usher, one of the worthies of the period, to see the Green pastured by none but freemen, and that proportionable.

South of the Green was the river, which here strayed westward in a wide reach, mudbanks on each side with a double channel embracing a great island, lizard shaped, six acres in extent, which ran from the old bridge at Athcliath to opposite the site of the royal barracks. This was Usher's Island, which was afterwards merged in the southern quays, but it still preserves memories that should not be lost, of one of the worthiest of our Dublin names. The Ushers were city magnates in Plantagenet times, John Usher, Mayor in 1561, merits a niche even in the Elizabethan Temple of Fame: statesman, philanthropist, promoter of learning, he won the confidence of Lord Burleigh and of Walsingham, and as one of the first who pressed upon them the project of the Dublin University, may be regarded as one of the founders of the College of which his greater kinsman was one of the first fellows. By him was published the first book ever printed in Irish type, of which only one copy is supposed to exist. It was the Church Catechism. Archbishop Adam Loftus writes to Walsingham in London—"my only suite to your honour is for the speedie return of Mr. Usher, the citie in these times standeth in such need of him." He was Warden of Oxmantown. His son, Sir William, followed in his steps, published the first extant version of the New Testament in Irish. The male line of this family failed, but from their ladies descend the great Duke of Wellington, and the Dukes of Leinster. But the name shall not die as long as learning lives embalmed in the memory of the great Primate of Armagh.

To the east of the Ostmantown or S. Michan's Street rose by the river side on the site of the old monastery of S. Saviour's. "the Innes" not, however, to be used as tribunals till when one hundred and thirty five years later, the Four Courts were thither removed from Christ Church, much to the disgust of the city houseowners, to erect the temple of British Justice in the centre of the homes of the Dublin Danes.

III.

THE SOCIAL STATE OF DUBLIN.

THE poverty of the city was complicated and intense, the misery not merely of the poor, the precipitates of misfortune or fault, who are always with us, but penury born of twenty years of terrible unrest which had spread through all society like a malaria. Dublin twice beleaguered and perpetually harassed, conflict within, and war without, her suburbs the scenes of many fights and of a desolating battlefield, found her commerce prostrate, her provincial trade paralyzed, her capital, public and private, vanished away, unable now to maintain her own natural population, much less the forlorn who flocked to her recurrently from the chaos utside. When the rebellion burst hundreds of "poor distressed English," with their families, repaired to the city "stript, denuded and destitute of everything. The Assembly Rolls testify gratefully to the unparalleled humanity of Ormonde at this time, though himself then a chief sufferer. After the first ten years, in 1651, half the houses in the city were destroyed, and Cromwell's Government were obliged to import a colony of artizans from England to rebuild. Numbers of houses were derelict, and the records are replete with petitions of the city lessees to be forgiven their rents or allowed to surrender; as they could not get a shilling from the occupiers. One of these is Francis Aungier, first Lord Longford, who owned the quarter in which ran the street still called by his name. In 1657 Lord Mayor Tighe, who had been sent as representative to Oliver's last Parliament, is clamouring for the unpaid £100 granted him by the city, but the salaries of the humbler city officers were left unpaid, and in the year of the restoration there is a plaint from all the city beadles, that they have had nothing for ten months, and are starving. The rebellion was, no doubt, chargeable with these calamities, but the retribution was terrible indeed.

For the Restoration at first only enhanced the trouble, when many thousands were looking to it as to a millennium, and motley throngs were crowding to the Courts of Claims, which would have needed such miraculous power as fed the five thousand to satisfy all. The Commissioners might have envied the lot even of the Land Commissions of our day, for their problem was a Gordian knot, which time only could unravel when the threads were out-worn. The position was something thus :—

The Cromwellian settlers were in possession *viva manu* of thousands and thousand of acres in the three nearer provinces assigned them, nominally for their arrears of pay, and they thus claimed by double title of conquest and purchase; many of them had resold, and the vendees thus had a further title by purchase. But the confiscated owners, whether exiled to Connaught or wandering at large, were not merely rebel Irishry; they comprised the lealest and noblest of the Royalists, such as Ormonde himself, his titled cousins, and Clanricarde, who were penalized by the Protector as delinquent. These, of course, must be restored. Then there were the Confederate Catholic lords and leaders, who, when the king was doomed, made peace with Ormonde in 1648, under articles providing for their restoration when the monarchy should be restored. These are known as the Article Men. Then there were the hundreds, women, children, lunatics, who could not have rebelled, and the relatives of rebel leaders entitled in remainder who had not taken arms, and then there were the Ensignmen, rebel warriors at first, who, allowed by Oliver to emigrate as soldiers of fortune, had joined Charles in his exile, and fought under his nominal ensigns in the low countries for France and against France, for Spain and against Spain, according to the shifting interests of our fugitive Prince. Many had served for years in battalions personally commanded by James himself, and several had become adherents of the phantom Court of Charles at Breda, and were thus more Royalist than the Royalists themselves. Beside these were a select list nominated by the king for favour and restitution. All were included in his Gracious Declaration of November, 1660, and were in high hope.

But restitution could only be at the expense of the Cromwellian settlers, and these were many-hued also. The regicides, of course, were outside mercy, and Cook, who as Solicitor General, had prosecuted the king in Westminster Hall, and had been made Lord Chief Justice in Ireland, Miles Corbett, who had been assigned the Castle of the Talbots of Malahide, and named Lord Chief Baron, and Colonel Axtell, Commandant of the halberdiers at the King's execution, who had been rewarded with the Kilkenny estates of the Butlers, were carried to London to be hanged, drawn and quartered at Tyburn. But the moderates who had worked with Henry Cromwell had joined in the recall of Charles on the express terms that their estates should be confirmed, and they now posed as the King's best friends.

Then there were the old Royalist families; settlers under James I. and Elizabeth, who had gone over to the Commonwealth when it prevailed, such as Roger Boyle, Lord Broghill, son of the first Earl of Cork; he joined Cromwell in person on his coming to Ireland, and had Lord Muskerry's Manor of Blarney, for his guerdon; and Sir Charles Coote, Chief Commissioner of Cromwell's plantation, now rewarded with a Galway estate of the Clanricardes, and Gormanstown Castle in Co. Dublin; such as Dr. Henry Jones, bishop of Clogher, and his brother, Colonel Theophilus, sons of the old centenarian bishop of Killaloe. Bishop Henry had consented to replace the Prayer Book with the Presbyterian Directory. He became Oliver's Scout-master General, and acted as herald of the engagement to the government as then established, without King or House of Lords, and his prize was Lynch's Knock, or Summerhill, near Trim, lately famous as the hunting lodge of the beautiful ill-starred Empress of Austria. Sir Theophilus, with Sir Charles Coote, had acted as Commissioners for punishing any who should promote the interests of Charles Stuart. He got the Sarsfield demesne at Lucan for his pains.

But there are "Vicars of Bray" whose government never goes out. Seeing how the cat jumped in 1659, Broghill, Coote and Sir Theophilus Jones seized Dublin Castle in December, and summoned a convention of the estates in February, 1660, to the Four Courts in Christchurch Place. They declared, like Monk, for an open Parliament, and treated personally with Charles for restoration on the terms of confirming their estates. Now they were seeking, not merely confirmation, but rewards, seats on the Privy Council, new dignities and ennoblement, and they got them mostly. Henry Jones was made Bishop of Meath, Sir Charles Coote Earl of Mountrath, Theophilus was sworn of the Privy Council, and behind these Cromwellians, noble and ignoble, were "Oliver's dogs," most formidable of all—Ironsides, who had not forgotten the use of pike and musket, and who were not to be displaced, but "that they would have a knock for it first." They were furious when they learned that any Irishry, new Royalist or Innocents, held the letters of the king. As to the Remainder Men, they said "they would know how to cut off their tayles." If a Cromwellian must be dispossessed, he must, at least, have reprisal out of the Connaught lands to be vacated by the return of the exiles or otherwise somehow.

Verily a motley flock, plaintiffs and defendants, thronging to the Courts of Claims.

Of these, there were three. The first, of thirty-six Commissioners, sat from March 1661, for nearly a year; their work was ratified by the Act of Settlement of 1662. But they chiefly represented the Royalist and Royalist Cromwellians, who were now dominant, and did little for anyone else, so by Ormonde's influence they were superseded, and a new court of five gentlemen sat in September 1662, to further consider the claims of the Innocents, Article, and Ensign men.

But there were more than eight thousand of these, and when many claims had been acknowledged, there were no lands available to meet the multitudinous residue, so the court was obliged to declare a closure after a twelve-months' sitting, and they did not re-open until 1666 to administer the Act of Explanation of 1665, the supplement of the settlement of three years before. Meanwhile the city swarmed with piteous crowds. These were not the claimants merely, but their wives and families, and their retainers, for, as Thackeray says, "there is never an Irishman so wretched, but he has some more wretched dependent hanging upon him." When Ormonde came back as Lord Lieutenant in July, 1662, he found the country "as divided and unsettled as is or ever was in Christendom." When the first Court was sitting, in 1661, Lord Chancellor Eustace writes to Ormonde of the unrestored Innocents, "our streets be full of those miserable creatures of all sorts, noble as well as of inferior degree." When the Law Courts opened next year, there were scenes fit for Lucian or Dante to imagine, tattered nobles and officers scarred and sunburnt, with buff coats patched, jack-boots and Bilboa blade, and broken-hearted followers around them, heart-sick with hope deferred; and so on for the miserable years, till for too many hope was dead.

Bourke, Baron of Castleconnel-on-Shannon, had fought under Ormonde, his relative, against Cromwell in 1650, and afterwards for five years trailed a pike in James's regiment in the Netherlands. As an Ensignman, he petitioned the king in 1662, stating he was in debt for food, raiment, and "unable to subsist if your Majestie relieve me not;" five years afterwards, he tells Ormonde, who had at last procured him a pension, that he had been forced to pawn his very clothes for twenty pounds to bring him out of Dublin, and was unable to appear for want of dress, "my wife and children ready to forsake house and home, and the little stock I had being taken for rent." MacCarthy Reagh of Bandon, connected by marriage with Ormonde, was a married Ensignman. He writes in 1665 to the Duke, that he, his wife, and seven children, had been forced for want of a home to come to Dublin; where they had not a penny or penny's worth to relieve them, and in a condition ready to perish with starving, with no other subsistence, but wandering from house to house, looking for bread."

The O'Dempsey, Viscount Clanmalier, of the Queen and King's Counties, had fought as a rebel, but was amongst the Article Men; he had been imprisoned by the Cromwell Government five years in Dublin, and so could not join the Ensigns abroad. He had nothing now to live on, but his claim was abortive, for his great estates had passed to Bennett, afterwards Lord Arlington of the Cabal, who formed the Queen's County lands into the Manor of Portarlington, for his distinguished self. Andrew Tuite, Lord of Cullanmore Castle, Westmeath, a Confederate chief, who had been imprisoned by the opposite Irish faction of the Nuncio, was reinstated at the Restoration by the king's letter, but, dying soon after, his son Walter was dispossessed by a Cromwellian claiming under the Act of Settlement. In 1666 his petition states he had been in Dublin twelve months with not sixpence for six months to relieve him;

two of his sons in the city, who from cold and want, had sickened to the point of death, whilst his mother, daughter, and two other sons were the Lord knows where, having not a bit to put in their mouths.

These were magnates. There was no land to reprize them; how was it with the starving others?

Charles and Ormonde have incurred the obloquy of ingratitude and breach of the promises which they were really anxious to fulfil, but the truth is this would have needed another Ireland, and a new army; for selfishness and rapacity were rampant. A general displacement of the Cromwellians would indubitably have evoked another Civil War; as it was they projected one, and a plot to seize Ormonde and Dublin Castle, and to restore the Covenant was only suppressed by the hanging of Colonel Alexander Jephson and his co-conspirators. In several instances restored Innocents were evicted by forcible entry, and the ejectors could never be displaced. It was hoped that the estates of the regicides and of some noted rebels still unpunished, might have proved large assets for redistribution, but to secure Court influence, the Cromwellian faction had the regicides' lands assigned to James of York, who, it was hoped, would have served his old comrades out of these, but he for whom they had bled, for whom, as king, the Irish afterwards staked their all, would not surrender an acre, and when five thousand acres of Oliver's own assignment in Meath were resettled on a Royalist, he claimed to be recouped elsewhere. Henry Cromwell had been so moderate, so generously kind, to the Duchess of Ormonde, that he was permitted to sell his great estate in Tipperary, and the purchasers were confirmed. So with many another expected reprisal.

So Dublin was filled with a ruined rabble of famished strangers, and natives little better off. This was the misery that led to the Letter of Lord Ossory, that led to the founding of the King's Hospital.

CHAPTER II.

THE FREE SCHOOL OF DUBLIN.

KING'S HOSPITAL was a rebirth or continuation of the old Free School of Dublin, which is thus a part of our story, and one which throws odd light and shade on the educational and financial conditions of the Caroline age, which might cause wonder to the Commissioners of Education and the School Committees of our time.

A lanelet still tumbles down the hill of Dublin, from High Street to Cook Street, like a turbid brook; there is a mound at one side of ruined masonry, the stones are the fossils of the old "Free Schole of the Cittie," this street was Rame Lane in the middle ages, it is called Schoolhouse Lane still, though the School ceased there so very many years ago.[1] The City Assembly Rolls in the reign of Henry VIII., and for a century after, have entries giving the names of the masters appointed by the Corporation and their salaries, these range from £20 English to £10 Irish, with the duty of teaching twenty children of freemen, and the rights of receiving from the parents from three shillings to eighteen pence a quarter, for each child; for anything beyond this they were referred to "the curtesies of the parentes according to their dysposycions;" they might, however, take pupils from the country for whatever they could get. They had residence in the garrets, over the big draughty School room, which would seem to have been held by the Corporation under covenant, to be kept continually out of repair, for there is an enquiry into the ruins of the free School house in 1615, and the complaints of the successive masters are piteous and recurrent. Yet these teachers were no hedge

---

[1] Gilb. *Cal.*, 2, 438.

THE FREE SCHOOL OF DUBLIN. 37

schoolmasters, nor were the pupils mere charity boys. The master was to "teach the children of the free citizens in humanytie, and others the liberal Sciences and frealtyes," and he did it, at least sometimes.

In 1588, the year after Mary Stuart's death, two Scotchmen, James Fullerton and James Hamilton, came here as secret emissaries on behalf of her son, James VI., to promote his succession to the English crown. But the king could not support them, and so Fullerton became master of the City School and Hamilton assisted there; clever Scotchmen can live on little.

When James became King of England, both had large grants of forfeited estates in Ireland. Hamilton was made Lord Clandeboye, his teeming posterity includes Lord Dufferin, Lord Holmpatrick, and the Hamilton Rowan family. Fullerton was knighted, became first gentleman of the Royal bedchamber, and was buried in Westminster Abbey.

But they had a pupil far greater than themselves, in that year, 1588, a little boy of eight years, James Usher, entered the School and remained there five years, and there was laid the basis, as the great Primate often acknowledged, of a learning perhaps the vastest and deepest of his day. He too lies in the great Abbey, not far from his old master of the Dublin Free School.

Poor as was the pittance, the office was deemed of great public importance, for, in 1642, Thomas Coffie is recommended as master by both houses of Parliament, yet, shortly after he complains that the slating of the roof is off. And the pittance was often in arrear. Even Fullerton had to petition " for £26 being dewe unto him as well for his stipent as his dyet," at last in 1651, at the close of Oliver's Conquest, the City couldn't even promise to pay anything, and appointed John Carr on the express terms that he was to have no salary beyond what he might get from the parents. We hear no more of him, and may hope he didn't starve; the school did.

So the new *regime* took up the question magniloquently enough at least. After electing their new Mayor, the

Assembly, in October, 1660, passed a law that the Reverend William Hill, Doctor of Divinity, shall have the place of Schoolmaster of the Cittie, and that the Mayors and Sheriffs be visitors, who, once a year or oftener as they see cause, shall see the said School well ordered and governed. At £15 a year, he was to teach twenty poor freemen's children to be nominated by the Mayor, for eighteen pence per child, per quarter, and other men's children as he can agree. The Dominie does not seem to have had a good time of it.

In the May following he is asking the Corporation to lay down a course for the speedy reparation of the roof; they ordered the Masters of the City Works to repair it, to be paid on the warrant of the Mayor, but though the warrant went the Treasurer had no money, and the poor Doctor was forced to spend £25 himself to make the place a convenient habitation for himself and family. It is not strange, therefore, that in 1664 he resigned, accepting a prebend's stall in St. Patrick's, glad, we presume, to be put back into the priest's office that he might eat a piece of bread. Yet, Dr. Hill, too, had an illustrious pupil. In 1662 Sir Winston Churchill was in Dublin as one of the Commissioners of the Court of Claims. His eldest son, John, was a boy of twelve, and was placed *sub ferula* of the Free School here. Hill was the Helicon at which the great Duke of Marlborough took his early draughts, and here was taught the hand that wrote the despatches of Blenheim and Ramilies. It is curious to think of this boy and of what he was thinking as he plodded daily by Christ Church and the precints of the now Synod Hall. His enemies in his greatness said he couldn't spell, and possibly this School is responsible, for Dr. Hill seemingly spells "School" and "repair" with final "ees," and "especially" and "speedy" end in "ie," but, as Lord Wolseley justly says, orthography was then fluctuous; it was Addison and Steele, Swift and Pope that fixed the standard, and even with Swift, "asparagus" is "sparrowgrass." At any rate, Marlborough shares this blame with Napoleon and Wellington.

Hill was starved out, but a place in Dublin is never vacant without many clamouring to fill it. The hint of Hill's resigning brought many rivals into the field. Mr. Fletcher was the fortunate candidate, his scholarship being approved by Primate Margetson, and in the grand language of the rolls, he was "invested in the said Free School and the Salary thereto belonging," which sounds queerly with the arrears due Dr. Hill still left unpaid. Fletcher fared no better than Hill, he is soon bleating over the repairs. "There is," he says, " a Schoolroom and a large fayre room over it, but the latter has no chimney, and it would be very convenient if the chimney should be built, which would not be very chargeable, for the tender children frequently made their address in cold weather in a strait little kitchen, scarce suitable for his own family." [2] There is pathos in that plea of the little strait kitchen sufficient for his own family, though scarcely so.

He seems to have come to grief, for in 1668 there was a petition for the appointment of Matthew Spring, M.A., founded on reasons "therein set forth," but which do not appear in the rolls; on this the grant to Fletcher was declared to be void, and Spring reigned in his stead, the Assembly ordering that the School should henceforth be visited by the Mayor and Sheriffs twice in the year, in June and September, instead of once as in Hill's time. But Spring, too, seems to have been a failure. Very shortly after his appointment, there is a rather angry order by the Assembly that no usher whatever be placed in the Free School under Matthew Spring, without the authority of the City, and in 1671 he was discharged. For the Corporation had meanwhile taken up the education question in real earnest. Early in that year they commissioned the Lord Mayor, Sir W. Davys, the Recorder, and the Sheriffs to confer with Lord Berkeley, the Lord Lieutenant, and the Lord Chancellor for establishing and regulating such a Free School as the Assembly desired. These gentlemen reported that His Excellency and the Chancellor were most desirous of the same, and would recommend that some dignity should be conferred on some

[2] Gilb, *Cal.*, 4, 522.

able Schoolmaster, and allow out of his revenue four score pounds for his support, and assign for the Schoolhouse the great house in Back Lane, called the Hospital, then in his hands, which, however, would cost £400 to repair. The report was ratified, the Dean of Christ Church, Dr. Parry, who became Bishop of Ossory in the following year, was appointed under the city seal, to contract with a Schoolmaster in England, and the Lord Lieutenant applied to the King for letters patent for a new Free School. Poor Matthew Spring was discharged, and the old School in Rame Lane was closed and for ever.

The King's letter followed to Lord Berkeley in May; it dates from Whitehall, and recites : " We are given to understand there is an extraordinary want of a good Schole in Dublin, the metropolis of our Kingdom of Ireland, by reason whereof our loving subjects of all ranks and conditions inhabiting in our sayd city and other places of that Kingdome are forced for the education of their children to send them to remote parts, and sometimes beyond the seas from their own oversight not only to the great hasard of their lives and health, but of having their youth corrupted with evil principles in religion by persons who may take advantage with their learning to instil erroneous, dangerous and destructive opinions." It then states the King's pleasure in conformity with the advice of Dr. Michael Boyle, Lord Archbishop of Dublin, and the Lord Mayor of our said city that there be for ever a Free Grammar School in the city, with fit and able Schoolmasters to be approved from time to time by the Lord Archbishop and Lord Mayor. To augment the Corporation grants and to insure masters "in a more than ordinary measure qualified for instructing youth after the best manner in School learning," the advowson of the first of the three dignities, Chanter, Chancellor, or Treasurer, of Christ Church which shall be vacant is to be settled for ever so that the Master from time to time, and no other, shall be incumbent. The Hospital in Back Lane, called Kildare House, for which it is stated the King pays £12 yearly to the Dean and Chapter, is allocated for the

EDWARD WETTENHALL,
First designate Chaplain of the Blue Coat.
Bishop of Cork, 1678; Kilmore, 1699,
Obiit, 1714; Æt. 78.
From an Original Picture by Vander Vaert.
London: Published by S. Woodburn, 1813.

School. Pending a vacancy in one of the dignities, the King will allow £80 a year for the chief Schoolmaster out of the Irish Exchequer. The Archbishop, Lord Mayor, Deans of Christ Church and St. Patrick's and the Provost of Trinity College for the time being, are made visitors, and Letters Patent are directed to issue.

Dean Parry went to England and secured a first-class man. This was the Rev. Edward Wettenhall, resident Canon of Exeter. He had been a pupil of that ideal swishtail, Dr. Busby, of Westminster School, thence he entered Trinity, Cambridge, but passing to Lincoln, Oxon, graduated B.D. there in 1669. He was a fine scholar, author of Wettenhall's Greek Grammar, which with Dorey's Prosody, and the Latin *Delectus*, held its place in English and Irish Schools for more than a century and a half. Resigning everything in England, he came here in 1672, with his family and an assistant Master, Walter Neale, to whom he was himself to pay £50 a year. But there was no School for him, nothing in the city coffers to pay his £80 salary, much less to transform Kildare Hall, or provide for the pupils. The Corporation, furthermore, were then building our Hospital and Free School, as we shall presently see, and had not enough for that. They were, however, ashamed of themselves and the Assembly in June considering it would tend much' to the loss and dishonour of the city if the master should be forced to turn into England again, ordered accommodation for the master and scholars to be provided in the new Hospital, if the Lord Lieutenant's consent should be obtained. Wettenhall must, therefore, be regarded as *de jure* our first Headmaster. But our Hospital wasn't ready, so meanwhile, he hired rooms himself, at £20 a year, where with Walter Neale "he taught School in the City in as publique manner as he could," as he tells in his petition in January, 1674, wherein he plaintively sets forth his wrongs, and prays for his arrears of salary, and that steps may be taken to give him a house and school somewhere. The Assembly ordered his arrears to be paid, and referred his petition to the Sub-Governors of our Blue Coat, of whom anon, and paid his rent out of the revenue of the City waters. In this year our Hospital was approaching completion, but there was no room for him yet. His petitions were entered in the Journal of the Blue Coat Governors; but Dublin could not afford two Free Schools, and he must wait for another year. He had held his ground, working like a man, and thinking while he taught in his temporary lodging, yet earning high repute as clergyman and scholar. But only a few months before our building was about to open and ready to receive him, he preached a famous sermon in Christ Church called "Collyrion" at a time when he needed a heart salve himself. And the King, as he told the City, kept his promise to him, for he was now installed Precentor of Christ Church in 1675, and Prebendary of Castleknock in St. Patrick's, and in 1679 with high acclaim became Bishop of Cork, eight Prelates taking part in the Consecration, the Primate Margetson, Archbishop Boyle, the Bishops of Meath, Kildare, Raphoe, Killaloe, and Dr. John Parry, his sponsor, now Bishop of Ossory. In 1699 he was translated to Kilmore. In both positions eminent, he rebuilt at Cork the old Bishop's Court, which he used as his palace; at Kilmore he built the Episcopal House at the west end of the Church, and began the restoration of the ruined Cathedral of St. Patrick at Ardagh. He died in 1713, full of honours, and lies in Westminster Abbey. Brave old City Free School, three of your memories amongst the ashes of the great.[3]

The collapse of the Free School was, in truth, because the City had in mind the combination of an Hospital with the School, to maintain which separately was utterly beyond their means, nor could they have attempted either, but for the allotment of Stephen's and Oxmantown Greens, a further breach of Strafford's ordinance, yet, one of vital and lasting moment to our Hospital, for it gave us a home and a

[3] This account of the Free School and Dr. Wettenhall is drawn from Gilbert's *Calendar*, Vols. IV. and V.; his *History of Dublin*, Vol. I. Sir James Ware's *Irish Bishops*; the Minute Books of King's Hospital. Lord Wolseley's *Life of Marlborough*, and Elrington's *Life of Usher* have been consulted.

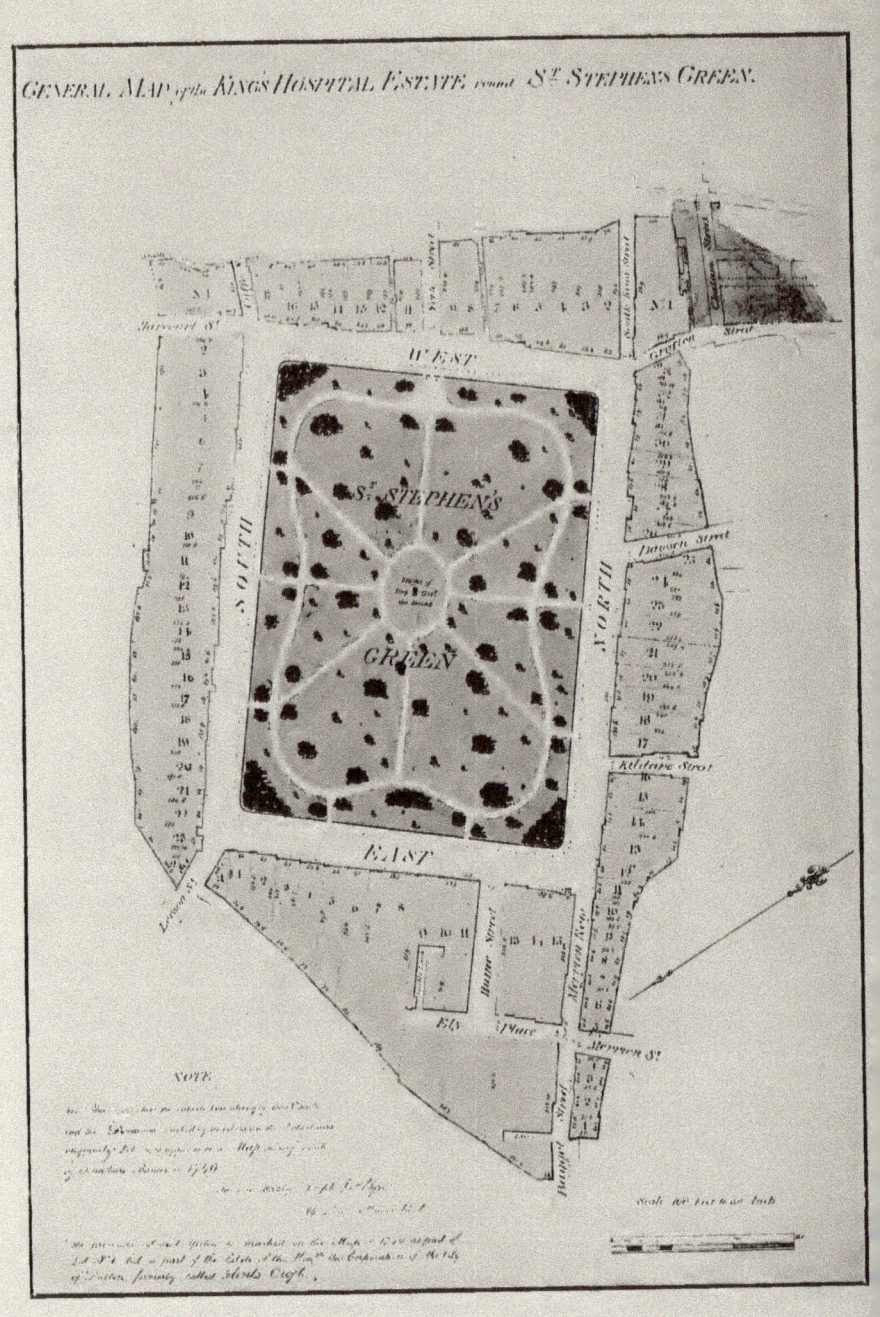

St. Stephen's Green, as allotted in 1664
(The adjoining Streets were inserted in the Map many years afterwards).

[To face page 43

THE FREE SCHOOL OF DUBLIN. 43

permanent endowment. In 1663 the Assembly, reciting that "by the late rebellion and long continued troubles of this Kingdom, the treasury of this Cittie is cleerly exhausted,"[4] resolved that by letting the outskirts of S. Stephen's Green and other waste lands, a considerable rent may be reserved. In the next year they had these skirts laid out in parcels, for which lots were drawn by the City Magnates themselves and other Notables, whose names appear in the Assembly Rolls. It may seem a mighty job, but the Corporation in fact had no money to build on, or even to enclose the wastes. Each allottee was to pay one penny per foot on three sides of the green, and one halfpenny on the south, or country side, and fines of ten shillings for each shilling of the ground rents. All were given grants in perpetuity, but each was bound to erect his portion of the boundary wall opposite his lot, and to plant six sycamore trees alongside. Next year Oxmantown Green was similarly dealt with, the allottees paying forty shillings fine and twenty as head rent, but in the lists we find Nos. 88 and 89 marked "Free School," showing what was in mind even then.[5] The space for the great market, now Smithfield, is also reserved and the residue of the green, at the instance of the Duke of Ormonde, was levelled as an exercise ground for his new regiment of Irish Guards, and the City Militia, after the City, who had nothing but waste lands, had presented to the Duke himself seven Irish acres. The feeling of gratitude towards him was intense, and the city wished him to have a palace and to live in Dublin. These acres are just to the west of the present Blue Coat playground, on the site of the Royal Barracks, erected in 1706; for the Duke's calls to London, and his son Ossory's death, prevented his building here, and the second Duke's life was chiefly in England.

The maps of the allotments which we insert may be of interest to some of the present residents, as they certainly are to the King's Hospital, part of whose title deeds they are, though, as with many Irish landlords, our rents are small. "The skirts" of Stephen's Green thus allotted, amounted

[4] Gilb. *Cal.*, 4-256, 271, 299.   [5] Gilb. *Cal.*, 4, 358.

to seventeen Irish acres, from which the aspect of the original expanse may be partially realized.

The outsider allottees in Oxmantown were more numerous in Oxmantown than in Stephen's Green, because Oxmantown was then becoming the fashionable West-end. Lots there were drawn by Lords Dungannon and Massareene, Chief Baron Bysse, who, as an old recorder, had asked leave to draw, Sir Hercules Langford, ancestor of the Rowleys, Lords Langford, and Warner Westenra, ancestor of the Lords Rossmore. He was then a member of the Corporation.

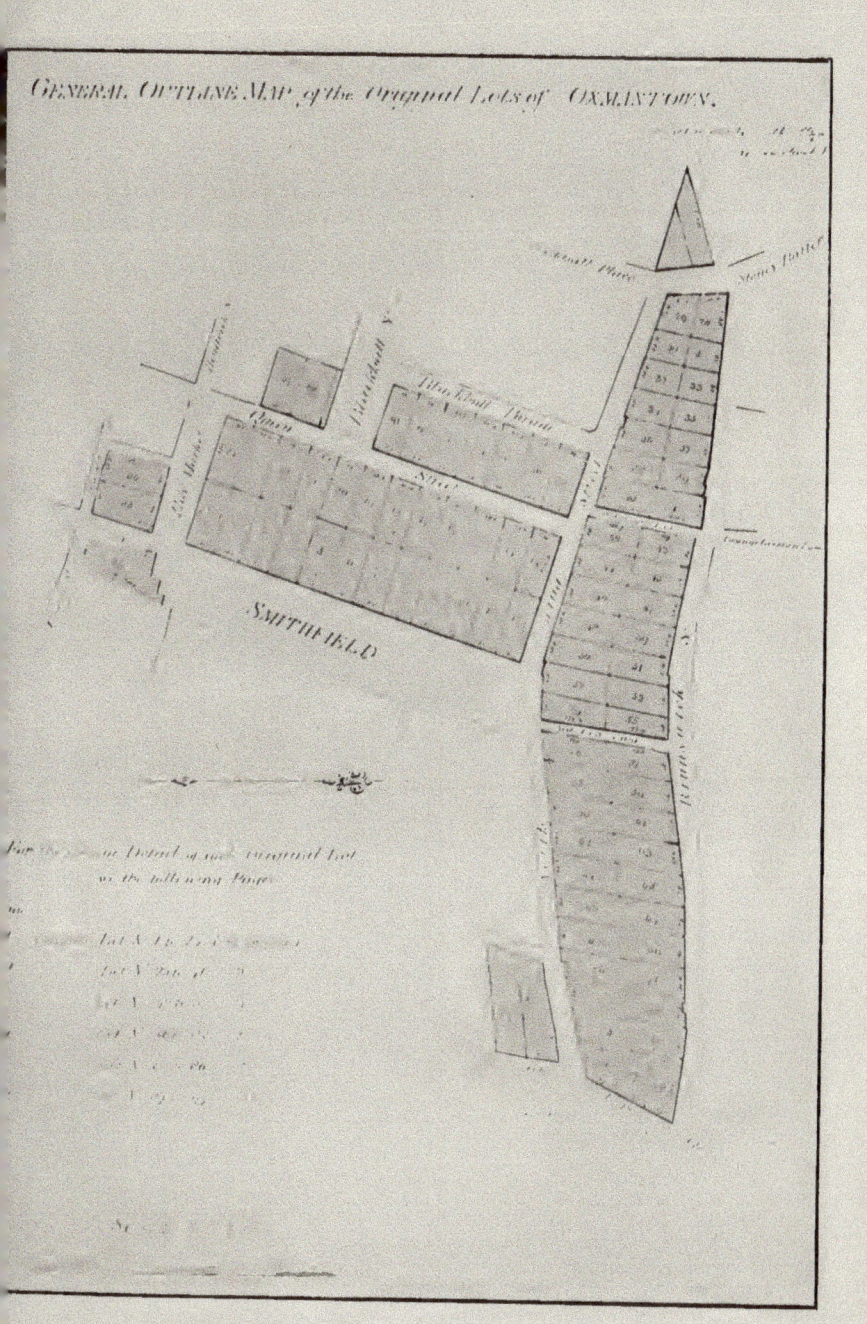

Oxmantown Green, as allotted in 1665

CHAPTER III.

TEMP. CHARLES II., 1668-1675, TO THE OPENING OF THE SCHOOL IN QUEEN STREET.

OUR Hospital bears the name of Charles II., but we may claim a purer eponymus than he, for its originating impulse came from one of the very noblest soldiers and statesmen of that not very noble age ; one of the choice spirits who rescue it from the shame of ignobility, Thomas, Lord Ossory, the Duke of Ormonde's eldest son, the darling, not only of courts but of nations, of navies, as well as armies. Paladin *sans peur at sans reproche*, *Laudatus a laudato*, his epitaph is written by John Evelyn—himself perhaps the worthiest of English worthies of his time, in a page which even now can hardly be read without emotion :—" No one more brave more modest ; none more humble, sober, and every way virtuous. Unhappy England in this illustrious person's loss; universal was the mourning for him, and the eulogies on him. I stood night and day by his bedside to his last gasp, to close his dear eyes."[1] He is immortalized by Dryden in *Absolom and Achitophel*, as one of the handful of statesmen who redeemed the times, and, deploring his early loss, he sings :—

" Yet not before the goal of honour won,
All parts fulfilled of subject and of son,
Swift was the race, but short the time to run."

Swift, writing to Pope fifty years afterwards, says:[2]—" The old Duke used to say he would not change his dead son Ossory for the best living son in Europe." In 1668 he was in Dublin, Deputy for his father, then Lord Lieutenant. Struck with

[1] *Diary*, August, 1680.   [2] Correspondence, 1735.

the dearth and misery in the city, partially depicted in Chapter I., he wrote on 8 February to the Corporation calling attention to the numbers of strangers who had crowded into the city, increasing the destitution of the native citizens, and suggesting that steps should be taken to banish the strange beggars, and to make provision for the poor who were entitled to be maintained in it. This letter, nearly a century afterwards, is styled by Charles Lucas as the laying of the first stone of the Blue Coat School. The Corporation responded with enthusiam. In the assembly of March, the subject was debated on a petition setting forth that for want of an hospital for the poor and aged men and women, and for the fatherless and motherless children without friends or estates to live on, the city is much annoyed with beggars, to its discredit and dishonour. It was stated that £200 was already placed in the hands of Alderman Mark Quin, Lord Mayor of the year before, and now City Treasurer, by a person who desires that the needful work should go on. A very strong committee was thereon appointed, consisting of the Lord Mayor, Sheriffs, all the Aldermen, and forty-eight of the Commons, to select a site for the hospital, appoint overseers, collect subscriptions, do all other matters for the speedy carrying on of the said good work, and to report to Lord Ossory and the Council, as also to the next Assembly. The committee was empowered to consider how orphan's property could be secured as in London, and they were to act under the advice of Sir Wm. Davys, the Recorder. Ossory's government ceasing with his father's in 1669, the Corporation presented him with the freedom of the city " as a monument of their gratitude and affection." In acknowledgment he writes :—" The beginning of my life, if infancy can be so called, was within your jurisdiction, and my first entrance into public employment was the care of that kingdom of which your own is the first and most considerable. I shall ever be to the city of Dublin a most faithful citizen and affectionate servant."

The Committee worked with a will; their first mandate was for an hospital, but they contemplated with this to combine a great city school as part of the project, and as they were of the whole House they had a free hand. They immediately selected as the site the Lots 87 and 88 on Oxmantown Green, which had been left unallotted in 1665, and then marked in the Maps as for the Free School, and without waiting for any report they began to work on this site on the 28 MAY, 1669, which may be regarded as the birthday of King's Hospital, for the first report to the Assembly of January, 1670, states that on that day "the pious work first began." This report gives a full account of the steps already taken, with lists of subscribers and of subscriptions, amounting to more than £1,100, which it asks to be made a record of the city " whereby a lasting memory may be perpetuated of the present benefactors, which will be an encouragement to others to follow their good example." The Committee, asking that their past dealing may be preserved from calumny, which, through ignorance, may be cast upon them, prays that a Charter be procured from the Crown *conformable to that of Christ's Hospital in London*, and that as an endowment the headrents of the lots in Oxmantown and St. Stephen's Green may be leased in trust for the Hospital for ever.[3]

The Assembly at once declared their good acceptance of the diligence and faithful actings of the Committee in carrying the good work so far forward through God's blessing, beyond expectation, and ordered the lists of benefactors to be recorded. An instrument prepared by Davys, the Recorder, was executed, conveying the headrents of both the Greens to feoffees to be named in the Royal Charter, which the City was at once to apply for, and the rents were ordered to be payable from the preceding Michaelmas.

Our founders were evidently in earnest, for the actual grant from the Corporation bears on it the very date of this Assembly, January, 1670. It is made to Alderman Richard Tighe and others, as trustees for the King's Hospital, and conveys all the headrents of the 99 lots in Oxmantown, and the 89 lots in St. Stephen's Green, to hold in perpetuity.

[3] Gilbert's *Calendar*, 4-485.

The primary list of subscribers was entered, as directed, in the Assembly rolls, and is printed in full in Sir John Gilbert's *Records*.[4] There are in all eighty-one donors. It has a column of annual endowments, totting to £82 10s., and a second for the money gifts. This latter does not include the £200, the primary subscription placed in Mark Quin's hands; this had been already invested at ten per cent, and appears in the first column as £20 a year; in our own records it heads our endowments as granted by "a person of quality who would be nameless," and who in all probability was Lord Ossory himself, for there is no other gift from him. His father the Duke gave £100 a year for several years, and Quin gave personally £100 and an annuity of £5 a year. Davys, the Recorder, and Aldermen Smith, Preston and Lewis Desmynieres gave their allotments in Oxmantown Green, six in all, in fee-simple, towards the perpetual endowment, but these, being still waste, yielded no present revenue. The general subscribers were chiefly aldermen and merchants, but Sir Edward Smith, Chief Justice of Common Pleas, subscribed £50, and Sir Henry Tichbourne £70. He was grandson of Sir Henry, one of the four sons of Sir William Tichbourne of Tichbourne, Hampshire, ancestor of the lost young Sir Roger, was personated by the base claimant Orson in the great Cause Celebre of thirty-six years ago. Sir William on the death of Elizabeth, as High Sheriff of Hampshire, had proclaimed James I., and the grateful King knighted all his four sons. Of these Sir Henry settled in Ireland, his grandson, our benefactor, was afterwards created Lord Ferrard. By the beginning of 1670 £1,200 had been spent on the building. The start was good, but the work begun in May, 1669 was not completed till May, 1675. The delay was not due merely to want of funds or size of the building, but in much to a civic conflict, which paralysed the Corporation, our governors, for more than two years; it therefore becomes part of our history, and whilst the Hospital is being built we venture to recall it.

[4] Gilbert's *Calendar*, 4-492.

Expulsion of Early Founders.

The commotion here was a vibration of the chords of court intrigue in London. In 1669 James, the King's brother, had secretly changed his religion, and Charles, inclining to follow him, but wavering to risk his crown for his creed, had imparted his doubts to his sympathisers in the Cabal, which was then in power. With them he was breaking off the Dutch alliance, and joining Louis XIV. as his pensionary in his war for the conquest of the Low Countries. Pursuing the policy of superseding the Duke of Ormonde here, Lord Berkeley of Stratton was sent as Lord Lieutenant in 1670, and with him as secretary, Sir Ellis Leighton. They were both supporters of royal prerogative, and inclined to favour the Catholics. The heads of the Corporation were almost loyal, and devoted to Ormonde, but many were opponents of arbitrary power, and still breathed the spirit of the Commonwealth; the City Commons numbered many Roman Catholics. Of the twelve aldermen who had subscribed towards the Hospital Mark Quin, Sir Francis Brewster, Enoch Reader, Richard Tighe, Daniel Hutchinson, Lewis Desmynieres, and Sir Joshua Allen had been or were to be Lord Mayors and chairmen of our board, and Davys the Recorder was an original benefactor. About this time there had been some riotous meetings of the City Assembly, of which the new government now took advantage.

By the Act of Explanation of the Act of Settlement the Lord Lieutenant in Council was empowered to make Rules with statutory efficacy for regulating all corporations, and the election of their officers and members, and in 1671 New Rules were accordingly published by Lord Berkeley.[5] As to him our Charter of the following year is addressed by the King, his name is perpetually connected with our Hospital, and gives us some interest in his career.

Pepys tells how he dined with him and Leighton in 1663, and "there was admirable good discourse of all kinds,

---

[5] These Rules are printed in Gilbert's *Calendar*, 5-548.

pleasant and serious."[6] Berkeley was somewhat of a swashbuckler, and would boast that he had fought more set fields than any man in England, and this was true enough, for he had great merit withal, and was one of the most slashing cavaliers in the Civil War.[7] He had fought the Scots in the Covenanter Campaign of 1639, and was knighted at Berwick by Charles I. After the war broke out in England he had a command in the west, where he defeated Cromwell, and won, he said, five pitched battles, overran Devon and part of Somerset, taking Exeter and Taunton, but after Naseby his career of victory ceased and he was obliged to surrender Exeter to Fairfax in April, 1646, departing, however, with the honours of war. He was one of the counsellors of poor Charles when he made his tragic visit to the Isle of Wight, for in his vanity he believed he could win over the Parliamentary generals. During Cromwell's regime he served under Turenne in the Low Countries, fighting Condé and the Spaniards. Then he rejoined the exiled Royal Family in Holland, was made Controller of James's household and was ennobled at Brussels in 1658, as Baron Berkeley, of Stratton, which was one of the chief scenes of his victories in Cornwall. On the Restoration he was made Lord President of Connaught, an office he held for life, master of the Ordnance, and a Commissioner of Tangier. His repute in London was that he had all along been a fortunate man, though a passionate and weak one in policy, and Lord Clarendon, whilst admitting his military merit, exposes his vacuity, want of tact, and ignorance of human nature. Pepys[8] tells how his friend Wren told him of how Berkeley *controlled* the household of James. Duke James had a perquisite of the Wine licences; these were farmed out at a high rent, but Berkeley found he could get a higher, and then perpetrated a job flagrant even in those days. The lessees surrendered for a fixed annual payment of £1,500, and the licences were re-let to the higher bidder, but the private arrangement was that the lessees were to have only £800 a year of the £1,500, Berkeley taking £700 for himself. He came here with strong leanings to the

---

[6] *Diary* 2, p. 141.   [7] *Ib.*, 345.   [8] *Ib.*, 4-175.

Catholics; he caused a scandal by lending the Castle plate to the Roman Catholic Archbishop Peter, for a religious function, and he told that prelate he hoped himself to see High Mass in Christ Church. He built in the sixties a magnificent palace in Piccadilly, where Devonshire House now stands, at a cost of £20,000, with glorious gardens behind. How much of this came from the revenues of Connaught and the wine licences? It was close by the still more splendid palace of Lord Clarendon. Both had tragic ends. Evelyn[9] deplores how in 1684 Clarendon's was demolished, and how at Lady Berkeley's request he himself laid out sweet Berkeley gardens for streets where Berkeley Square is now. The house was reserved. Princess Anne lived there when William was King, but it went away in fire in 1733. After his return to England he was sent ambassador to France to negotiate the treaty of Nimeguen. He died in 1678; his three sons succeeded to his title, but the peerage became extinct in the third generation.

Leighton, the son of a Scotch divine, once pilloried for malignancy towards the Crown and the bishops, was brother of the saintly Archbishop Leighton of Glasgow; he was not a saint himself, rather a scampish courtier of the Sedley type, though with a Scotsman's eye to the main chance. Sir Ellis had begun his career as a soldier, but in the exile, became secretary to the Duke of York in Holland, and was knighted there. His real Christian name was the old testament Elias or Elisha, which he softened to the more mundane Ellis when a man of fashion. After the Restoration he was made secretary to the Duke of York, and to the Prize Office in connection with the Admiralty, got himself called to the Bar, made a doctor of laws, and practised in the court of Admiralty. In a note to Evelyn's *Diary* he is said by one to be "a mad freaking fellow," by another, "one for a speech of forty words the wittiest man that ever he knew, and one of the best companions at a meal in the world." He was counsel for Pepys, as Secretary to the Navy, in an Admiralty cause in 1667, and made, Samuel says,[10] a very silly motion

---

[9] *Diary*, 2-197.   [10] *Diary*, 27th March, 1667.

on our behalf which did neither hurt nor good; but in the Castle Tavern by Exeter House that day, 'I find him a wonderful witty ready man, for sudden answers and little tales and sayings, very extraordinary witty.'" He was certainly very versatile. Evelyn[11] in 1663 goes to see Sir Elias Leighton's project of a cart with iron wheels, and Pepys also tells how he saw at Lord Berkeley's new house the new experiment of a cart with little wheels in the axle tree to make it go with half the ease. He also was said to favour the Roman Catholics, probably from his connection with the Duke of York. He came here seemingly with the intent, attributed by Dr. Johnson to Scottish immigrants, of living on the natives without *animo revertendi* to his native land.

So, riots having occurred in our Corporation, "Lord Berkeley's Rules" were issued to curb the Commons. These ordained that all Assemblies should be held with due respect to the Lord Mayor and Aldermen without clamour, disturbance, or contention. The Lord Mayor, Recorder, Sheriffs, Town Clerk, and Auditors were to be elected by the Lord Mayor and Aldermen only, subject to the approval of the Government. Nothing was to be debated save on a petition previously submitted to the Aldermen. All members, including the Commons, were to take the Oath of Supremacy, and the famous Oath of Non-resistance, then devised by the Cabal, declaring abhorrence upon any pretence whatever of taking arms against the King or those commissioned by him. The sanction of the Rules was disfranchisement of any who disobeyed them.

The Rules of course increased the popular commotion. A cry was raised that they were passed to enable Davys the Recorder to get a lease from the Corporation of the city water rates and to exploit these in his own interest. Perhaps there was some truth in the cry. With the Recordership Davys held the lucrative office of Clerk of the Tholsel, equivalent to Town Clerk, but he was a magnate, son-in-law of Archbishop Michael Boyle, who, as Lord Chancellor, then dominated the

[11] *Diary*, 17th September, 1663.

Privy Council. Sir Ellis Leighton utilized the opposition ; he got at Sir John Tottie, the Lord Mayor, and a little plan was formed by which Sir Ellis was to be Recorder, and Sir John Clerk of the Tholsel, *vice* Davys cashiered. So in April, 1672, an Assembly was held, afterwards decided to be wholly illegal. There were only four Aldermen with the Lord Mayor; on a petition of some of the Commons Davys and eight Aldermen were charged with crimes and misdemeanours ; they were not summoned to make defence, they were not heard, no proofs were adduced, but they were all expelled. Sir Wm. Davys, our subscribing governors Mark Quin and Sir Francis Brewster, Tighe, Hutchinson, Reader, Desmynieres, and Sir Joshua Allen were, in modern phrase, fired out of the Corporation, though they had loyally accepted Lord Berkeley's Rules. Sir Ellis was proclaimed Recorder, and Tottie clerk of the Tholsel.

But if any of the Corporation thought Leighton was their tribune they reckoned without their host. On 4 April he made a charming inaugural speech to the Corporation,[12] he told them that he, as their good Recorder, would be their good counsellor, and then that corporations are the creatures of the monarchy, bound to depend upon and to uphold it; that the aldermen were the creatures of the Corporation, an abstract of the wisest and wealthiest amongst them, whose duty it was to ease the Commons of the burthen and disturbance of numerous assemblies, but especially it was their duty to depend upon the King, to have no politic maxims of their own, no headiness or restiness but leave all affairs of State to the piety and prudence of the prince. The ejected members he jauntily alluded to as a few who affected an oligarchy, and linking to themselves factions, bred in the Commons an unnatural stiffness, contrary to the temper they should show to his least intimation of the King's pleasure.

But Davys and his father-in-law, Boyle, to say nothing of our aldermen governors, were not the men to submit to all this. Mandamuses were at once applied for in the King's

[12] Gilbert's *Calendar*, 5·558.

Bench, and petitions to King Charles were addressed by the evicted officers and backed in London by Ashley, Lord Shaftesbury, who had now become arch champion of the Protestant interests. The result was that Lord Berkeley's Viceroyalty ceased in May, 1672, and Arthur Capel, Earl of Essex, succeeded, not, however, coming over here till August. To him and his Council the King in Council in London referred the petitions, with a counter-petition of the newly constituted Corporation.

The cause came on before the Privy Council here on 11 September. There was a strong board of fourteen members, including Primate Margetson, Archbishop Boyle Lord Chancellor, the Earl of Arran, and several other peers, Jones, Bishop of Meath, and Sir John Bysse, Chief Baron, *ci-devant* Recorder. Little chance for Leighton in such a court. At the first hearing the new Corporation were silent, but they then petitioned to have counsel assigned, and to be allowed to prove that the evicting Assembly was a lawful one, and that the evicted had been expelled for just cause. Six counsel were accordingly assigned them, Sir Nicholas Plunkett, who had been a chief of the Confederates in the Civil Wars of the forties, was their leading counsel. The case was resumed in the Privy Council on 18 September, from nine o'clock to two, and on the 20th from nine to six, when the Council unanimously decreed that the expulsions were illegal, that Davys and our seven other founders should be restored, and the intruders expelled in turn, and that all their acts should be expunged from the city records. The costs of the evicted tenants were to be paid by the City Treasurer, in which office, Enoch Reader was now reinstated. He had been forced to give up the keys on pain of breaking open the doors of the Treasury. The election of Tottie to the Mayoralty for the second year was annulled, and Alderman Deey appointed for 1672-3.

Leighton now disappears from our scene. The scars of this warfare are still apparent in our city records, for two parchments were removed from the Assembly Rolls under the expunging order of the Privy Council, though this was disobeyed for two years, and there is a gap of twelve months in the annals now.

Berkeley's successor, Arthur Capel, first Earl of Essex of that family, remained Lord Lieutenant to 1677. In September, 1672, he issued New Rules superseding Berkeley's. These proved of lasting historical moment in the city for more than a century, notably when James II. was King, and in the agitations of Charles Lucas. They are printed in the Public Statutes, appended to the Act of Explanation. They are very accurately framed and are known to have been drawn by Chief Baron Bysse. By them the Common Council was to consist of twenty-four aldermen, sitting apart, eight being a quorum, the Commons were to sit in a separate room, the sheriffs presiding, forty-eight being sheriffs' peers, and ninety-six members chosen triennially by the city guilds. All members were to take the Oaths of Allegiance, Supremacy, and Non-resistance, but the restrictions of debate to subjects sanctioned by the aldermen contained in Berkeley's Rules is not repeated. The election of Lord Mayor, Recorder, Sheriffs, and Town Clerk are made subject to the approval of the Lord Lieutenant and Privy Council, which if not accorded within ten days of presentation a new election must be held, and so from time to time. The choice of Lord Mayor, Sheriffs, and Treasurer, was vested in the aldermen alone. But on the side of liberality the *Oath of Supremacy could be dispensed with by the Viceroy*, and all resident traders and artificers, irrespective of creed, and even if foreigners and aliens, were to be admitted to the freedom of the city on payment of twenty shillings and taking the Oath of Allegiance alone. The rumblings of this civic earthquake muttered on for a good while and angered Lord Essex much. His Rules were denounced from many quarters, by the great jurist, Dudley Loftus, as unconstitutional, by the strong Protestants, because allowing dispensations from the Oath of Supremacy to be given by the Viceroy to some Catholics, by Presbyterians of the Covenant, as containing the doctrine of passive obedience. Then some of the Guilds presented a gold chain to Sir John Tottie for his pains in supporting the privileges of the city, and two of the Leighton corporators, though expelled, had silver cups cast with the inscriptions :— " Made in the year when Philpot and Gressingham were aldermen." Then the Privy Council Order to erase the mutinous records of 1672 long remained unexecuted, for Tottie, who seems to have been a general favourite, was reinstated in the clerkship of the Tholsel, and as such refused to expunge them. Lord Essex, in 1674-75, writes to Sir Henry Coventry, now principal secretary of State, and to Lord Arlington, his predecessor, who was now the King's Chamberlain, complaining of Philpot, the haberdasher, as one of the ringleaders of mutiny, and that his silver cups were being constantly used in the feasts of the city. Of Tottie he speaks " as a person of as much disloyalty as any about in this city, which he has brought into a mutinous temper." He bitterly describes how, when in obedience to a second order of the Privy Council to erase the illegal records the Lord Mayor and Aldermen were ready to comply, the Commons had refused, and when the third order menacing penalties came, and the aldermen proceeded to obey, the Commons tumultuously broke up the Assembly. Lord Essex advises the council that there will be no peace till the chief incendiaries smart for it, and that it will be necessary for the Crown to revoke the City Charters. This threat brought the opposition to their senses, and the cancellation was effected at last in 1675.

There were certainly counter currents at work in the movement, and it is not quite clear how far old political animus had inspired the expulsion of these eight founders. Five of them had indeed been members of the Corporation of the Commonwealth, but Sir Wm. Davys had been made Recorder on the Restoration, and Sir Francis Brewster and Sir Joshua Allen had become aldermen afterwards, but two of the other five at least had been Cromwellian notables. Richard Tighe was Mayor in 1651, and was succeeded next year by Daniel Hutchinson. Tighe and Hutchinson were summoned to represent Dublin in Oliver's two parliaments of 1654 and

1656. When Henry Cromwell came to Dublin Castle as Lord Lieutenant, he, in 1659, formed two regiments in the city, in view of a suspected Royalist uprising; they were of ten and nine companies respectively, with the Mayor for the time being Commander-in-Chief. Tighe was named Colonel of one, and Hutchinson Captain of the Horse, with power to nominate his own officers, but with these they joined in the celebration of the King's coronation on Oxmantown Green. Enoch Reader, another of *The Evicted Eight*, was a Captain in one of the regiments. Richard Tighe acquired large estates, and is ancestor of the eminent families of Woodstock, Kilkenny, and Rossana, Wicklow, and a large progeny of distinguished people, amongst whom we may include Mary Tighe, the graceful poetess of Psyche. John Preston also had been Mayor in 1653 in the Cromwell regime. He, too, acquired large estates in Meath and Queen's County, and was ancestor of the Prestons of Ballinter, of whom his namesake, John, was created Lord Tara in 1800, on the Union. John Preston's name is memorable in the Blue Coat still. He granted to the Hospital a charge on his Queen's County estate, originally yielding to the School £20 a year, but which more than a century after brought upwards of twenty-fold more, in a startling litigation to be noticed in due course.[13] And his original allotment in Oxmantown Green, which he bestowed at once on the Hospital, is still amongst our endowments. It adjoins the site of the present school. Hutchinson also made a fortune purchasing from a Cromwellian adventurer, and afterwards obtaining a grant of lands in King's County and County Down under the Act of Settlement. He, however, left daughters only, and his name cannot now be further traced. He was member for Queen's County in the Irish Parliament of the Restoration from 1661-1666. He bequeathed £300 to the Hospital by will. Lewis Desmynieres, another of the eight, was a Dutchman, and had with his brother John been in the Corporation of the Commonwealth, John serving as Sheriff in 1654, but Lewis, with the Westenras, also Dutch merchants, were

[13] *Infra, Final Chapter.*

naturalized by Act of Parliament in 1662, John became Lord Mayor in 1666, and Lewis in 1670. He did not make a fortune, for we find him a few years after a supplicant for aid from the city.

Sir Joshua Allen was one of the most distinguished citizens of the period.[14] His father, an eminent Master Builder, favoured by Strafford, was of Dutch origin. He left a good estate, which, in his son's hands, became a large fortune, and thus he was the founder of a noble family, which, in the female line, is still represented by the Earl of of Carysfort. He acquired the great property which his son, Colonel Allen, enlarged into the finest demesne in the County Dublin, reaching from Foxrock and Carrickmines to Blackrock and the sea, part of which has been known in our times as Stillorgan Park. Sir Joshua remained for many years a useful governor of the Blue Coat; he was a strong adherent of the Protestant interest, to which he probably, though a royalist, owed his expulsion by Leighton, and to this was certainly due his flight from Dublin in the acme of the Tyrconnell regime in 1688, when he retired to his wife's family in Chester. Here he joined William III. in the embarkment of whose army to Ireland, he took a prominent part, and returning home after the Battle of the Boyne, he was, at once, nominated High Sheriff of Dublin by William, though he does not seem to have actually taken office, for he was in ill-health and died in the next year. His son, Colonel John, who was M.P. for Dublin, and for Wicklow, was created Baron of Stillorgan and Viscount Allen, to be followed by five of the family in succession till the peerage became extinct with the sixth Viscount, Joshua William, Colonel in the Guards, who fought at Waterloo, and died unmarried. But the sister and co-heiress of the third Viscount, who was M.P. for Carysfort, married in 1750 Sir John Proby, to whom she brought a large share of the Stillorgan and Blackrock and Wicklow estates, and he, in 1792, became first Lord Carysfort. Joshua, the second

[14] See a very interesting account of the Allens in F. Elrington Ball's *History of the County Dublin*, Vol. I., 120.

Viscount, is the Troilus of Swift's *Lampoons*. They had been friends, but when, grateful for the Dean's fierce fight for Irish Manufactures, the city presented him with the freedom of the city in a gold box, Lord Allen, who belonged to the alarmed court party, violently assailed him as a Jacobite in the House of Lords, and so aroused the wrath of the past master in ridicule and invective, who could never endure any criticism of himself. The last Viscount was a "character," and a hero of clubs, in which he was known as King Allen. He had lost the remnant of the Dublin estates and became insolvent. A sketch of him in Burke's *Romance of the Aristocracy*, tells how having raised a loud laugh in his club by a sharp joke on a brother member, a banker, the latter next day retaliated with a once famous repartee. Addressing Allen amid a large audience, he said :—" Why, Allen, I find you are only half a king." " How is that," said the Viscount, angrily. " Because I have heard you have just compounded with your creditors for ten shillings in the pound, so you are only Half a Sovereign." This was the end of the Allens.

Mark Quin, to whom Ossory wrote the initial letter, and to whom he entrusted the primal donation which he followed himself with £100, and a perpetual annuity of £5, personally organised the work in 1669. He did not live to see it completed, he died in 1674, but he must be held a primary founder, and claims an obituary notice here, especially as his memory has been unjustly consigned to a grim immortality by Swift in one of his most savage pasquinades. The Dean had himself no grudge against him, but used his tragic fate as a weapon to wound his arch-enemy, Quin's grandson, Chief Justice Whitshed, on his principle that any stick was good enough to beat a dog. He was in truth one of the worthiest citizens of his day ; chosen alderman in 1654, Lord Mayor in 1667, and Treasurer in 1668, he was in the Corporation thirty-two years, to his death. He lived in the High Street, opposite St. Michael's Church, the site of the Synod Hall, and was its chief parishioner ; the church plate was kept in his house for safe custody ; a successful merchant, he left an estate of £1,000 a year, a large fortune in those times, but his domestic felicity was not in proportion. Mrs. Quin was fair but frail. The alderman, maddened with jealousy, and rushing from his house one morning at ten o'clock, bought a new razor and, withdrawing into Christ Church Cathedral, cut his own throat in St. Mary's chapel. His fortune passed to his son James, who was a graduate of Trinity College. This son became a member of the Bar in England, where he married a presumed widow, a lady whose husband had been absent and unheard of for many years. In 1693 she bore James Quin an only son, also James, but shortly afterwards the supposed dead husband reappeared, and, unlike poor Enoch Arden, re-entered and reclaimed his Penelope, thus illegitimatising her son, young Quin. Old Mark's next heirs were the Whitshed family, the children of his daughter. They appealed to the law, taking advantage of the illegitimacy, for they were a family of lawyers, and succeeded to the Alderman's estate. In 1720, Sir William Whitshed, Mark Quin's eldest grandson, was Lord Chief Justice of the Irish King's Bench. In that year Swift, in fury at the English policy which, having prohibited the export of Irish woollen goods, went on to prohibit the Irish from even weaving woollens for themselves, emerged as a patriot giant in the land of his adoption. He hurled forth his proposal for the universal use of Irish manufactures, in which he suggests that Ireland would never be happy till a law were made for burning everything that came from England, except her people and her coal. Prospero had raised the storm; the Government took alarm; the printer was prosecuted. Swift writes to Pope that one in high office had personally gone to the Chief Justice and asked that the prosecution might be pressed with the utmost rigour of the law. And so it was: the Chief presided, but the whole country was with the printer and Dean. The jury returned a verdict of not guilty. The Chief Justice raged; he sent the jury back nine times and kept them twelve hours till he tired them into giving him a special verdict to be argued in bank. Swift tells Pope that the judge had put his hands to his breast and solemnly avowed to the Protesant jury that the printer's design was to bring in the Pretender. The case never came on for argument. Public opinion in Ireland was all one way, and, the Duke of Grafton succeeding as Lord Lieutenant, the Government entered a *Nolle Prosequi*. The Dean's second duel with the judge was shortly after, when Harding, Swift's printer, was prosecuted for the Fourth *Drapier Letter*. Swift circulared the Grand Jury in his own style the night before the trial. They ignored the bill next day, despite the vehemence of the thwarted judge, who discharged the Grand Jury, again in a rage. The lawyers of the day regarded this as unconstitutional. Through both these contests the Dean assailed the judge with all his matchless prowess of logic and lampoon, rapier and bludgeon, shafts, feathered with fun and poisoned with rancour, till he is supposed to have driven him to a premature grave. He raked up the buried griefs of Mark Quin, which would have touched his better nature in themselves, to smite his grandson.

Witness this Trilogy.

The judge speaks :—

1.

I hate the Church, and with good reason,
For there my grandsire cut his weason :
He cut his weason at the altar,
I keep my gullet for the halter.

The Dean speaks :—

2.

In Church your grandsire cut his throat,
To do the job too long he tarried.
He should have had my hearty vote,
To cut his throat *before he married*.

The judge speaks :—

3.

I'm *not* the grandson of that ass, Quin,
Nor can you *prove* it, Mistre Pasquin,
My grand dame had gallants by twentie's,
And bore my mother by a prentice.
This when my grandsire knew, they tell us he
In Christchurch cut his throat for jealousy.
And since the Alderman was mad, you see,
Then I must be so too, *Ex traduce*.

Swift's editors curiously have not identified his ass, Quin, with our worthy Founder. In vindicating his memory now, we may recall that that other grandson, the illegimatised young James Quin, lived to be the greatest actor and wit of his day. Intended for the Bar in Dublin, when he was disinherited he went on the stage. His jokes set London tables in a roar for a generation, and he was one of the greatest Falstaffs that ever trod Drury Lane; a fine figure of a man; a great elocutionist; he lived to hear George the Third's first King's Speech, and the old man cried " I taught the boy to speak." He was sometimes coarse and overbearing, but he is a creditor of Literature, for he once redeemed Thomson of the *Seasons* from a debtor's prison, paying the debt in honour of the Poet, for personally he didn't know him. And as to the grandson, Whitshed, it is fair to remind that even Swift acknowledges that, politics apart, he was a fine judge. His memorial was the last which remained in old St. Michael's when the church was taken down thirty-five years ago to build the Synod Hall; a slab, with a Latin inscription that any judge might be proud of, telling how, as Chief Justice, first of the King's Bench, and then of the Common Pleas, he was "*Judex indefessus perspicax incorruptus*, who so bore himself as a man, who both believes there will be a Supreme Judge and hopes it."

The civic shock may now read as a tempest in a teacup, yet it was, as we have said, the vibration of one that shook the crown and ministry and parliament of England in 1672-75 on the doctrine of passive obedience, the prerogative of the dispensing power, and the Test Act. The Oath of Non-resistance imposed by both the Berkeley and the Essex rules, agitated the House of Lords with one of its most memorable debates, that lasted for seventeen days in 1674, seeming to involve the fate even of the dynasty. It gave occasion to Shaftesbury's famous *Letter from a Person of Quality to a Friend in the Country*, to escape prosecution for which were called out all his consummate arts in keeping up the agitation. This oath was framed by the great Lord

Clarendon in the first loyal outbursts of the Restoration, but that heat was cooling, under the intrigues of Charles and his Cabal, not only in England, but here too.[15]

But before Berkeley left us the Charter had been drawn by Davys, and read before Charles in Council, and to the Lord Lieutenant came a royal letter, dated at Whitehall, 24 Oct.,1671,[16] directing him to cause Letters Patent, under the Great Seal of Ireland, to pass conveying to the Mayor, Sheriffs, Commons and Citizens of Dublin, the parcel in Oxmantown Green on which the Hospital and Free School is already begun, "to be held of us, our heirs and successors in common soccage as a mansion house and abode for the relief of poor children, aged, maimed and impotent people, by the grantees, who are to be incorporated as a body politique, by the name of 'The Governors of the Hospital and Free School of King Charles the Second, Dublin.'" The Letters Patent are to empower the Governors at their will and pleasure from time to time to place therein such master or masters and such numbers of poor people and children and such officers and ministers of the Hospital and Free School, as likewise an able, learned, pious and orthodox minister, to be approved by the Archbishop of Dublin for the time being, who shall read Divine service and preach and teach the word of God to such as shall reside, and catechise such of the children as shall be in the school. The Governors are enabled to hold lands to the value of £6,000, notwithstanding the statutes of mortmain, and to make leases of buildings for 41 and of lands for 21 years, and the letters are to contain such clauses and privileges "as in the Charters granted by our Royal Predecessor, King Edward Sixth to the Mayor and Commonalty of London for the erection of Christ's Hospital and Saint Thomas, his Hospital and Bridewell."

This was followed by our Charter. It is dated the 3rd

---

[15] The materials of this chapter have been mainly found in Gilbert's *Calendar of City Records* and his preface to Vol. V. The *Journal of the Hospital*, the *Diaries of Evelyn and Pepys*, and the *Dictionary of National Biography*. There is a confusion in both the Diaries, made more confounded by the indexes between Lord Berkeley of Stratton, and Lord Berkeley of the great Berkley Castle family.

[16] *Pat. Roll Chane.*, 23, Cor. 2, pt. 1. (f. m. 25.)

December, 1671, and slightly amplifies the royal letter. It is in effectual force to-day, and is set forth in full in our appendix.[17] The original is now in the Public Record Office; engrossed in old English text on a parchment roll, two feet square, it is illuminated in gold and tinctures, the Royal Arms with the harp in the third quarter, separated from the supporting lion and unicorn by roses and thistles, tulips and carnations, which surmount the text. The great initial C of the King's name encloses a good portrait of his Majesty in ponderous periwig. In the left margin are the city arms blazoned in azure, with an unblazoned oval below, probably left for our seal when chosen. On the margin of the second skin, a lady under a canopy leads a naked boy and bears a naked baby at her breast—though presumably a distressed widow, she is clothed like the King's daughter in a red petticoat and a green gown, and some might think the group more disreputable than pathetic, yet, it has been the cognizance of our seal ever since. The instrument, however, is a very interesting sample of the Royal Charters of the day. The Great Seal of Ireland is attached, a waxen circle of five inches. This is of the pattern used by the English Kings from the very early times. On the obverse the King in armour gallops on a caparisoned steed with a greyhound beneath. On the reverse he is enthroned under a canopy, the harp and crown are on both faces, the legend round each circumference:—*Carolus II., Fidei Defensor Dei gratia Magnæ Britanniæ Franciæ Hiberniæ Rex.* The Charter bears *teste* " 3rd day of December, in the three and twentieth year of our Reign," and is simply signed Domville. Sir William Domville was then the distinguished Attorney-General, an office he held for twenty-eight years, and a Privy Councillor, and is the progenitor of the eminent family of Santry and Loughlinstown, but it is more likely that our signatory was one of his two sons, who then jointly were patentees of the clerkship of the Crown and Hanaper, for though Sir William was a very worthy public servant and general favourite, he knew how to take care of himself; by

[17] *Appendix.*

grants in reversion this clerkship of the Crown and Hanaper remained with his descendants for one hundred years.[17] But traffic in offices did not shock much in these good old times.

Meanwhile, peace being restored, our founders resumed activity. In Oct., 1673, a grand committee of "Sub-Governors and Trustees" was named, consisting of 117 members :—Sir Joshua Allen, Lord Mayor, and Davys, Recorder, all the aldermen, both Sheriffs, forty-six Sheriffs' Peers, the forty-four Masters of the City Guilds, and the twenty Churchwardens of the eleven City parishes. Their names appear in the first entries of our first Minute Book, and include Tottie, and Philpot and Gressingham of the silver cups. This appointment of Governors is noteworthy, for it was an act of the whole Corporation, and from it arose the usage of co-opting from outside the Corporation, which we shall see was afterwards challenged by Charles Lucas and others as illegal. They are empowered by the City Assembly of Christmas, 1673, to address the King and the Lord Lieutenant as they deem fit for benevolence to forward the good work. By the end of 1672 £4,000 had been subscribed, the second list including £100 from Lord Berkeley : £60 from Primate Margetson ; £50 each from Archbishop Boyle, Chief Baron Bysse, and Sir Ed. Smith, late Chief Justice of the Common Pleas ; £20 each from Sir John Temple, Master of the Rolls, Sir Robt. Booth, Chief of the King's Bench, and Capt. James Stopford, son of the ancestor of the Earl of Courtown. The City gifts comprise £150 from Sir Francis Brewster ; £75 from Sir Joshua Allen ; £108 from Mr. Williams, Brewer, and £50 from Aldermen Tighe and Hutchinson, and the Farmers of the City revenues. The first business before our Grand Committee was Wettenhall's petition and the Free School, but, as we have seen, they could do little for him pending the building of the School, for they were in straits themselves—they had expended their subscriptions already. Early in 1674 the Hospital was nearing completion, but money was wanting to finish it, and as it was planned for three hundred and fifty residents,

[17] See *Liber Munerum*.

how was it to be filled, and how, when filled, was it to be maintained? They found that for annual revenue they had only the headrents of Oxmantown and St. Stephen's Green, £170 a year, and £114 of secured annual subscriptions, they had, no doubt, six of the lots in St. Stephen's Green, and three in Oxmantown, granted to them in fee-simple by the allottees, but all still waste, and of their rents and of the headrents, £850 was now in arrear. £450 of promised subscriptions were still unpaid, and nearly £600 was due to the builders. So the Committee appealed on a great scale in March, 1674. First they petitioned King Charles in person, reciting Lord Ossory's letter to the Corporation of 1668, and the reply of the City, with the project of the Hospital; they state the Privy Council had directed them to begin with all speed possible, promising to contribute their endeavours to so good a work; that by the blessing of God the structure is now almost finished, capable of receiving three hundred and fifty persons at the least, with a fair chapel, garden and walks walled about, with all schoolrooms and offices requisite, at the expense of near £4,000; they remind the King of his own Letters Patent directing the Hospital and Free School to be called for ever by his own Royal name, and alleging the stately structure to be empty for want of a suitable revenue, they implore the Royal bounty for such maintenance as may enable the Hospital to continue to succeeding ages "as a monument of your Majesty's undoubted piety and charity."

But they did not trust to those well-known royal qualities alone. They enclosed the petition in a letter to one whom they held in true trustful affection, the Duke of Ormonde, then in the Court in London, asking him to procure its favourable admission with the King. They recall the Duke's constant favours to the city, and, reminding him that Lord Ossory had given the first encouragement to the erection of the Hospital, and thus assured them of his Grace's furtherance, they ask him now to crown the first beginnings of his noble son. They would remind his Majesty, "who takes the proper measures of this kingdom from your Grace's better prospect of them, how glorious to posterity Kings of England have made themselves by like foundations;" and they pray him to refer their petition to the Lord Lieutenant in Council for a report from what branch of the public revenues a fitting maintenance may be secured for a work of so great charity, so great honour, and so public an use. "To whom," concludes this letter, "can we humble ourselves but him who has so long and so well known Joseph."[18]

That pathetic allusion to Joseph sounds rather mysterious. How were the Corporation like Joseph? Was it that as a body they wore a coat of many colours which their brothers sometimes tore? Ormonde and Ossory, however, seem to have understood it, for in 1670, when conferring on Lord Ossory the freedom of the City, the Corporation wrote that his name would be second on the roll next to his illustrious father, who stood first, "your lordship being, in truth, the second edition of his Grace, whose services to the city during the calamities of rebellion and civil war had thus known, pitied, and relieved *Joseph* in all his miseries."

This letter to the Duke, of March, 1674, referring to Lord Ossory, speaks of "his preservation from those mighty dangers which his valour, so greatly celebrated, lately exposed him to and which we heartily congratulate."[19] This refers to the great sea fight with the Dutch in 1673, when Ossory, lately made Rear Admiral of the Blue, was in command of the first-rate "St. Michael." Admiral Sir E. Sprague, who, Commanded-in-Chief, was killed and his ship disabled. Ossory defended her through the day, and brought her off safely at night, every man on his own quarter-deck being slain save himself, his page, and Capt. Narborough. For this he was made Rear-Admiral of the Red.

If these alluring letters of the Corporation and one they addressed to Lord Lieutenant Essex also, did not bear much fruit in endowments, they certainly had a royal reception. There was a Council at Whitehall, 8 May, 1674, at which our petition was presented. King Charles pre-

[18] Gilbert's *Calendar* VI., 497.
[19] *Historical Manuscripts* 6 Rep., 719, Note b.

sided in person. Beside him was his cousin, Prince Rupert, with the Chancellor Finch, Danby, Lord Treasurer Arlington, still Principal Secretary of State, the Dukes of Ormonde and Lauderdale, The Lord Privy Seal, the Earls of Ossory, Bridgewater, Northampton, Carlisle, Bath, Craven, Tweedale and Carbury, Viscounts Halifax and Faulconbergh, the Bishop of London, and Lords Mainard and Newport, the Chancellor of the Exchequer, Sir H. Coventry, second Secretary of State, the Vice Chamberlain, Mr. Montague, and the Speaker of the House of Commons. This Committee of twenty-six of the Lords of the Universe ordered Arlington to prepare a letter referring the petition of the Blue Coat to the Lord Lieutenant and Council in Ireland, who were to report what was fit for his Majesty to do in the matter. This letter was sent by Arlington on 12 May.

Essex in Council considered it on 1 June, when they appointed the Primate, the Archbishop, and Chancellor Boyle, Chief Justice Booth, Chief Baron Bysse, Jones, Bishop of Meath, Sir Thos. Stanley, and Sir Chas. Mere to consider fresh proposals of the Corporation for a maintenance for the Hospital, and to report to the Council accordingly.

So in July the Committee sent to Lord Essex a well thought out scheme, estimating £400 as necessary to complete and furnish; £600 to pay the builders, and for annual maintenance of three hundred and fifty inmates, an endowment of £2,795 a year. For the £1,000 cash they proposed that an immediate grant should be made by the Treasury, and for the annual revenue a perpetual charge on the excise of ale, beer and strong waters, and the hearth money of the city, and they reiterate the claim given them by Lord Ossory's first letter and the Charter granted by the sovereign himself.

But pending these treaties they determined to open the Hospital, whether endowed or not. They were without funds, and knew that to fill it was out of the question, so resolving to begin with not more than eighty inmates, they sent circulars to each of the eleven parishes, and each of the City Guilds, requesting each to furnish the names of three boys not under six years, and not sickly or maimed, and to provide three pounds ten yearly for maintenance of each child, promising that any benefactors securing this should have the status of First Founders and be so recorded. At the same time they posted the Exchange and all the City Gates with printed offers of leases of our six lots in the two Greens, and they sent out a strong deputation to perambulate the City begging for bounty, and to remove all objections and doubts that might be made. Dr. Wettenhall having now become a church dignitary, the Governors appointed as our first *de facto* chaplain, the Reverend Lewis Prythirch, nominated by Archbishop Boyle at a salary of ten pounds a year with diet and lodging, Mr. Thomas Howard, as agent, at £20 yearly, Dr. Ralph Howard, as Physician, Mrs. Williams, Schoolmistress, to teach the children to read, £6 a year with her keep, a steward, butler, messenger and porter, a governess, Mrs. Leech, an aged matron, to oversee the nurses and servants, two nurses, each with charge of thirty children, and "two drudges" to wash and scour, at the election of the Governors, who it is to be hoped elected.

This original staff reads modestly enough, so shortly after that court at Whitehall with the King in the chair and Prince Rupert, and the Dukes, and the Earls, and Chancellor of the Exchequer, and great Ministers of State, but even Oxford and Eton had modest beginnings.

On 27 April it was reported to the Assembly that the chapel and ground over the water, commonly called the King's Hospital, was fitted and prepared for consecration, and thereupon a deed of donation was duly executed and ordered to be presented to his Grace, Michael Boyle, Archbishop of Dublin. He was great-nephew of Richard the first, and called the great, Earl of Cork. He was raised to the Primacy in 1678.

The Hospital occupied 170 feet in length, fronting the west side of the present Queen Street, covering the space from the present No. 69 and thence running north over most of the broad roadway of the present Blackhall Street, thence it stretched back with its gardens in a parallelogram 300 feet in depth. It was built on the original lots 87 and 88 Oxmantown Green, which had been reserved for a Free School in the original allotment, and No. 90, Sir William Davys' lot, which he had made over as his subscription in 1669, and which is now part of the thoroughfare of Blackhall Street, but to these a large space from the Green had been added by the City for gardens and cartilage. There was a chapel at the south end with a single rounded window to the street and an infirmary on the north side, and between these ran the front facade, a long structure of two stories with six pigeon-house windows in the slanted roof of the upper one, three at each side of a wooden cupola surmounting the vestibule which projected across the narrow courtyard between the building and the street, from which it was fenced by a high wall with a good entrance gate in front of the vestibule and hall door.

And so at last on 5 MAY, 1675, just twenty-three days less than six years from the turning of the first sod, our Hospital was opened, sixty children being admitted, of whom three were girls. We append the table of the names of these, our FIRST PUPILS, with their nominators, thus helping to fulfil the promise that the benefactors should be chronicled as amongst our First Founders.

BLEW COAT BOYS HOSPITAL.

Original School, as completed 1675.

[To face page 70.

CHILDREN SENT INTO THE HOSPITAL BY Yᴇ SEVERALL BENEFACTʀs HEREAFTER NAMED.

Benefactoas' Names.	Names of the Children
Sr. ffra: Brewster, Kt., L.Ma.	John Rames John Goddin
City of Dublin	Barthol. Davis Wm. Arnill Charles Swetman George Orr
Trinity Guild of Merchts.	David King Jeremy Woodall
Corporation of Cordwainers	Bery. Edsol
Corporation of Coopers	Wm. Williams Peter Dillon
Parish of St. Michan's	Charles Camponsky Allex Williams
St. Werburgh's Parish	James Saunders
St. Michael's Parish	Robt. ffarr
St. John's Parish	Robt. Shelton Wm. Stranger
St. Kath. & St. Paul's	Robert Paton
St. Andrewe's Parish	Christr. & James Mortimer
Mr. Giles Martin	Thomas Smith Henry Chennel Edward Williams Daniel Lee Thomas Williams Joseph Gough
Dame Brewster	Mary Archbould
Samll. Mollinous, Esq.	Richd. Kennedy
Dame Jane Stanley	Edmond Brookes Jonath: Whitnoll Ambrose Johnson Markt Elligton

Benefactors Names.	Names of the Children.
Robt. Shapcote, Esq.	James Rames
Ald. Danl. Hutchinson	{ Thomas Sprinkle { John Barker
Ald. Enoch Reader	{ John Bennett { Richard Carey
Ald. Rich. Hanway	Thomas Banks
Mrs. Mary Tighe	{ John Toy { Thomas Burgis
Mrs. Parry, wife of Dr. Ben. Parry	Joseph Tunn
Mr. Abel Ram	John Hutchinson
Mr. Richard Lord	John Shorr
Mr. Richard Young	Christr. Harris
Mr. John North	Alexandr ffusland
Mr. Thomas ffrancis	Thomas Purtill
Mr. Robt. Brady	John Ogilvy
Mr. Richd. Baker	Osborne Kitteringham
Mr. Piriam Poole	John Cooper
Mrs. Joyce Seile	Anthony Gaghagan
Sr. Joshua Allan	Hugh Ward
Ald. John Preston	John Harris
Ld. Bishop of Ossory	Thomas Hunt
Sr John Torey, Knt. Ld. Chief Justice of the King's Bench	Henry & ffolliott John
Mr. George Warburton	Charles Jenkins
Mr. Wm. Bragg	Grace Tunn
Ld. Bp. of Ossory, his lady	Mary Running
Hewit, one of the boys	John Hewett
Walter Harris	Michll ffennel

CHAPTER IV.

FROM THE OPENING OF THE SCHOOL TO THE END OF CHARLES II.'S REIGN.

WHEN the School opened, the Lord Mayor, Sir Francis Brewster, was our chairman. He had been one of the Evicted Eight. The work of the Governors in the early years was of immense difficulty. None of them were educationists—expert educationists were unknown then. Crippled as to means, with some seventy children in a great building, four of them little girls, most of them of tender years and more fitted for the care of nurses than of schoolmasters, and yet including older boys, for in 1676 we find a boy admitted aged fifteen, classification, generally difficult, was then impossible. The essay of their 'prentice hands may merit a note. The Board, then consisting chiefly of business men, began by directing that the training should be industrial, and to fit the children for trades, so they were all to be taught the making of shoes, knitting stockings, and spinning, and materials for this end were procured accordingly. The teaching of knitting was entrusted to the nurses, to whom the order humanely allows "a drudge" to ease their housemaids' duties. Six hours are allotted for handwork and four for lessons. This scheme, as might be foretold, broke down in a few months; the order was rescinded in October, the shoemaker and spinner were discharged, and the chaplain Prytherch directed to instruct, assisted by a female teacher. Then it was found that the number of Sub-Governors, being more than one hundred, as constituted by the Assembly in 1674, was quite unwieldy, and the Corporation were petitioned to modify the order, which they did in July, 1675,[1] and ordained

---

[1] Gilbert's *Calendar*, 5, 78.

that henceforth the Lord Mayor, Sheriffs, Aldermen, and Sheriffs' Peers, with such other Sub-Governors as they might think fit, should constitute the Board. The quorum was to be seven, of whom the Lord Mayor and one Sheriff were to be always two. This clause was more than once the cause of trouble and controversy in after years, for no lawful meeting could be held in the Lord Mayor's absence, as he was the necessary chairman so long as this order stood, but it had the salutary effect of identifying the School with the government of the city for a century and three-quarters afterwards.

But instead of committing instruction and the control of the house to the chaplain and headmaster Prytherch, allowing him to select the necessary staff, the Board limited his teaching functions, and themselves appointed the assistant masters, the officers, nurses, and servants, all at the wretched salaries and wages to which their own meagre income confined them; but boards even now are apt to love patronage and to retain functions which they cannot adequately discharge. Thus James Rigby was appointed to teach writing and arithmetic to the whole school daily, attending from 7 to 11 a.m., and from 1 to 5 in the afternoon, at a salary of £5 a year " till the revenue of the Hospital be greater," along with his lodging and diet. He taught from the opening of the School for two whole years, so we can read without surprise the entry in 1677 that poor Rigby's post "is void by his confinement in the Blackdog," the diabolical debtors' prison by the old Newgate in High Street, whose horrors are detailed in Gilbert's *History of Dublin*. Thereupon Miles Bateman took his place on the same terms, but he only lasted five months, when we find him " removed," and replaced by Robert Ingram in November—his tenure was even less than Bateman's. In March, 1678, he, too, is " removed," and John Carrington placed in his stead, who held on for eight months. It took more than a century since to teach us that teachers are not the menials of mankind. At last, in November, 1678, the Governors were fortunate to find an admirable master in English and Mathematics, who remained in the School for thirty-two years, and was largely instrumental in its successful development. This was James Mead. Similarly we find three successive stewards in the first three years. The Governors had separated this office from that of the agent, Thomas Moland, appointing John Tear at £12 a year, yet, they entrusted him first with all the supplies to the Hospital and tradesmen's accounts, and then, in addition, with complete control over the children, who are subjected to his moral discipline in all things, so, in June, 1677, we have an inquiry of the Governors, who find that he has improvidently managed the trust reposed in him, and he is discharged. Allen, succeeding him on like conditions, holds on for less than a year, and then resigns, and in April, 1678, Wetherall is appointed, the Governors now seeing the expediency of giving him a salary of £16 with maintenance in the house for himself and wife. Yet, though he continued for four years, there is "a full hearing" of the Governors in 1682, on divers matters laid to his charge, and he is found to be a person not fit to be any longer continued in the employment. Perhaps that *wife* had something to do with his downfall, for the dismissal order goes on to command that Mrs. Hollins, "and all other women in the Hospital that are no way useful to the house have notice forthwith to depart." Eve caused Adam's eviction from Eden.

An entry of July, 1675, gives a glimpse of the quaint old city streets. Casting about for revenue everywhere, the Governors resorted to an Act of Assembly of the year before, which empowered the Lord Mayor and Corporation to treat with the "encroachers," as they were called, who lined the streets and down to the river with stalls, porches, stands and chairs, and stating that nothing had yet been done, they asked the Assembly to place these trespassers under rents, these to be applied for the first seven years to the School, and then to revert to the City estate.[2] And this was acceded to. These encroachments continued for two centuries more or less, and a few years since were made subjects of prosecution

[2] Gilbert's *Calendar*, 5, 71, 76.

before our City Magistrates. Booths and tents blocking the footwalks, fruit stalls obstructing carriage ways too. Most of these were swept away; the orange women that sat round the semicircle fronting Trinity College, and at each side of Carlisle or O'Connell Bridge, survived to late in the Victorian age, till trampled out by the march of a ruthless civilization; yet, our entry shows some colour of a legal origin which might have saved some if our entry had been made known to the justices who suppressed them.

Whilst awaiting aid from the Crown, the City resorted to another device, which would sound strangely in the King's Bench to-day.[3] A former Act of Assembly had imposed a tax upon all brewers and other owners of drays and carts having iron bound wheels, of ten shillings per cart, to be paid towards repair of the city pavements, but at the January Assembly, 1676, they ordered "as a great help to the King's Hospital," that in lieu of this tax every such brewer and owner should deliver to the Steward of the Hospital, "a barrell of table beer for each carre, and two barrells for each dray, yearly." What would the auditor and the temperance associations think of this?

Three months after the School opened, William Smith became Lord Mayor, and our chairman for 1675-6. He was an original Founder and favourite Governor for nine years. He was the Whittington of Dublin, and his unique career, during which he was Chief Magistrate in eight several years, casts a strange, yet vivid sidelight on our City in the agony of the Civil Wars.

The Whittington of Dublin.

Shortly since, our present estimable Chaplain and Headmaster, Rev Mr. Richards, exploring a stratum of forgotten records, came on a slab below, seemingly of stone, grey and oxidised, 18 inches by 12, but the weight of which, when handled, proved it to be of metal, and the face, when

[1] Minute Book, Gilbert's *Calendar*, 5, 94.

burnished, disclosed a fine brass thus inscribed, clear as when it left the hand of the graver :

NEERE THIS PLACE
WAS BURIED THE BODY
OF WILLIAM SMITH, ESQ., AN
ALDERMAN OF THE CITY OF
DUBLIN IN IRELAND AND WHO
WAS SEVEN SEVERALL
YEARES MAYOR (AND LORD MAYOR THE YEARE 1675) OF THAT CITY
HE DIED THE 31ST
DAY OF OCTOBER
ANNO DOMINI 1684
AETAT SUÆ 82.
25 OF JULY 1684.

This Brass was presumably taken from the wall of our original chapel, when ruinous and forgotten, into the new building a century after his death. The inscription is surmounted with his arms : On a bend dexter three lozenges between two Unicorns' heads with the City Arms in the dexter angle. The crest is a Unicorn's head on a ducal crown, and the motto *Deus liberabit*. The graving, black on brass, does not indicate the blazonry, but the family arms seem almost identical with those of the Cusack-Smiths, one of whom was so long the Master of the Rolls in Ireland some 40 years ago, shewing the unicorns azure armed or, on a field of argent.

This epitaph is simple, but between its lines we can read in the whole story of the Dublin of the times as if it were a cypher.

William Smith, at thirty-four, was elected sheriff of Dublin, 1636, when Wentworth was at the zenith of his reign, and he took part in some of the great viceroy's civic reforms. The next year he was made one of the Masters of the City Works, and in that following was one of the aldermen in whom then was vested almost the entire civic power. After Strafford was flung to the wolves of the factions, that beset him from opposite sides, the Irish rebellion burst forth in autumn, 1641. Almost connived at by Parsons, the Lord Justice, and creature of the refractory Parliament, who used it to promote the Covenant, to discredit the King and to create forfeitures, in the course of the winter it had flooded all the land. When Ormonde's victory at Kilrush, and the raising of the Siege of Drogheda, had extorted the praise of Parliament, and he became Marquess, Knight of the Garter and Commander of the King's forces, Alderman Smith was made Mayor at Michaelmas, 1642; the senior alderman, Kennedy, had, according to usage, been elected at the spring Assembly, but in the agony of the rebellion, the city, moneyless, in danger and dismay, crowded with half-starved fugitives, its revenues unpaid, could scarce find a candidate who could accept the chief magistracy. In his first year Parsons was still Lord Justice, and Lambert, Lord Cavan, who commanded the Government forces in the city, assumed the civic government also, but Smith withstood him to the face, and the Corporation, under his leadership, maintained their charter rights before the Privy Council. Lambert then claimed from the Council to undertake alone the city defences, with power to enforce the labour of the citizens, unless the Mayor and City would guarantee the duty at their own sole charges. The Council referred this to the Assembly, who, despite their penury, boldly undertook to construct the defences by the citizens in batches, with right to call the aid of the army to distrain defaulters "freed," as they said, "from the extreme pressure of levying the defaults by authority from the Lord Lambert."

At the spring Assembly, 1643, Carbery, the senior alderman, was elected Mayor, but the penury continued. The £200 then voted by usage to the Mayor was still unpaid to Smith, as was that voted to his predecessor in 1642, so that at the Michaelmas Assembly, Smith remained in office for his second year. Parsons had now been removed from the Government, and Ormonde became Lord Lieutenant in January, 1644. "In the extremity and dearth people were then dying of hunger, to the great grief of the Corporation," and Smith was put at the head of a Commission "to send away such as the town are not able to relieve, and to take a course for the relief of the native Poore." He was now senior alderman, and at the Spring Assembly was duly elected Mayor " for his own term according to the law of succession " from Michaelmas, 1644-1645. During Ormonde's armistice with the Confederate Catholics there was less confusion in Dublin, but the reigning dearth may be seen in such facts as that the great Lord Lieutenant, who, being refused a guinea from the Parliament, had mortgaged his own estates, was forced to borrow £184 from the City, an asset which had fallen to them by a chance. One Delaporte, had slain a brother merchant, Panckart, and fled. The City Sheriffs seized his goods as forfeited by the felony, and realised £184 8s. by their sale, which went to the credit of the City, and even of these assets, one part consisted of City plate, pledged to Delaporte by Wakefield when Mayor in the year before Smith's first election. And in this his third year, of the three £200 voted him by the City, £472 was unpaid, for which the city could only give him a lease of their lands in Baldoyle, the rent of which he was to retain for the debt, yet, even this, too, was conditional, on their evicting the tenant, one Fitzsimons, who held possession *more Hibernico*. In Spring, 1645, Watson, senior alderman in rotation, was elected Mayor, but, he being also unable to take office, Smith was again continued at Michaelmas, for his fourth year.

In this he had a conflict with Lord Brabazon, whose father, the Earl of Meath, had, in the previous reign, unsuccessfully claimed exemption from all civic authority within his Liberties of S. Thomas and Donore. In those curfew days the keys of the City gates were kept by the Mayor from sunset to morning. Lord Brabazon at midnight demanding the key of the West gate that led to his manor, could not get it, so he smashed the windows and doors of Smith's Mayoralty house. The City ordered prosecution in the Exchequer, and petitioned the Lord Lieutenant for redress. The citizens were not then bound to insure against malicious injuries out of the City rates.

But in summer, 1645, the Royal cause was borne down at Naseby, and Ormonde heroically holding out for his master, could now only hope by a treaty with the Confederate

Catholics to raise an army to combine with Montrose, his compeer Marquess, in Scotland, and for this he struggled two long years. Herein he was thwarted by Rinnucini, the Pope's Nuncio, who, dreaming of a Catholic Conquest, inspired Owen Roe O'Neill to attack the Parliamentary army, which he destroyed at Benburb in June, 1646, and then urged him on for the capture of Dublin. O'Neill beleaguered the City in the autumn with 18,000 wild Irish. Ormonde was with his army in Meath. Under him Smith was the commander of all the City forces, for which he nominated all the Captains of companies. Ormonde gave orders that all the citizens, of every rank and sex, over fifteen years old, should work at least one day in each week till the defences were complete. His own noble wife (she was his cousin, the Lady Elizabeth Preston), led the defenders with ladies of the first quality, who, with their own fair hands, carried baskets of earth to repair the fortifications.[4] The Marquess, like Wellington, at Torres Vedras, had ordered the country round Dublin to be denuded, and on the report of succour from England, the Irish, unfed, withdrew, dissolving as a storm cloud. No Assembly that year could be held at Michaelmas. At Easter, Lake, senior alderman, was elected Mayor, but Smith was continued to January, 1647, when he was again elected for the fifth time to hold to Michaelmas following.

But the Royal cause was now lost. His treaty, denounced at once by the victorious Parliament, and by the Nuncio, Ormonde was forced to the choice of to which he should abandon Dublin. He chose the former. His intention being rumoured in the city, Smith came to the Privy Council, and boldly told the Marquess who presided, that he, as Mayor, was entrusted with the King's sword of this city, and that he would not resign it to the rebels. Ormonde obliged to seem offended, ordered him to withdraw, but after some conference, the Council called him in again, and the Lord Lieutenant graciously commended him for his resolution to maintain his Majesty's authority. Then he personally read

[4] Gilbert's *Calendar*, xix, iii.

to him the King's letter, requiring his Lord Lieutenant to deliver up the sword to the Commissioners of Parliament, and then the brave Mayor reluctantly acquiesed. It was no ignoble ending of his five years magistracy, covering all the unparalleled period of the King's struggle and of Ormonde's first ascendancy. In the twelve years of Cromwellian supremacy which succeeded, Smith did not time-serve the new regime, as many old Royalists did, but he earnestly discharged his aldermanic duties, serving as city auditor in seven, and as city treasurer in four, successive years, and he acted as a leading member on all the important city committees, on those for preserving the revenues and rents, lost, some for ever, in the prevailing confusions, on those for dealing with the prevalent destitution, on that for securing from the Parliamentary Commissioners repayment of the loans forced from the city to support the Cromwellian army. But when the army had declared for a free Parliament and then for recall of the King, the City Assembly in May, 1660, reciting that the city had always been firm and faithful to the English interest and very instrumental in defending itself against the Irish rebels, resolved that two aldermen be employed into England to attend his Majesty, "and to manifest the city's detestation of his father's murther, and their joy in his happy access to his royal father's crown and regiment of his native kingdom." Alderman Smith was the first of the two delegates named. With them are associated Sir Maurice Eustace, Lord Chancellor, and £450 was voted by the city to support their embassy.

In 1662 Ormonde came back Duke and Lord Lieutenant. At the Spring Assembly of 1663, Cooke had been elected Mayor, but the summer meeting resolved that "being sensible of the very great confusion of the years past, they deemed it necessary that an able, loyal, well-experienced person should be chosen, and one well known to the present Governor of this Kingdom." And "finding that the Duke of Ormonde and Council have a desire that Alderman William Smith should undertake the Mayoralty for the ensuing year," he was elected, for the sixth time, to hold to

Michaelmas, 1664. Alderman Cooke was permitted to resign, but as he did so to meet the wishes of the Duke, he was given standing as if he had served, and his expenses in preparing for office, Smith being granted £400 to maintain his dignity. During this, his sixth Mayoralty, he was chairman of the committee which made the allotments and enclosure of the great city common of St. Stephen's Green, and of that appointed to conduct the petition to the Duke and to the King for royal grants in aid of the distressed finances of the city which bore fruit next year. At the Spring Assembly, Sir Daniel Bellingham was elected Mayor, but praying to be excused, Smith was yet again continued at Michaelmas, to hold for his seventh Mayoralty to Michaelmas, 1665.

In this year Ormonde presented the weighty petition to the King which evoked a most gracious reply from Whitehall, acknowledging the eminent merits and services of the city to his father and to himself at the restoration, and contemplating the great poverty to which the city was reduced by loyalty, Charles announces "his royal judgment to confer such favours as may deliver to posterity for their honour the gracious sense we have of their services, merits, and sufferings." These consisted of a grant of the ferries of the Liffey so valuable then when there was only one main bridge, and a perpetual grant of £500 a year to the Mayor, to be paid from the Civic list, he further forgives the crown rents then due and reduces them permanently to £20 a year.

One of Smith's last official acts this year was to read the city petition to the crown against the merchants of London, who, with banal selfishness, were seeking power from the King to ban Dublin and Ireland from its trade with the Canaries, whither the petition states Ireland was then sending feeding commodities of the best vend, for which a fleet was then freighted by the city merchants. Bellingham was now obliged to take the Mayoralty; but in the last days of the tenure, Smith had a letter from the Duke referring to a charter of Charles I. in 1641, which had not been acted on by which the title of Lord Mayor had been conferred on the

Chief Magistrate. The Assembly before which Smith laid it, resolved that this would be for the honour and good of the city, and so Sir Daniel Bellingham and not Smith became first Lord Mayor of Dublin, yet these two years of office were not without honour, for in these he wore the Cap of Maintenance and the splendid collar of S.S. which Charles had sent the city immediately on his restoration, and he was colonel of the first city regiment of foot.

It might now be though his civic life had ended, especially as the odious intrigues of the Cabal ministry shortly after effected the recall, and brought about the political fall of of his great patron, Ormonde.

Nevertheless after the Cabal had been broken, and Lord Berkeley, its representative in the Irish Government removed, and Essex sent as viceroy to restore order in Dublin, Smith once again was summoned to the civic chair, just ten years after he had last left it. If he heard the bells of Christ Church chiming. "Turn again, William Smith, Lord Mayor of Dublin," it was not to come back as a turncoat, but to complete his career of loyalty, consistancy and good faith. He was now old and impoverished; his rent to our Hospital for his own allotments in Stephen's Green was in arrear ten years, and for this he could only assign his allotment in Oxmantown as portion of the site of our original edifice, yet he managed to contribute £20 to the building fund, but his unparalleled career, as he opened for the first time, the assembled school in 1675, is a contribution to our annals richer than a large pecuniary subscription. Born in 1602, his life links our story with the spacious days of great Elizabeth. He was one of our most deligent governors, presiding at all the eleven meetings of his Mayoralty, and he ended his days with us the only intern governor we have ever had, for now poor and old the Board in 1679, directed that he should have such lodgings in the Hospital as he shall make choice of in the upper story of the south isle, he to undertake the government of the house and trouble of keeping the children in order. And so he ruled to his death in 1684, a little before our founder, King Charles.

In 1675 the Hospital acquired what proved to be its richest single endowment, the fee simple of the lands of Nodstown, in the parish of Ardmayle, and barony of Nethercross, County Tipperary, situate near Cashel, adjoining the Suir, and then including more than eight hundred acres chiefly of prime land. This gift to the Hospital was the outcome of a domestic romance, in which the female element, of course, prevails. Mr. Gyles Martyn had acquired this estate a few years before from one John Upton, who held under patent from the Crown, and thus becoming a landed proprietor, was anxious to transmit it to his heirs. But Mrs. Martyn was childless. She had a sister, however, who was not so, and when the next confinement was expected, Mrs. Martyn, in league with her, feigned pregnancy, and in due time, presented her sister's babe to her husband, Gyles, as his veritable son and heir, to the supposed father's delight.[5] And thus Nodstown would have gone to this child, but that the lady conspirators quarrelled, and the angry sister disclosed the truth to Martyn. In rage and disgust, he went to his lawyers, and thereupon executed a deed, granting the whole estate, in trust, for King's Hospital. Mrs. Gyles Martyn shortly after died, childless, and the widower marrying again, had a numerous family, some of whom vainly endeavoured to recover the estate. The grant to the Hospital reserved to the Martyn family the nomination of six boys to the school perpetually. Martyn's son, many years after, petitioned the Corporation for some redress, as the family had sunk into poverty in the revolutionary troubles of James II. The rents of Nodstown were then small, but the Corporation voted him an annuity of twenty pounds a year, and after his death, on a petition of his mother, Gyles Martyn's widow, in 1702, asking a grant in lieu of the nomination of boys, the Assembly granted her thirty pounds on those conditions; but it is satisfactory to find that nominations by the Martyn family were always honoured afterwards, so long as they were sought for. The action taken by the city, in this Martyn case, was by the

[5] Whitelaw's *History of Dublin* by Walsh, Vol. I., 573.

Corporation itself, and not by the Governors, and illustrates the union between school and city in this period.

Through all the changes and chances of Irish land tenure. Nodstown has remained with us, its present rental is over £400 a year. The rise and fall of its rents and land value in all this time has reflected the varying economic and political conditions of the country, and the estate has afforded striking examples of the mismanagement to which lands are often exposed when the owners are corporate bodies, obliged to depend entirely on their agents, and living at a long distance, for, till the railway times, it was as far a cry from Dublin to Cashel, as now from Dublin to Canada. The acreage under the crown patent was 888. Of these two-thirds were superior land, the residue adjoining the Suir was swampy and then unprofitable. When granted to the Hospital it was under a long lease to one, Leary, at a rent of less than £100. In 1724 this lease was renewed by the governors, the acreage stated been 607 only; the figures are over an erasure, and the map to which it refers, has been abstracted, so that it is hard to escape suspicion of some foul play, though, perhaps, the tenant may have insisted on excluding the unprofitable acres; that would not, however, have conferred those acres on him, and a nearly contemporaneous entry gives the contents as 703. This confusion was made the subject of adverse comment before the Commission on Educational Endowments in 1856, when Mr. Mallet, then an eminent citizen and active governor, indignantly complained of the neglect by which a large part of that valuable estate had been lost. He described his personal visit to Nodstown, where he found a deep trench severing the river side portion from the rent paying land. This portion had then been reclaimed, and was in the ownership of the brilliant Irish parliamentary orator, Richard Lalor Sheil, and the title under the Statute of Limitations could not be assailed; though had steps been taken in due time, the tenant could have been debarred from any claim founded on encroachment on the adjoining waste lands of his landlord. We have not, however, great reason to lament, for as shewn in a subsequent page, this estate became immensely enhanced in the latter years of the eighteenth century.

The old Duke of Ormonde had, in 1677, been reinstated as Lord Lieutenant. He was to the end the constant friend of the Hospital. For seven successive years he had contributed £100 towards its maintenance. In 1676, whilst he was still in London, Sir John Temple, then Solicitor-General in Ireland, wrote to the Lord Mayor, his old protege, William Smith, that at the instance of the Duke, His Majesty the King, had consented to provide a yearly endowment for the School, to which, Smith replying with the grateful thanks of the Corporation, asks His Excellency to secure that the grant may be placed on the Civil List.[6] That, however, was overcharged by the poor King now, and it was nearly two years after that Ormonde obtained in the Privy Council the following Order, which places the Hospital in relation to the Church and State, on the level of the great cathedral which Sir Christopher Wren was then erecting, and which has proved a large source of revenue for some generations; it is here set out in full [7] :—

By the Lord Lieutenant and Councell.

Ormonde. Whereas, we, the Lord Lieutenant, are given to understand that his Majestie, taking notice of the great expenses the Bishops of England are now usually at in making of Feasts at their Consecrations, did think fitt that the making thereof for the future should be forborne, and that the Bishops at their Consecrations, should, in lieu thereof respectively pay fifty pounds towards the building of the Cathedral Church of St. Paul. And, whereas, it is observed that the Archbishop and Bishops in this kingdome, doe, usually upon their respective Consecrations, make great Feasts. Now, we, the Lord Lieutenant and Councell in imitation of what is done in England, as aforesd., do think fitt hereby to recommend it to such Archbishops and Bishops as hereafter shall be consecrated, that they forbear putting themselves to any expense for a Feast upon their Consecrations, but that, in lieu thereof, they will pay to the governors of the King's Hospital, lately built, near the Citty of Dublin,

[6] Minute Book, p. 76.   [7] Minute Book of King's Hospital

the sum of thirty pounds for the use of the said Hospitall which we look upon to be a most commendable act and less chargeable to the said Archbishops and Bishops than the ffeasts. Given at the Councell Chamber, Dublin, the 7th day of March, 1678-9.

> Mich., Armagh. John, Dublin. Arran, Hen. Midensis, Robt. Fitzgerald, Carey Dillon, Chas. Meredyth, Jno. Bysse, Jo. Davys. Ol. St. George, Jo. Cole, Richd. Gething, Theo. Jones, Wm. Fflower.

We had good friends on the Council who gave this boon, the Primate Boyle, Lord Chancellor, already a benefactor, John, Dublin, is Dr. John Parker, just appointed Archbishop, in his stead a benefactor too, Earl of Arran, is Richard, brother of Ossory, and who was now Lord Deputy in his father, Ormonde's, absence shortly after. Chief Baron Bysse was one of our founders, Davys was Secretary of State, a brother of our Recorder, now Chief Justice; Sir Charles Meredyth had negociated the affair at Whitehall, Carey Dillon was uncle of the poet, Lord Roscommon, whom he succeeded as fifth Earl, and was our neighbour in Oxmantown.

This Order had no actual legal sanction, but the word of the Privy Council was law in those days, and the practical sanction was that all future bishops were appointed by the crown on the faith of it. Though the aggregate of the payments made under it is very large as the then great number of bishoprics led to continuous promotions and vacancies, many bishops from time to time without daring to repudiate the obligation, kept the governors dunning them for years, and once or twice compelled them to apply to Government for a renewal of the ordinance, but the majority paid with alacrity. The second sum ever paid was by our friend Dr. Wettenhall on his consecration to the See of Cork.

In 1677 the governors obtained under the will of Mr. Ratcliff, the lay impropriator of the tithes of Mullingar, the valuable gift of the rectorial tithes in fee simple, our entry states they were estimated at £100 per annum. Through all the changes in Church Law since, this gift has remained to us, in part, at least, to the present, for the rights of the lay tithe owners were preserved by the Disestablishment Act of 1869. The usage then was to farm out the tithes for terms of years at rents to lessees who collected the tithes from the land occupiers, and our records for a century and half are replete with entries showing how those rents varied with the conditions of the country from time to time. The lay impropriators held under the same obligation to the parishes which had bound the ecclesiastical bodies and monasteries who had first appropriated the parochial tithes before Henry VIII. captured and distributed them at pleasure to laymen. The obligation was originally to provide for the cure of souls, but this was often compounded for by a fixed sum or *modus* to maintain the fabric of the chancel of the Church. This later charge was imposed on our governors frequently. In 1682 the Board have a missive from Arthur, second Viscount Granard, stating that the chancel of Mullingar is very much out of repair, and asking them to arrange with his father-in-law, Sir George Rawdon. Accordingly, the Lord Mayor, Sir Humphrey Jervis, thereupon agreed with Sir George that £20 in full should be paid over to the Bishop of Meath to cover the repairs. This Lord Granard was a distinguished soldier, he commanded the 18th Old Royal Irish, and served under Turenne, but proving a Jacobite, was dismissed by William III. Sir George Rawdon was ancestor of the Earl of Moira and Marquises of Hastings. The Bishop of Meath was the famous Anthony Dopping who became an historical personage afterwards.

The division of functions of Chaplain and Master broke down, and in the end of 1680 Mr. Prytherck's chaplaincy ceased. The Rev. Benjamin Colquitt was appointed under a very strict order, which is noticeable as showing the purely denominational character of the foundation, and because its enforcement often caused trouble, notably when Dean Swift compelled its observance in 1731. The chaplain and headmaster is carefully to instruct the boys in English and Latin, and every morning read Divine Service at 10 o'clock, and at 4 o'clock in summer, and 5 o'clock in winter in the

Hospital Chapel; he shall carefully instruct them in the catechism of the Church of England, and examine them publicly thereon every Sunday after evening prayer, also in the chapel, and shall preach in the chapel at least once each month, he shall constantly reside in the Hospital and bring therein neither wife or child, but may choose one or two of the children to attend him in his chamber. For this his salary is £40 a year with full maintenance, and he is to have James Mead as his usher in teaching.[8]

It is curious to find Latin in the curriculum of such a School, but the old Free School had trained great scholars. The governors had, however, early and wisely resolved that none be put to learn the Latin tongue " but such pregnant youths as they shall from time to time approve, and not before they can first write and cast accounts very well. Luke Lowther was Lord Mayor and our chairman when this order passed. He seems to have been a disciplinarian, for at the time, he ordered that one alderman and a sheriff's peer should attend him every week to see that the children had a due proportion of victuals, and to inspect the steward's account's; and he issued a curfew order for locking all gates and wickets at given hours, eight, nine and ten o'clock, according to the time of year, the steward to keep the keys all night, and bells to ring a quarter before each, curfew hour. And Sir Humphrey Jervis, his successor, followed his steps with an order which illumines the then state of discipline, " that Mrs. Hollins and Mrs. Draper, widows, with their children and servants, and all belonging to them, do depart the house, and that such of the Nurses and other the servants that are married, be forthwith removed, and no servant for the future be entertained but who are single, and that this house be not encumbered with any that shall not be useful and serviceable to it, and that all such in the Hospital as have a key for the street door do bring in said key to my Lord Mayor, and no one else to have one save porter all day, and steward at night.

[8] Minute Book, p 90, 20 March, 1681, 21 February, 1686.

Essex Bridge.

Jervis was chairman for two years, being chosen Lord Mayor for 1682 and 1683 an original founding governor, he so remained for thirty-six years, to his death in Queen Anne's reign. A large ship-owner and merchant, he amassed a fortune, and founded a family. Though one of the chief city magnates, he was for years embroiled with his colleagues, but he was one of the makers of Dublin, and this with his high services on our Board, may excuse the following esipode, especially as it has not been, we believe, told in detail before. He was *Pontifex Maximus* here, for after the centuries in which the Liffey was crossed by a single bridge, he built two, Essex or Grattan, and Ormonde, now known as the Four Courts bridge, by which alone the city was able to spread over the prairies of Mary's Abbey and wastes of Oxmantown. Keen as was the need, these bridges were no project of the civic authorities, erected rather in spite of their fierce opposition, for they were mainly interested in the house property within the walls now enhanced by the very need of expansion, and they eyed with sore jealousy the opening of the north side. The quarrel lasted twenty years after the bridges were up, in the course of which Jervis was imprisoned, and, if he is to be believed, half ruined, with the martyrdom which often befalls reformers. The story has some comic features, for it would seem that though he posed as a philanthropist, Jervis's motives were quite as personal as those of the monopolists he opposed, and it throws humourous light and shade on the doings of those days. The merits are somewhat obscure as the records of the Privy Council were lost by the fire in the Bermingham Tower in 1711, but they may be fairly judged by a comparison of the Case presented to the Irish Commons in 1695, with the Answer of the city and the decision of the house.

Sir Humphrey petitioned Parliament in August, 1695, setting forth his doings and praying pecuniary relief. The claim was afterwards embodied in his "Case," which tells how, in 1675, Lord Lieutenant Essex made order for building Essex Bridge, and assigned a fund for same, appointing five overseers, of whom Sir Humphrey was one, all of whom, save he, began to make excuses, whereupon His Excellency " Deeming the work necessary for the Public Government," persuaded him to assume the duty alone, and encouraged him with a donation of £100, promising to find money for the completion.

Lord Essex is thus the founder and true eponymus of the bridge. Henry Grattan and the Grattan's had never anything to do with it.

He proceeded, he tells, with all imaginable diligence, but Lord Essex unhappily went away before the work was half done. Ormonde came back in 1677, and Sir Humphrey petitioned his Grace in Council for means to complete. He had, he says, only a verbal reply that there was little money in the Treasury, but if he proceeded, he would be honourably dealt with. On completing the bridge in 1678, his accounts were passed in the Privy Council, who reported his expenses in excess of his receipts as £1,407, which he had had to borrow, paying interest ever since, he repeatedly asksd payment from Government, but never could get any satisfactory answer.

He tells how, at this time, the north bank was laid out in lots for projected streets, and that the Duke learning that the plans showed the reres of the houses and warehouses facing the river without any quay, the Council appointed Sir John Cole, Sir George Rawdon, and Sir Oliver St. George, baronets, to persuade him, Sir Humphrey, to front the houses to the river, " with a quay for the greater beauty and ornament of the city "; this, he told them, would cost him £1,000, but he would comply if recommended to the King for his balance. So he made the embankment which was named Ormonde Quay from the Duke, with the Market behind similarly named. Still he could get no satisfaction, though the convenience of the bridge, he says, is worth ten times the cost.

But his foes were not content with his being unpaid. The bridge had been formed with a drawbridge to allow the crafts to pass to and from the existing Wood and Merchant Quays, with two houses on the north bank for the keepers.

In 1684 the city magistrates, he says, egged on the masters of ships and gabbards to Petition the Privy Council against him for not having men, night and day, to raise the drawbridge, and the Lord Mayor and Corporation appeared to support the charge. His plea was that he had built the two houses on his own land, and for seven years had given them rent free to the bridge keepers, but when unable to obtain his balance, he thought himself entitled to take these houses to his own use. As, however, he had charged the cost of these to the bridge account, the Duke and Council, were, he says, "exasperated to that degree," that they ordered him forthwith to make over the houses by deed to the city. He offered to do this on condition that the drawbridge was changed to an arch, and that the houses should be restored to him, but the Council peremptorily ordered him to assign within forty days. His lawyer told him the decree was illegal (probably it was), so he petitioned the Council, assisted in this, he says, by Sir John Temple, the Master of the Rolls, this petition was rejected, and he was summoned again.

The Duke was now in England, and Boyle, now Lord Primate and also Lord Chancellor, sat at the hearing as Lord Justice, there was no prosecutor, but the despotic prelate bid him obey the former decree or answer at his peril. Then by the advice of counsel, he petitioned again, praying that the city should be left to prove their rights in a court of law, but, if we can believe him, the spirit of the Star Chamber was not yet dead. The new petition was held a contempt, and on 23 December, 1685, the pursuivant arrested him in bed, and lodged him in prison, and the primate refused him leave even to go to church on Christmas Day.

The results, he says, were disastrous. His city foes spread reports that he was broke; his credit was destroyed. He was a large owner of ships. One, the "Dublin," was then chartered for Lisbon to Bartholomew Van Homrigh (Vanessa's father). On the rumour of his ruin, John Hayes, the captain, absconded with the "Dublin" and her freight, with a total loss to Jervis of £2,200. Following suit, his factor in the "Virginias," ran away with £1,600 worth of tobacco. Then, Thomas Stretton, master of the "Catherine," ran away with her and a cargo of iron worth £500, whilst Stephen Simmons, her master, similarly abducted the "Mary," value £600; and his goods in places abroad, were seized by his creditors. Then losses like Antonio's in the *Merchant of Venice* "enough to press a royal merchant down," reached £7,000, a terrible disaster in those days.

Of Ormonde Bridge, the "Case" states, that the city grand jury presented a timber bridge from the upper end of Wood Quay, at Winetavern Street, to the upper end of the Pill, and assessed £400 on the city for this. Owing to the opposition, however, this assessment was respited, but Sir Humphrey persevered and built the bridge at his own expense of over £500. The enemy then thrice presented the bridge as a nuisance in the King's Bench, and would have pulled it down if the judges had not vacated the presentments. Then they combined not to pay the assessment, of which £20 only was ever raised. Sir Humphrey bluntly attributes this combination to Sir John Davis, then Secretary of State, whom he roundly charges with influencing his brother, Sir William, now Chief Justice, to refuse him justice on his appeal to the King's Bench. The motive assigned gives delightful point to the charge of corruption. Sir John, he says, joined the opposition, not because he was averse to the connection of south and north, but because he was himself negotiating to buy the new Ormonde Market, which he would get much cheaper in the agitation, and this was seen afterwards, for when Sir John's purchase was completed, he procured a new presentment in his brother's court for a stone bridge in lieu of the timber, with power to appropriate Sir Humphrey's displaced materials, and this was fiated by the court. This charge, however, needs higher proof than Jervis's assertion.

Sir Humphrey's "petition" came before a Committee of the Whole House of Commons in October, 1695. Their report was adopted, finding £1,407 partly due to Jervis for Essex, and £380 for Ormonde Bridge, and, allowing him ten year's interest, declared him entitled to £3,434 in all, to be raised by a tax of one shilling per ton on all coal entering Dublin, and they ordered the heads of a bill to be drawn accordingly for approval of the Privy Council in England.

But this bill, transmitted to London under Poyning's Law, was rejected by the Council, on the ground that it proposed to put a duty on the products of England.[9] Nothing is said of its imposing a duty on the consumers in Ireland. The proposal was, curiously, exactly that adopted by Sir M. Beach, when Chancellor of the Exchequer, as one of the aids for the South African War. The result, perhaps, shows that the veto under Poynings Act, was sometimes salutary.

So Sir Humphrey came to Parliament again in 1697, and a Special Committee reported in August that £3,434 was justly due, and that it was highly just and reasonable to take speedy steps for payment. But the city was now in arms : they claimed to be heard by counsel concerning Jervis's demand of a tax for building the bridges. This was conceded. His case was answered by " the Case of the city of Dublin," caustic and pungent with humour, conscious or not. It exposes the springs of Sir Humphrey's patriotism showing how, before the bridges were built, the sites of Ormond Quay and the New Market were wastes, the passage of the river being by ferries, yielding large rents to the city, when Sir Humphrey, with his partners, bought twenty acres of the wastes and laid them out in twenty-eight building lots, which, without bridges, they could turn to no account ; he then, say the city opponents, set himself, first to get the leave of the city, and then to provide a fund. This was a difficult matter for the river belonged to the city, and as the case naively adds, " the improvement of the north side would certainly, in a great measure, ruin the old city, whose inhabitants were always on their guard to discountenance and prevent it." The Grand Jury, indeed, presented for a bridge, but this, the city says, was because Alderman Peter

[9] See *Journal* of House of Commons.

Wybrants, the foreman of the jury, lived on the north side of the water. The next thing was to get the money, so first Jervis accosts his partners but they would only subscribe £250 or £10 per lot; so he then approaches the Lord Lieutenant, telling him his undertaking would be very splendid, that the bridge would be called Essex Bridge with the Earl's arms set up there, and the street beyond, a large noble one, called Capel Street, which should perpetuate his memory. On this the Earl gave him a £100. Like compliments he used with the Ormonde family, calling the embankment Ormonde Quay. He now, they say, thought himself strong enough to practice with the city of which he was a sworn freeman.

The Government shortly before had granted the city the customs of the city gates, reserving, however, the income for the first seven years. The greater part of these he induced Lord Essex to assign him for the bridge fund, which, in seven years, should be worth £2,000, enough to build the bridge. Impeaching his accounts, the case tells, how, in 1690, Sir Humphrey was committed by the Lords Justices for receiving money from papists, for certifying they had taken the Oath of Allegiance, which they had, in fact, refused to take. Thrice indicted for this in the King's Bench, he was fined on his submission, £200; in view of the balance still due him the fine was remitted, and the city therefore say it is just and reasonable that this £200 should be deducted from his balance. And as to his two bridge houses his claim should be reduced, for he had charged them in the bridge accounts, yet retained them still for himself.

"To move your compassion," the city case goes on, "Sir Humphrey tells you a long (but not a true) story about his being imprisoned by the Lord Primate for petitioning that the city should be left to the law as to its title to the houses, and how he was taken and kept close prisoner on Christmas Day, and how his confinement ruined his credit, and made five masters of his ships run away with them, and several other terrible things happened him; but had he justly told his case, it would have appeared, he was justly committed for preparing a petition *in which were several expressions reflecting on the Government ;* that he was in the pursuivant's hands only from the 24th to 28th December, and then, on his asking pardon, was discharged, " his confinement being only during the holidays when no exchange was open or business done, so that part of his case is rather a libel on the Lord Primate and the Council than anything else."

As to Ormonde Bridge, the city urges that this project, too, was for Sir Humphrey or his partners' own private advantage, the presentment being obtained during his mayoralty against the consent of the city, as proved by their presenting it as a nuisance. They charge him with procuring his second year of office, and using his power to drive the markets from the old city into his new grounds, imprisoning many for continuing the antient markets until he had ruined these.

The city case concludes by suggesting that if Sir Humphrey is to be re-imbursed it should not be at the cost of the city which had lost its ferries, its markets, and half its rents whereon the wastes across river now yielded a hundredfold. " Hard," they say, " it would be to cause several bridges to be built over the Thames, and then to order the charges to be paid by the watermen of London. If Sir Humphrey is to have this money that he cannot tell who owes him, we hope it may be laid on those that reaped the benefit. For his dealing with the papists about the Oath of Allegiance and his false suggestions and reflections about his confinement, he ought to be no object of compassion, and otherwise he has no pretence."

Jervis lodged a reply. Admitting the north bank was waste, he and his partners had paid £3,000 for this part of the abbey lands, purchased from the Earl of Tyrone, but as the sea overflowed a great portion, it cost several thousands to wall in the strand and embank it with earth before any house could be built. Further their purchase was after Lord Essex's promise to provide a fund, and the Earl, persuaded of its utility, had recommended Ormonde, his successor, to procure money from London to finish. He concedes the hostility of the city, adding dryly " lest their rents for lodging for gentlemen when they came from town should fail." As to the customs of the city gates, he was obliged to lease them out and then raise capital on the rents, so that they yielded him only £900 in all.

His defence as to the Catholic oaths has historic interest, emphasised by controversies of the present day. The oath, as he actually administered it, ran " you shall swear that from this day forward you shall be true and faithful to our Sovereign Lord and Lady, King William, and Queen Mary, their heirs and lawful successors, and faith shall bear of life, and members, and honour, and shall neither know nor hear of any ill will or damage intended them that you shall not defend, so help your God." The oath as it was said he should have administered, it was : " I do sincerely propromise and swear that I will be faithful and true *allegiance* bear to their Majesties, King William and Queen Mary. So help me God." He says his counsel advised that this oath, though enacted for England, was not made obligatory in Ireland till 1691, so he traversed his indictment, but afterwards, to save charges, as he says, he submitted to a fine of £200. No wonder he did so for he makes the fatal admission that he was aware the word " allegiance " was not in the oath as taken before him, but that many others so administered it. As to this latter fact, he calmly adds : " the papists were not aware of this, but thought he had omitted the word ' allegiance ' in favour to them," he says nothing as to the charge of taking money for the deception.

In proof of his loyalty he adds a paragraph quite refreshing in its unconsciousness of any perfidy. How in the days of King James and Tyrconnell, David Stuart, one of his mariners, was commissioned by the King to carry a Captain Shuttleworth to a gentleman in Wales, as he had previously taken another secret emissary to Duke Powis. Stuart informed Jervis that the Castle officials had, for three weeks, been writing commissions for Shuttleworth to raise commotions in England, and that he, himself, was offered £24 to take Shuttleworth across channel. Sir Humphrey says he told Stuart he was in danger to be hanged if the Government changed, *yet advised him to save himself by accepting the employment, first getting his £24 in hand, to leave this with his wife, but, on landing, to get Shuttleworth arrested and his papers seized.* This was done. Shuttleworth, with all his commissions, was carried to London, and many men of note were lodged in the Tower and Newgate. "If," he adds, "Stuart had discovered, Jervis has certainly been hanged." That was true enough when Dick Talbot ruled. Sir Humphrey, however, was addressing the Williamite Parliament.

The cause was heard before a Committee of the Whole House on six several days in September, 1697.[10] Their report retreats very far from their former finding of £3,434, for they now found £1,500 *and no more* to be a full satisfaction and discharge for all Sir H. Jervis's demands. They evidently considered that his personal interest in the bridge well compensated his loss of interest on outlay, but that the promises of Lord Essex on which he had acted made it fair to repay him the principal. Yet even this would seem never to have been paid him. The House referred it to a Committee (they were very alert to do this) to provide a fund, but the journals never show that it was raised, and in 1698, we find Sir Humphrey once more knocking at the gates of Parliament. Perhaps he got as much as he merited, for he left a large fortune, and Jervis Street still pierces his twenty acres from the river to Great Britain Street, where his descendents are still the landlords of a considerable portion. His daughter, and sole heiress, married Mr. White of Bally Ellis, and is ancestor of the present baronet family of Jervis-White. Sir Humphrey, himself, came from a Staffordshire stock, from which descended Sir John Jervis, the famed Earl of St. Vincent, who, with Nelson, broke the Spanish fleet in February, 1797.

Our Chairmen from the foundation to King Charles's death, were the Lord Mayors—1767-8 Mark Quin, 68-9 John

[10] *Journal* of House of Commons.

Forrest, 69-70 Lewis Desmynieres, 70-1 Enoch Reader, 71-2 Sir John Tottie, 72-3 Robt. Deey, 73-4 Sir Jos. Allen, 74-5 Sir Fran. Brewster, 75-6 William Smith, 76-7 Chris. Lovett, 77-8 John Smith, 78-9 Peter Ward, 79-80 John Eastwood, 80-1 Luke Lowther, 81-2-3 Sir H. Jervis, 83-4 Elias Best, 84-5 Sir Abel Ram. Under these, beside the enclosures of the Greens and the two bridges, the evolution of Dublin went on. In 1882 the vague shore between Queen Street and the Duke of Ormonde's wall, at the present barracks was granted to Mr. Ellis, on the terms of his forming the quay which still bears his name, with a road behind to the Park, then another road in the line of Barrack Street, to be planted with trees for a citizens' walk alongside the fine Bowling Green, lately formed to the north, and which now is merged in the playground of our present schools; it then lay west of the original school, and was still long known as the Bowling Green after it had become ours; all this was a large accession to our vicinage. Then the quay was formed from the Four Courts site, the Inns by the new bridge with a market behind ever since bearing Ormonde's name, and far eastward the slobs along the North Strand were allotted from Mabbot's Mills, still marked by Mabbot Street. South of the river, the Wood Quay was extended to Essex Bridge in line of a slushy shore called the Blind Quay, and the Dam and point at Dames Gate, south of the creek were covered. Behind the Green and the Hoggen Mount was a recreation ground called Tib and Tom, which was now pierced with William Street by Mr. Williams, under treaty with the city; and where the Theatre Royal now stands, Mr. Hawkins, under similar treaty, built a wall to protect his houses on Lazie Hill (Townsend Street), but still leaving the tides to flow round it over the site of Westmoreland Street to the strand of Fleet Street. And all this time the old city towers were disappearing, first let to private persons and then to be trampled in the march of reform. Fair Isoult's Tower by Essex Street went down in 1681.[11]

[11] With regard to the question asked in Chapter I, page 13, as to Isoult and the Arthurian Legend, the following surmise is ventured:—The

Arthurian Legend, as it now survives, lives in the *Morte D'Arthur* of Sir Thomas Malory, written *tempore* Edward IV. Here La Belle Iseult is daughter of Anguish (Angus) King of Ireland, who claimed to take "truage" or toll from the Cornish King, and sent his brother-in-law, Sir Marhaus, to enforce the claim by knightly battle from King Mark of Cornwall. Mark's nephew, the young Sir Tristram of Lyonesse (South Cornwall), as his champion, fought Sir Marhaus, and wounding him fatally, Sir Marhaus returned to Ireland to die with a splinter of Tristram's sword in his skull. He had given Tristram a wound which was said to be poisoned and could only be cured in the country whence Sir Marhaus came. So Tristram, changing his name to Tramtrist, came to Ireland to the Court of King Anguish, was cured, won favour, fell in love with the beautiful Iseult, and she with him. Once and again he returned to Ireland, and took away Iseult to be the wife of his uncle, King Mark, but they never forgot their first loves; she left the Court with Tristram and lived with him in *Joyeuse Garde*, whilst he still wrought as Knight of Arthur's Round Table, second in glory to Sir Launcelot only. Now Malory tells us he took his *Morte D'Arthur* from the tales and songs of the French *Trouveres* or Troubadours, at their acme, in the times of the Crusades, whose knights came from all Western Europe: thus the Troubadours drew from the traditions and myths of many ages and many lands, and copiously from the bardic relics of Wales, Cornwall, and Armorica, or Brittany, colonised by the Celtic Britons, driven westward by the Saxons and called Lesser Britain by Malory. In the sixth century, and after, Wales had close connexions with Ireland through St. Bridget, and St. David, who is said by Geoffry of Monmouth, writing in the time of the Crusades, to have been the nephew of King Arthur, with Caerleon on Usk as his first See, which he changed to Menevia, thence called St. David's, by St Bride's, or Bridget's Bay. This connection was revived at the Plantagenet Conquest by Giraldus Cambrensis and Strongbow's companions of South Wales. Following these was Sir Armoricus Tristram, who, with his brother-in-law, De Courcy, captured Howth in 1177, and became its first Lord. He, with De Courcy, was knighted at Rouen *tempore* Richard Cœur de Lion, and he took the name St. Lawrence. He was slain with his thirty knights in Connaught by O'Connor, King of Ireland, and his sword has traditionally hung in Howth Castle for nearly six centuries and a half. Is he not Sir Tristram de Lyonesse, and have we not here the germs of the Romance of Tristram and Iseult, which forms a full fourth of the *Morte D'Arthur?* Is the sword at Howth that which was shivered in the skull of the Irish knight? Armoricus seems to point to Armorica and Brittany. I can find no suggestion of this in Dr. Somner's exhaustive "searches" after the origin of the Arthurian epic, but it is pleasant even to dream of a connection of Old Dublin with the Old Romance which has inspired the genius of Spenser and Tennyson, and is now enshrined for ever in the *Idylls of the King*.

CHAPTER V.

1685-1702.

TEMP. JAMES II. AND WILLIAM III.

In the years following the death of our royal Founder the journal of the Hospital is rather jejune. It was not now a favourite with the Government at the Castle. The school work, however, went on as before. Sir Abel Ram was Lord Mayor and Chairman in 1685, Sir John Knox in 1686, and Sir John Castleton in 1687, and several of the original governors are still on the Board, including Sir Josua Allen, Sir Humphrey Jervis, the two Desminieres, Sir Francis Brewster and Enoch Reader, but none of the distinguished co-opted governors seem to have attended. In October, 1685, Mr. Benjamin Colquit resigned, and the Rev. Nicholas Knight became Chaplain and Head-master. His letters of presentation by the governors to Francis Marsh, Archbishop of Dublin, pursuant to the Charter, are inscribed in our minute book in Latin, quaint, if not very classical. The Lord Mayor and Corporation style themselves,—*Dominus Major, Vice Comites, et cives Civitatis Dublin, indiubitati patroni Hospitii*, of the late Lord King Car. II., and they supplicate his Grace, whom they address in the vocative,—*Reverendissime Pater*, to admit their beloved Nicholas Knight, *clericum*, to exercise all the duties in the Hospital. *Dei Verbi predicatoris, puerumque eruditoris.* Knight so continued up to May 1687, when "on his preferment," as our minute book runs, the Rev. Thomas King became Chaplain and master in his stead. Of King we hear more anon. In September, 1686, we have our first entry recording trouble with our boys; it gives a sample of the summary discipline then in vogue. Some twelve boys were detected in taking money out of the Hospital poor box. It couldn't have been much, but Master Andrew Roulston the ringleader, ran away for a week, and the others for two days. So Roulston is condemned, " that as a terror to the rest from falling into the like miscarriage, he be to-morrow whipt in the great hall, in the presence of the other boys, by the keeper of the Bridewell's servant, and that he be stript of his Blew Coat, and be turned out of doors, never to be admitted again." The other eleven are to be admonished by the Chaplain, but the admonition is to be endorsed by a whipping in presence of the school. By what law the official aid of the Bridewell keeper was thus invoked does not appear.

In 1687 our minute book shows that there was no meeting of the governors after September, or in the nine months following, and in the three years and four months to May, 1691, five meetings only, being two each in 1688 and 1690, and one in 1689. At these no school business seems to have been done; three deal only with one of our Endowments, the Tythes of Mullingar, and two with a change in the agency of the Hospital. And yet these meagre entries, closely looked at, are, perhaps, the most interesting in all our annals, for they disclose the connection of our school with one of the greatest events in the history of England and Ireland, the Revolution and reign of King James the Second. To decipher the cryptogram, however, it must be read in the light of the contemporary facts of the strange eventful story as they affected Dublin, whose civic governors were our governors too.

When King Charles died, in February, 1685, the Protestant Corporation at once addressed the new King in terms of almost servile loyalty, for passive obedience was then taught almost as dogma in the Anglican Church. Composed by Sir Richard Reeves the Recorder, and one of our governors, the address blesses God for the accession of " our only true and lawful sovereign whom we will ever obey and serve with our lives and fortunes with an untainted allegiance, and with all obedience of your Majestie's most humble and faithful and dutiful subjects."[1] The King's first act in Ireland was to withdraw the venerable Duke of Ormonde from the Lord Lieutenancy appointing Lords Justices, and placing Richard Talbot, newly created Earl of Tyrconnell in command of the army in Ireland, then numbering some 8,000 men. This was ominous, but in that year Tyrconnell seems to have confined his acts to the army, for the King during spring was occupied in punishing his enemies of the Rye House plot, in obtaining subsidies from Louis XIV., and in controlling the elections which returned him a Parliament, of which eleven-twelfths were his own devoted Royalists and Cavaliers; and in the summer his hands were full with the suppression of Monmouth's rebellion. His ministerial changes which were drastic enough, did not cause general alarm as in his first speech in the Privy Council, he promised to uphold the Established Church.

The only symptom of a new policy in civic Dublin which the City Rolls record this year, is a petition in November of Roman Catholic citizens for their freedomes which the Privy Council ordered to be heard by the two Chief Justices, Sir Wm. Davys, and Keating, the Chief Baron Henry Hene, and Sir Richard Reynell of the Common Pleas. This assembly, regarding—" as a matter of very great moment which will influence all the Corporation in this citie," direct that Counsel shall be retained for the hearing. The precise nature of this petition or its result, we do not now know; but if any decision was pronounced by these high Judges, it could not have been favourable to the Jacobite Government, for had it been, it would surely have been used by Tyrconnell when the question was raised acutely in the following year; and we know that next year Davys was turned out of the King's Bench, and Hene from the Exchequer, replaced by Nugent as Chief Justice, and Rice as Chief Baron.[2]

But when after the Bloody Assizes the King was paramount he declared for a standing army and officered the new

[1] Gilbert's *Calendar*, 5, 356.   [2] Lib. Mun.

regiments, of which fifteen were raised in Monmouth's rebellion, with Roman Catholics discharged from taking the statutory oaths. Then alarm spread, increased by the Revocation of the Edict of Nantes in France in November, so that when the King invited the Houses reassembled that month to repeal the *Habeas Corpus*, and Riot Acts, he was met with remonstrance, and, proroguing parliament he embarked on the fatal policy of Prerogative versus Law, sure to lead as it did to his ruin. In the close of the year he sent here as Lord Lieutenant his brother-in-law, Lord Clarendon with Tyrconnell as Commander of the Forces. Soon it proved that the Commander of the Forces was commander of the Viceroy too. Clarendon was of the moderate section in the Cabinet, supported by all foreign powers, including Pope Innocent XI., Tyrconnell was leader of the Forward section ; he passed over to Whitehall where he remained till June, 1686, James's Chief Confidant and Arch instigator of the policy that scoffed at statutes. Hence he directed the Government in the Castle, brow-beating and undermining the Lord Lieutenant. In June Lord Clarendon writes to the Corporation in obedience to the King's commands in the previous March, stating that his Majesty, being informed there was no law warranting the usage of requiring Roman Catholics, seeking admission to the city franchises and offices, to take the oath of supremacy, now commanded, that not only should they be admitted freemen on the simple oath of allegiance, but if when admitted they were chosen to the Mayorality or any City office, their names should be returned to the crown :—" That we may dispense with the oath of supremacy." The question of the legality of this test in Ireland at that time, has not, we believe, been hitherto fully examined, either by English or Irish historians, and may be stated here. In England the law was explicit ; there the Act of Supremacy, 1 Eliz. C. 1, made the oath obligatory on all candidates for office, ecclesiastical or temporal. The Irish statute followed it in the next year. A doubt, however, was raised in England as to whether the oath could be enforced unless it was actually tendered, and by an amending Act of 5 Eliz., the tender of the oath to all officials and professional men too, was made compulsory with a death penalty in case of a second refusal to take it. This amending act was not followed in Ireland, where the sanction of the statute still remained doubtful. Macaulay thinks the doubt well founded, and that there was no enforceable test then in Ireland at all, herein disagreeing with Archbishop King, who, in his Statement of Ireland regards the doubt as *Jesuitical*, and the act had *de facto* certainly been operative here; for example, in 1604, Skelton elected Mayor was superseded on declining to take the Oath, and the Corporation had gone much further. In 1678 the Assembly ordered that no one should thenceforth be admitted a freeman, without first taking the Oath of Supremacy. This was, indeed illegal for the Act of Supremacy referred to officers only. Catholics usually declined the Oath, as it abjured all ecclesiastical as well as temporal authority outside the realm, and thus it was practically an effective test, though many of them were in fact admitted freemen, probably without any tender of the Oath. But Lord Macaulay was, seemingly, not aware that under the Acts of Settlement as mentioned above, powers were given to the Government to make Rules and Orders, having Statutory effect, for the regulation of Corporation, under which Lord Essex' Rules in 1672, commanded the Lord Mayor to tender the Oath to all officers of the Corporation, and the masters and wardens of the City Guilds, whose refusal would entail disfranchisement, though the Lord Lieutenant could give a dispensation in any special named case. The Royal command in June was therefore warranted as to the admission of freemen, but not legal in giving a universal dispensation in respect to all officers to avoid the statutory law. The fluttered Corporation replied in terms of humility. They did not plead either the statute of Elizabeth or their own order of 1678, they yielded submissively as to the freemen of whom they said there were already four or five hundred Catholics on the

[3] Gilbert's *Calendar*, 2, 430.

roll. But shocked at His Majesty's imputation of illegality in requiring the Oath in the case of officers they pleaded the rules of Lord Essex as binding on them. Little chance there was for such a plea with Tyrconnell to whom the mention of the Act of Settlement was the red flag of the taureador to an angry bull, and when in England, the King in the teeth of direct statute law was seizing colleges in Oxford, and appointing Roman Catholic Deans to Anglican Cathedrals. And yet had this plea been accepted the Jacobite Government might soon have constitutionally emancipated their co-religionists, for under the Act of Settlement it was open to them to supersede the Rules and Orders, and to enact new ones dispensing with the Oath of Supremacy. But that would not suit the hot haste of James, bent on using his own dispensing prerogative wholesale. So in July came a letter from the Viceroy to the city, stating that he was not satisfied with their explanation, and commanding immediate and implicit obedience in the King's name. The Corporation, doubtless aware of what was proceeding in England, did not dare to rejoin, and forthwith directed that the Oath should no longer be tendered or enforced.

Here was another chance for a moderate and progressive change, but Tyrconnell would brook no delay. He commanded Sir John Knox, the Lord Mayor to admit to all franchises and offices forthwith, and on his refusal he resorted to his own more excellent way. Knox was a loyalist; in the previous May sitting, as Chairman of our Board he had ordered that on St. James' day, the 1st May in each year a sermon should be preached in our Chapel of King's Hospital, and that the Lord Mayor, Aldermen. Sheriffs and Sheriffs' peers, and all other Governors should attend in state in their gowns, and that new clothes should be provided for the blew boys. But this was not the loyalty Tyrconnell wanted. Continuing his intrigues against Clarendon in Dublin, and his brother Rochester, Prime Minister at Whitehall, he persuaded the King to dismiss them both, and in February 1687, came back to the Castle as Viceroy himself, with the lesser title of Lord Deputy, but with complete control over church, state and army.

One of his first steps was to withdraw the Royal Charter, in Dublin and through Ireland, that stood in his way. *Quo Warrantos* were accordingly issued from the Exchequer where Stephen Rice now presided as Chief Baron, known for his boast that he would drive a coach and six through the Act of Settlement, and from that court no writ of Error to England lay as in the King's Bench and Common Pleas The dismay was general, hundreds of families crossed the channel with Clarendon. The Dublin Corporation implored the Lord Deputy for grace in vain, and sought to appease him by hastening new admissions to the franchises. The *Quo Warrantos* went on, but as some hundred charters were being suppressed the proceedings took some time, and it was only in October that the King's new Charter for Dublin was published. Then Sir Thomas Hackett became Lord Mayor, Reeves was dismissed from the recordership and replaced by Sir John Barnewell to whom Reeves was commanded to deliver *The White Book*, containing the ancient Charters and Customs, and all other records in his custody.[4] Thomas Kieran and Edmund Kelly were named Sheriffs, and so became governors of the Blue Coat : by the end of the year all the thirty sheriffs of Ireland were Roman Catholics, save one, who was said to have been named in mistake for a namesake.[5]

Still it was necessary to form the lists of the new burgesses, which were only complete in the spring of 1688. Thus we can decipher the hiatus in our minute book, showing no meeting of the Blue Coat Governors from September 1687 to June 1688, as also the composition of the Board which then met. James this year had changed his first idea of an alliance with the Church of England against the Presbyterians and the sects to that of an alliance against the Church of England with all the nonconformists, whom he had hitherto assailed with the bitter

[4] Gilbert's *Calendar*, 5, 464.
[5] See the list in King's *Statement of Ireland*, opp. 52.

hostility of which his angry refusal in 1686 to repeal the act which made it death to attend a Presbyterian conventicle is but a single example.[6]

He now declared it his desire to treat all denominations with impartiality. Accordingly several of the old corporators were now re-admitted, including Sir Josua Allen, Sir Humphrey Jervis and Sir Abel Ram, three of our former chairmen, and Bartholmew Van Homrigh, then an eminent Dutch merchant of Dublin, whom we see admitted to the new franchise in April 1688, with his little daughter, Esther, Swift's Vanessa, then a child. This fair-play was, however, only a semblance, for the Protestants were everywhere in a powerless minority. At the Blue Coat Board, on 8th June, Sir T. Hackett was chairman, and beside him, William Dongan, Earl of Limerick, one of the five nobles who had patents from James whilst still King of England. He was a gallant soldier, and then in command of one of Tyrconnell's new regiments of dragoons, as was his son of another. They both fought bravely for James at the Boyne, where the young man was slain. This Lord Limerick merits a memory in Dublin, for with King James he was a joint founder of the Workhouse in St. James' Street, our original Poorhouse and basis of the South Dublin Union. Its site was partly on Dongan's estate in the suburbs, and partly on that of the King which was portion of the confiscated lands allotted to him under the Act of Settlement. They both assigned to the new foundation, the city adding part of the city estate.[7] On James's downfall his lands were conferred on Lady Orkney and those of Lord Limerick on General Ginkell, now Lord Athlone. Hereupon one Brian Poole, Esquire, who had somehow got possession, finding a difficulty raised by the forfeitures *more Hibernico* refused to admit title, and it was only when the new city regime obtained confirmations from Lady Orkney and Lord Athlone that possession was enforced, and the Workhouse restored. With Lord Limerick, sat on the Blue Coat Board the new

[6] Macaulay's *History of England*, 1, 374.
[7] Gilbert's *Calendar*, 6, 218.

Sheriff, Kelly, and several of the new Aldermen, with several of the old Governors, including Aldermen Ram and Otterington. But it was futile to suppose that a Protestant school under a clerical headmaster could be managed by a predominently Roman Catholic Board. No scholastic business was done at this meeting nor at that in the following week, and no others were held in 1688. We find, indeed, in October the Master of the new Workhouse in James's Street, one good thing established by Tyrconnell's Government, petitioning the Corporation to allow him "the clothing of the Hospital boys," to be made by the workhouse inmates who were then set at weaving, but we know not if there was any result.[8]

But the King's forward policy was now moving blindly apace, until the seizure on Magdalen College in Oxford and ejection of the Fellows, the bringing over Irish troops to England, the wholesale dispensations under the second Declaration of Indulgence, the trial of the Seven Bishops who refused to proclaim it in their charges, and their acquittal, were followed by the advent of William of Orange in November, James's flight to France in December, and the election of William and Mary as King and Queen. All Celtic Ireland rose now in arms, fifty thousand regulars, fifty thousand irregulars, with swords, pikes, scythes; even many women wielded skeanes. The gates of Derry were closed in December, and thither and to Enniskillen the Protestant population fled as to cities of refuge, beleagured by the Irish Army till the relief of Derry on 1st July, 1689. And though after that Ulster was safe, the wrath of the three other provinces waxed, for James was now with them as their King, and the population rose *en masse*. The Protestants were disarmed, hundreds were imprisoned, thousands fled. Amongst these Sir Josua Allen as mentioned above. These were no times for a Protestant Corporation School in the city. In 1689 there was only one meeting of the Blue Coat Board, at this Alderman McDermott, deputy Lord Mayor, presided, with Barnewall, the Recorder, Sir Thomas Hackett, and five other

[8] Gilbert's *Calendar*, 5, 485.

Aldermen: the single item of business done reflected the state of the country; it was in July, when the army was still before Derry, and the Governors had to deal with a petition of Sir James Leigh to whom at the two meetings in 1688 they had arranged for a lease of the Tythes of Mullingar, asking to be relieved of his lease as he had been unable to collect the tythes. This the Governors refused but offered if he paid the arrears to abate the rent in the last half year. For the Government was now in the deepest straits for monies. Trade being paralyzed, they must raise it or create it anyhow. In the ten months after the relief of Derry the factiousness of the English Parliament gave the Castle and the Irish Parliament a free hand which they used to carry on the war. Then the King coined copper money, making four pence worth legal tender for a sovereign and seized on all property they could. Most Protestants who had any and could do so escaped. Then by the Sullan Proscription Act, known as the great attainder, they were ordered to return forthwith on pain of being hanged and quartered for high treason; this they no more dared do than the French emigrants dared return to Louis XIV. Sir Josua Allen, Van Homrigh, and Otterington thus ceased to be Governors of our school, and in November, 1689, Tyrconnell seized on our Hospital and " turned out all the poor Blew Boys who were still there to the number of sixty, with all the servants and officers, and all the bedding goods and all the household stuff which were carried away to the great Hospital at Kilmainham (lately founded by Charles II.) for their wounded soldiers."[9] No funds were granted to the school by the new regime, and up to this time it had been kept alive only by subscriptions collected by Moland the steward and the chaplain, Thomas King; the latter was now imprisoned and kept there ten weeks, " for no other reason," as he says, " but to disable him from attending the charge of the Hospital, and out of malice, because Mr. Moland and he by borrowing money and the charity of good Christians kept the Hospital from dissolving till it was done by force."

[9] Hospital Minute Book.

There was a meeting of the Jacobite governors in January, 1690, and a final meeting in March, Terence M'Dermott, Lord Mayor, in the chair, but these were held only to appoint Thomas Hewlett as agent and steward in Moland's room, with an order to the latter to deliver up the Charter and all the books of laws, orders, property, and accounts, and Hewlett is directed to take charge of all the outstanding debts and rents of the endowments.

King William was now expected in Ireland, and Louis sent over a French contingent of 7,000 men to the army of James[10] then, as our minute book has it, " the Hospital was by King James given to the French to be an hospital for their wounded officers and soldiers, and so continued till the Rout of the Boyne, then they hastily forsook the same, and the old governors re-entering, found great quantities of linen and bedding the French had left behind them, which the governors intended to use in lieu of the household stuff formerly taken away by the Lord Tyrconnell, but these were ordered by the new Lords Justices to be removed to the Hospital of Kilmainham.[11] For when William entered Dublin on the morrow of the battle, the place was a chaos, and was now occupied as a corn store for the victorious army.

All things now changed; the Ins were Outs and the dread policy of *Vae Victis* which had raged three years swung to the other side to harden into penal laws. Sir Chas. Porter resumed as Chancellor, *vice* Fitton; Reynell became Chief Justice of the King's Bench, *vice* Nugent; Sir Richard Pyne of the Common Pleas, *vice* Keating; and Hely, Chief Baron, *vice* Rice. Our exiled governors returned, Motley became Lord Mayor to September, succeeded then by Otterington, Van Homrigh, who, as a Dutchman was *persona grata* to William, was made commissioner of the public revenues. But it was not till May, 1691, the governors could meet in the Blue Coat, and all was a scene of dilapidation still. Allen and Ram, back from exile, were there, and several

[10] See Minute Book 21st September, 1694.
[11] Gilbert's *Calendar*, 5, lviii.

other displaced members: but the spirit of patronage is strong in spite of ruins, the board had before them a letter from Archbishop Francis Marsh of Dublin, also a late refugee, and from Thomas Conyngsby, one of the new Lords Justices, pressing for the appointment of Mr. Francis Higgins as chaplain. Conyngsby, who had been member for Leominster, and who Macaulay calls a busy and unscrupulous Whig, had accompanied William and fought by his side at the Boyne; left behind at the Castle in high places of trust, which it is said he abused. He was nevertheless ennobled here, and afterwards advanced in the peerage in England. The reply of the governors to these letters was that taking into consideration the low estate and condition of the Hospital, the Lord Mayor and Governors cannot, at present, maintain a chaplain, nor is there as yet any occasion for such a person to be employed therein.

In spring, 1692, the school being still uninhabitable, poor Thomas King, our late imprisoned chaplain, wrote to the Board, detailing his losses, as quoted above, and asking some relief. The governors had then no assets available, but they assigned over to him in lieu of his unpaid salary, the £30 payable by Doctor William King, who had just been consecrated Bishop of Derry, and who was his uncle. He, too, had been imprisoned by Tyrconnell twice in the Castle, for he was leader of the opposition and a fighting man. He was then Dean of Christ Church, and on King William's entry he preached the sermon in Christ Church in the King's presence. It is said that when sending him to Derry, His Majesty, who seldom joked, asked him what was the difference between them, and the Bishop failing to answer the riddle, explained "you are William King, but I am King William." We shall have to refer to King again when Archbishop of Dublin and one of our greatest governors. He now at once honoured our assignment of the £30. He was generous to a fault, and is noticed in our books as the only prelate who at this time paid the £30 tax in lieu of consecration feasts.

It was not till April, 1692, the governors could appoint as chaplain, Mr. Thomas Hemsworth; they were seeking to collect their arrears and debt to rehabilitate the house, but owing to the desolation of the country, they were forced to remit much. There is an entry in May that the circumstances of the several tenants in the late troublesome times, differ much from each other, some being forced to fly from their habitation, whilst others lived all the while in their houses and were not sharers in the late calamities, and the agent is, therefore, empowered, if it appear that their losses and suffering have been great, to make an abatement as he shall think reasonable, not exceeding one year and a half.

Though the Hospital was still in a wretched condition, the governors, in July, brought back twelve of the children expelled nearly three years before, and a few weeks afterwards admitted twenty new boys. Big people again took an interest in the School, one of the recommendations for admission is by Sir Richard Reynell, and one by Lady Porter, the Lord Chancellor's wife. Mr. Hemsworth, the chaplain, was now appointed schoolmaster also, his salary was slightly raised, though many of the arrears were now pronounced desperate, and the Board were still struggling hard to make the buildings inhabitable whilst most of their rents were in arrear.

In their straits at this time the governors had uncheerful relations with the greatest scholar of the times, Dr. Dudley Loftus, polyglot writer in twenty tongues, who was then the most learned orientalist in Europe. Syriac, Armenian, Ethiopic, to say nothing of Hebrew, to him were alike familiar; then he was a great Jurist, a Theologian, and an Antiquary. Some might say much learning had made him mad, and one did say :—" he never knew so much learning in the keeping of a fool," but he had mother wit enough for, successively, royalist, Cromwellian, royalist again, Jacobite, and Williamite, he lived in Dublin through the revolution, and on under William, respected by all the five regimes. He was Cromwell's judge advocate-general, and Charles II.'s vicar-general. But he owed King's Hospital £800, for which they threatened to sue him in 1692; it was still due when he died in 1695, and was only realized far in Anne's time, our books through all the interval being dotted with entries of his arrears. It might be too much to expect that one who wrote reams in Ethiopian could think of such small things as debts. Our security was his house on the Blind (now Essex Quay), where he lived and wrote; money was very scarce; yet he left a fortune. He was a cadet of the eminent family, descended from Adam Loftus, Queen Elizabeth's Primate, ancestor of the Marquises of Ely, and his brother was owner of Rathfarnham Castle, the seat of the Marquises till Victoria's reign.[12]

In the year 1692 an apparent source of revenue was granted to the Hospital, which illustrates some of the then conditions of the city. The coal ships were still discharged at Ringsend, whence the cargoes were still carried up river in gabbards to the Wood and the Merchants' Quay, where only they were allowed to land. The merchants had now combined to delay the gabbards in the tideway and on the quay, refusing to sell till they had unduly raised the market prices, so the city passed ordinances creating two new landing quays, Ormonde and Arran, which marks the extension of the town on the north side, and compelling the merchants to discharge at one of these four wharves within six days under penalty of two shillings per ton per day demurrage, one half of which was assigned to the Blue Coat. These merchants had further charged exorbitantly for the carriage from Ringsend; they were now confined to twelve pence per ton under penalty of thrice that sum for extorting more, one half of which was likewise assigned to our Hospital. This, however, brought little present income, if it ever brought any. Meanwhile little could be done, and the meetings of the Board for two years were few and far between. But in 1693-94 Sir John Rogerson was Lord Mayor and our Chairman, and one of the most eminent of our citizens in his long public life. He found the shock of the revolution still paralyzing the Hospital structurally and financially, as it continued to do during all the reign of William. In this year

---

[12] There is an admirable sketch of Dr. W. Loftus' career in George Stokes, *Some Irish Worthies of the Irish Church.*

there were fourteen meetings of the governors, at all of which he presided. The front of the Hospital was so mutilated that it was essential to replace it, and the governors themselves subscribed for the restoration; the royal arms of William and Mary were erected with an inscription " Anno Domini, 1694. This frontispiece was rebuilt at the charge of the benefactors, Sir John Rogerson, then Lord Mayor, John Page, and Robert Twigg, Sheriff." But all our endowments were in arrear, the building on St. Stephen's Green had ceased during the troubles, and the rents on the Lotts belonging to the Hospital were in arrear, as were those of the the tythes of Mullingar, the Dean's orchard, the Oxmantown, and the Nodstown estates and were either irrecoverable or could only be reached by large abatements and reduced rents in the future. The Earl of Roscommon who had undertaken the block between Hume Street and Merrion Row, could not pay, and asked the governors to accept a surrender, and when the new tenant of Nodstown was trying to rally he was sued in a writ of dower by a Dame Upton, claiming as widow of the man who had sold the estate to Gyles Martyn our benefactor years before. This, the governors, of course, must defend, they held the claim to be vexatious and false, and the minute states the direction of counsel that the Hospital should plead that the doweress *had never been married*. The litigation went on for years, and though it came to naught it added to burdens already scarce bearable. Rogerson dealt with them bravely, liberal arrangements were made with all our debtors in which he was well aided by Nehemiah Donellan, our new Recorder, who now came *vice* Thomas Coote, appointed by the restored regime in 1690, and now advanced to the King's Bench. Then the Board petitioned the Lords Justices setting forth their losses of the last six years, as detailed above, which prevent them fulfilling their duty under the charter to the Hospital built for three hundred children; they enclose a copy of the ordinance of the Privy Council of 1679 as to the Consecration Feasts, and pray that this may be now revived and reinforced, as the newly made prelates had ceased to pay, saving only William

King, the new Bishop of Derry. The Privy Council assembled and in September, 1694, passed an order in Council accordingly. This is signed by Lord Chancellor Porter, Narcissus Marsh, now Archbishop of Dublin, and Sir Richard Reynell, now Chief Justice of the King's Bench.

This year was appointed one of the best officers the Hospital has ever enjoyed; Bartholomew Wybrants, steward and agent, *vice* Thomas Howard, who had broken down under the stress of the troublous times. Wybrants held office for thirty-six years and will be referred to again.

A curious entry of this year marks the care then taken of the religious training of the pupils. An order directs the schoolmaster and the porter " to take them each Monday morning to Christ Church to prayers in a decent and orderly manner. The nurses to take care that their heads be combed, their clothes clean, shoes tied, stockings and garters." The state of the chapel made this necessary.

The entries in 1695-97 deal chiefly with things of routine, for the Board was still crippled from want of income. Our chairmen were successively Lord Mayors, George Blackhall, William Watt, and William Billington. Donnellan, the Recorder, was chosen a Baron of the Exchequer, of which he was made chief in 1703, and Sir William Handcock now became our Recorder in his stead. One entry in 1696 may be noticed as bearing on discussions of the Board in our own time as to the limit of age in retaining pupils, sixteen having been adopted by the governors for many years. This entry directs that seventeen years should be the limit. Modern ideas recognize this as essential if boys are to be trained beyond the mere elements, and it has been again adopted in our Hospital in the last few years.

But 1697-8 was a notable twelve months. Bartholomew Van Homrigh was now Lord Mayor and proved to be one of the most notable of our chairmen. He, like Rogerson, presided at every one of the many meetings of the Board in his year. Being an eminent shipowning merchant himself, he strenuously promoted the training of boys in the mathematics essential for navigation as already encouraged in the

School by the Merchants' Guild; order is given that every boy should be thus trained, who, on examination, was found capable of learning. At this time, Mr. Henry Osborne, of Dardistown, Co. Meath, gave the Hospital £1,000 which had far-reaching consequences. He gave it by a deed reserving to himself and his heirs for ever the nomination of ten boys, and to this the governors assented, for they sorely then needed £1,000. At his death many years later he devised this right to the Lord Bishop of Meath and his successors. It is very doubtful whether the governors had any power thus to alienate to strangers their duty as trustees over admissions, and further whether under the reservation to his own heirs he could treat it as a fee simple, devisable to an ecclesiastic corporation, but the governors have ever since loyally adhered to the bargain, and honoured the nominations of the Bishop of Meath to the present day. For a single gift of £1,000 hundreds of boys have been trained free during the two centuries since elapsed. It is satisfactory to know that these episcopal nominations have been well selected almost always. Osborne was a *persona gratissima* with the governors, they asked to have his portrait painted and placed in the Hospital for ever.[13] This honour he declines in a quaintly gracious letter; "such preserving of memories," he says, "are due only to princes and great men; if extended to some benefactors others would expect it, and if only given to some, he humbly asks to be excepted." "I am old," he adds, "and going to the place where such things are forgotten, and desire I may do it silently." Then he promises to befriend the Hospital in the future. By his will he left it a large legacy of £1,500, which, however, appears never to have been received. Perhaps this promise was an element in the governor's gratitude. This £1,000 throws light on the then financial state of the city. Part of its estate had been mortgaged, there was no money to redeem the debt for which the city paid eighty pounds yearly, so the corporation applied to our governors to lend them this Osborne £1,000. Van Homrigh and the Board assented,

[13] Minute, 24 March, 1703.

they to have eight per cent on the loan, which gave the School for many years a virtual annuity of eighty pounds.

In 1698 we have the first admission to the School of a son of one of the French refugees, Stephen Verger. They now formed a considerable colony here; they were industrious, useful, citizens, and were welcomed. The city rolls give the names of more than 150 admitted to the freedom of the city by special grace, with full liberty to trade, and in our journal through the next fifty years it is interesting to note the great number of our boys who were apprenticed to silk and ribbon weaving, and the serge and poplin manufacture, introduced by these skilful Frenchmen, whose work, Swift, a century afterwards, so laboured to promote through Queen Caroline in London.

In 1694 the French Emigrées purchased, for their Cemetery, Lott No. 10 on the north side of St. Stephen's Green. The price was £16. They thus became the tenants of the Blue Coat, in so far as they became subject to the head rent granted to the School as its original endowment. Mr. T. P. Le Fanu has kindly given the writer some interesting notes on this subject.

Van Homrigh left his mark on the city. Through the favour of his countryman, William, he now held high office in the state. He was M.P. for Derry city from 1692-95, and in this, 1698, we find him enrolled as one of the first members of the Dublin Philosophical Society,[14] founded by William Molyneux. He used his royal favour by petitioning the Government that the ancient, loyal and metropolitan city of Dublin, might, in everlasting memory of the great services of William III. to its Protestant inhabitants, and as a mark of his royal grace and favour, be honoured with a collar of SS. and His Majesty's effigies on a medal to be worn by the Mayor of the city. The King was then in Flanders, and there at his court at Loo, on the 28 Oct., 1697, he signed a royal warrant under which the Lords Justices here were to authorize the making of the collar and medal as prayed to be presented to Bartholomew Van Homrigh, Lord Mayor

[14] Dr. Stokes' *Worthies of the Irish Church*, p. 140.

of Dublin, to be worn by him during his continuance in office and by the succeeding Mayors for ever as it has since ever been. The cost, £770, was to be paid out of the Irish revenue and collar and medal were "to be made in England by the most able and skilful artists in things of this kind."[15] The medal was executed by James Roettier, and is considered one of the finest of his works. On the obverse is a bust of the King in armour, and inscribed in capitals :—" Gulielmus Tertius. D.G. Mag. Brit. Fran. et Hib. Rex, James R. fecit." On the reverse :—" Gulielmus III. antiquam et fidelum Hiberniæ Metropolin hoc Indulgentiæ Suae Munere Ornavit Barth Van Homrigh Arm. Urb. Prætore, MDCXCVIII." After paying for collar and medal, there was a surplus of £250, and this, in July, 1701, the city voted should be applied for the purchase of three gold chains for the Mayor and Sheriffs of the city in succession. "They to give security for the re-delivery of them as usual." Gold chains are tempting. The former SS. Chain, presented to the City by Charles II. had been abstracted by somebody in the revolutionary troubles.

In Van Homrigh's year the city may be said to have been lighted for the first time. Hitherto there were but a few lanterns in the principal streets, and these were put out at nine o'clock, when, as if a curfew tolled, the shops were closed. Now a plan was adopted following that in use in Holland and in London, from Kensington to Whitehall, for erecting lights in all the streets and lanes at intervals of from six to eight houses, which burned from six to twelve o'clock through all the winter months. There were then presumably few burglars in Dublin, for we do not find much record of felonies, and yet the city was in darkness from midnight to morn.

So much for Van Homrigh. His name has been made classic by Swift's Cadesus and Vanessa, which surround it with the glamour of a sad romance.

Of 1698-9 we have little to record. Thomas Quin, Lord Mayor, was our chairman. Our chaplain, Rev. Thomas

[15] Gilbert's *Calendar*, 6, viii.

Hemsworth, now gently announced that he intended changing his condition, which the then rule enforcing celibacy and residence forbade. But he soon after obtained preferment, and in the beginning of 1700 resigning, the Rev. Charles Carr became chaplain and schoolmaster, but under strictly expressed conditions that he was to hold under the same obligations as to celibacy residence, the entertaining of the boys, the preaching in the chapel, expressed in the Order of 1681, when Benjamin Colquit was appointed, and on these terms his name was sent by the governors for confirmation by Archbishop Narcissus Marsh, pursuant to the Charter.

The new century opened well for the Hospital, our chairman and Lord Mayor, 1699-1700, was Sir Anthony Percy. Our finances were at last improving, and the governors now raised the number of the boys to eighty. A legacy of £600 bequeathed by the late Chief Baron Bysse, was now paid in, and by Lord Mayor Percy's aid, was lent to the city, which was still deeply in debt, and who now agreed to pay the Hospital an annuity at eight per cent, or forty-eight pounds, whilst the loan remained outstanding. Percy's mayoralty has left a memorable mark in Dublin. Under him the Assembly resolved to erect a statue of William III. in copper or mixed metal. A contract was made under authority of the Lord Mayor, with the celebrated sculptor, Grinling Gibbons, for £800. Gibbons or Gibbon, Evelyn gives it both ways, was discovered by the great Diarist in 1670, in a wretched shanty near Deptford, carving a splendid copy of Tintoretto's Crucifix, and he at once perceived the man's genius. He introduced him to his friend, King Charles, as "this incomparable young man;" he proved to be the greatest wood sculptor England has ever seen, and the most prolific: he was a great statuary, too. His works still adorn many of the great cathedral sedilia and stalls, and many palaces and houses. From Evelyn alone we have notes of his decorating Windsor, St. James's, Whitehall, and of his equestrian statue of Charles II. On 1st July, 1701, anniversary of the Boyne, his statue of William was inaugurated in College Green, the ceremonial, as witnessed by a contemporary, is described in the preface of the sixth volume of Sir John Gilbert's *Calendar*. All the civic authorities were there, with the military and city bands, grenadiers, militia, and crowds immense. At the statue they received the Lords Justices in State, Archbishop Narcissus Marsh, and the Earls of Drogheda and Mount Alexander. Then all marched together thrice, nobility and gentry joining in, all uncovered. Kettledrums, trumpets, and all kinds of music resounded from a stage hard by. Then our Recorder, Handcock, made a florid oration setting forth the great deeds of the King, after which there was a volley from the great guns. Then the Lords Justices, the nobility and gentry, with the Provost and Fellows of Trinity College, were entertained by the Lord Mayor in an improvised building, and when the King's health was drunk the grenadiers fired the great guns again, and hogsheads of claret with baskets of cakes were opened for the multitude. The great people then adjourned to the Mansion House, where the Lord Mayor gave a splendid banquet, ladies being present, and the night closed with fireworks, ringing of bells, illuminations and bonfires. A tablet on the north side of the statue is inscribed:—Inchoatum An. Dom. MDCC. Antonio Percy Equite Aurato Praetore, Carolo Forrest, Jocob Barlow *vice* Comites. Absolutum An. Dom. MDCCI. Marco Rainsford equite aurato Praetore Johanne Eccles Rudolpho Gore, vice Comites.

Sir John Gilbert states that the execution of this statue by Grinling Gibbons had been unnoticed previous to the publication of his *Calendar*. The inaugural ceremonial throws light on the periodic march of the College students around the statue on festival days in the two centuries since elapsed. Our modern crowds would bear this more patiently, perhaps, if the wine were flowing and the cakes were throwing as on that 1st July, 1701.

In this year two *ex officio* governors were added to the Board. The Masters, Wardens, and Brothers of the Trinity Guild of Merchants, voted £24 a year to the Hospital in consideration of having three nominations of boys so long as this annuity continued. The then Masters of the Guild, Joseph James, and Thomas Pleasants, were at once co-opted as Governors during their term of office, to be succeeded by their successors, Masters for the time being. In the next year, 1701, Samuel Walton, being Lord Mayor and our Chairman, the Master and two Wardens of St. Anne's Guild, Charles Wallis, Christopher Borr, and John Quin, were similarly co-opted, *ex officio*, that Guild having voted £40 a year to the Hospital some time before.

In 1701, Sir W. Handcock, the Recorder, died, and John Forster was chosen in his stead. One of the first duties of his active Recordership, was to draw up the address of condolence on the death of King William the Third, "of blessed memory," and of loyal congratulation to the new Queen Anne. The address is given in full in Sir J. Gilbert's *Calendar*.[16] It bears date only five days after the King's demise, on the 8 March, 1702.

Osborne's gift brought to the Blue Coat the association of names much loftier than his. The gift was inspired by his friend, William Molyneux, philosopher, patriot, mathematician, metaphysician, the correspondent of Locke, who said he was proud to call him his friend. Representative of the family of Castle Dillon, Armagh, he was now M.P. for Dublin. Sent, when young, to report to the Government scientifically on the fortresses of Holland menaced by Louis, he was made, on his return, a fellow of the newly formed Royal Society, and came home ambitious to form a similarly great institution here. In 1653, he, accordingly, formed the Dublin Philosophical Society, which, though broken up and exiled in James II.'s revolution, ultimately evolved into the Royal Dublin Society as it now exists, for restored from exile, after the Boyne, he resumed his scientific labours, and also entered the field of politics, wherein, too, he attained high fame. Our governors, grateful for his services in the Osborne gift, elected him a governor, and we find him at our Board in April, 1698, sitting beside his friend, Bartholomew Van Homrigh, then Lord Mayor. It was in this year he

[16] Vol. 6, 262.

published his famous *Case of Ireland Stated*, oft quoted even now, but he sat little in public places again; he died in the following October. He brought with him to our Board, his brother-in-law, Dr. John Madden, and his brother, Thomas, whose scientific eminence approached his own. Madden and Thomas Molyneux were amongst the most distinguished physicians of the day. They had been colleagues of William in the founding of the Dublin Philosophical, which Thomas lived to see merged in the Royal Dublin Society, and helped the merger. He was physician-general to the army in Ireland, and was made a baronet in 1730. Dr. Madden, when becoming a governor, most generously offered his services as standing physician to the School. He is ancestor of the Right Hon. Mr. Justice Madden, Vice-Chancellor of T.C.D., and was father of Dr. Samuel Madden, the eminent scholar and founder of the great fellowship premium in his University.

The names of Molyneux and Madden recall the connection with the King and Queen's College of Physicians, inaugurated by them, which existed for very many years after, and which adds a memorable grace to the Annals of the Blue Coat. Dr. John Madden had been President of the College in 1694, 1697, and in 1700. Sir Thomas Molyneux held the same position four times, in 1702, 1709, 1713 and 1720, and was a Governor of our School in all these years. In 1717 the Blue Coat Board passed a resolution that all Presidents of the College, for the time being, should be *ex officio* Governors. Of these Dr. Bryan Robinson, President in 1708, 1727 and 1739, and Dr. William Harvey, President in 1784, 1791, 1797, 1802 and 1814, were in turn the acting medical officers of our Hospital.

Our chairmen in King William's reign, were, Lord Mayors, 1690-1, John Otterington; 91-2-3, Sir Michael Mitchell; 93-4, Sir John Rogerson; 94-5, George Blackhall; 95-6, William Watt; 96-7, Wm. Billington; 97-8, Bartholomew Van Homrigh; 98-9, Thomas Quin; 99-700, Anthony Percy; 1701-2, Samuel Walton.

During the revolution, and for some years after, the extension of the city was checked, for its chiefs were more occupied in filling the wastes already taken in than in enclosing others. In 1699, reciting the great increase of the city " which is now much greater in the suburbs than within the walls," the Assembly resolve that the ancient gates are now of little use or security, and so decree that the old Damas gate, the principal entrance to the city, shall be pulled down, as some others have been by toleration of the Government." So down went the historic approach to the Castle through which the Plantagenet pageants had passed.[17] Reform is ruthless, yet the Order vindicates its vandalism, stating the entrance to be uphill, and only nine feet across, whilst the removal will give fourteen feet at Crane Lane, and so let two carriages pass. Crane Lane to-day where Dame Street narrows at the Lower Castle Yard, marks the site of the mediæval tower.

[17] Gilbert's *Calendar*, 6, 222.

CHAPTER VI.

1702-1714. *TEMP. QUEEN ANNE.*

AN entry in our books in Queen Anne's first year, indicates that she acknowledged the loyal address of the City by a royal gift to King's Hospital. It runs : "£200 given by the Queen out of the quarter's vacancy of the Primacy." This is noteworthy, as suggesting a remnant of the Prerogative by which during the vacancy of a See or Diocese its revenues vested in the Crown. It was by this assumed right, William Rufus left bishoprics vacant for years, seizing the income meanwhile, and this led to his murder, for murder it was, in the New Forest. When King Henry VIII. became *Caput Ecclesiasticum*, this prerogative again attached to the supremacy and went to his successors, and it was used by Charles II., when needy, or his ladies were greedy. In December, 1702, Primate Michael Boyle died after a reign at Armagh of twenty-four years, and in Spring Narcissus Marsh was appointed, Dr. Wm. King of Derry being translated to Dublin. Thus there was a vacancy of three months, during which Dr. King administered the revenues under the Crown, and probably prompted our royal gift. The loyal city for some time afterwards styled our School, "The Queen's Hospital." One of Anne's best, because sincerest, characteristics, was her devotion to the Church, as evinced by Queen Anne's Bounty, and the surrender to the Church of the First Fruits or first year's revenue of benefices which Henry had taken from the Pope in his own supremacy. This grace was soon after conferred by the Queen on the Church of Ireland, mainly owing to Swift's mission and exertions.

King's Hospital just now obtained a parish church with parochial rights. Hitherto St. Michan's covered the whole north side of the river from the Park to the North Strand, with houses few and far between. But after the Restoration the City spread, and many nobles now had villas in Oxmantown. By Statute of 9 William III., c. 16, reciting that from the late increase of buildings and inhabitants in the Parish of St. Michan's in *the suburbs* of Dublin the cure of souls had become too great for a single minister, it was divided into three—St. Paul's, taking Oxmantown Green from the Park to Smithfield, St. Mary's, extending east from Capel Street to the sea, the centre being reserved to the mother parish, St. Michan's. In 1702, St. Paul's was ready for consecration. At this ceremonial a deed of gift in perpetuity was always exhibited which on the petition of the new Parish, the City now granted, but thereby reserved " a seat in the Church for the Lord Mayor and his successors, and a place for the Blew Boys of King Charles's Hospital," which then lay almost adjacent to the new Parish Church. Dr. Ezekiel Burridge was first rector of St. Paul's—he was one of our benefactors.

As its own Chapel and Chaplain were part of its Chartered Constitution, the Blue Coat did not often need to claim its statutory rights in St. Paul's, though the boys were sometimes sent there when our chapel was not available. And when in 1821 St. Paul's was being re-built, our governors granted the Blue Coat Chapel to be used temporarily as the parish church, in response to a memorial from the Rev. Mr. Radcliffe the rector of St. Paul's.

This year the number of boys was increased to 82, the patronage of the two city guilds proved a great stimulus to the Governors and the staff. The training in mathematics was specially committed to Moland, our steward, who was also surveyor and accountant of the Corporations and to Mead, our second master, who was with us from the beginning, and who was this year specially thanked by the Board, and his salary raised. The Trinity Guild of Merchants recognised the carrying out of the policy by raising their annual contribution to the Hospital to £50, which they paid for many years. In 1710 they, by leave of the Governors, formed a Mathematical class-room in a gallery of the Hospital, they had a Navigation school of their own, and in 1711 arranged with our board to train in this, four of our best lads, sending to our class four boys of their own nomination, and a few years after they gave a further grant of £20 yearly for a master to teach eight of our boys the art of navigation.

The return of Archbishop King to Dublin was a momentous event for our Hospital, for the many years in which as builder of churches, reformer of abuses in church and state, organiser of charities, promoter of education, he wrought with a generous energy which has never been rivalled, up to his death in 1729.[1] His influence operated everywhere, for with the Corporation it was immense. We can trace it thus early, though unseen, in the advance our School now makes. In 1704 all our boys were trained in Church music systematically, and we find them two years after placed under a skilled musician, Neville Fane. This step taken two centuries ago in a Dublin Charity School, is noteworthy, when we think of how little the example has been followed since, or even in these days of universal education of all classes in all things. This, with the progress of our Mathematical classes, brought us new governors, as always happened when the school throve. The Hon. Sir Charles Fielding, Colonel of the King's Regiment of Guards, and a Privy Councillor, now joined the board. He was brother of the Third Earl of Denbigh, and grand-uncle of the great novelist, Henry Fielding. At his death a few years afterwards he left us a legacy. With him came William, second Viscount Charlemont, to remain a governor for the rest of his life. Then we have nominations by the Duchess of Ormond, the wife of the Lord Lieutenant, second Duke; she was Mary, daughter of the Duke of Beaufort; and by the Lord Chancellor, Sir Richard Cox.

And yet at this time we find the sequelæ of the Revolution still seriously weakening us in the general want of

[1] On his return his nephew, Thos. King, our Old Chaplain, Tyrconnell's prisoner, was chosen Prebendary of Swords in S. Patrick's Cathedral.

money; our waste grounds in Stephen's Green and Oxmantown still unbuilt on, and our rents of these and through the country deeply in arrear, owing to what are now called the late troublous times. So our governors were obliged to look out on all sides for ways and means.

A source of income had been devised by letting the great hall for public entertainments: this was now put an end to. A rope dancer had given us one benefit night in 1703 for the use of the hall, which yielded just £20, but the Governors decreed that—" such diversions were very prejudicial to good government, causing the boys to be disorderly, to break the glass windows and cause scandal,"—so the rope dancing ceased, doubtless much to the disgust of our boys, and a Board Order forbade the future letting of the Hall save by special leave of the Governors. This seems to have been given some time after, when the great Italian Opera singer, Nicolini, came to Dublin. He had taken London by storm, he was the Mario of his day, and was known in Naples as Cavaliere Nicolini, and Addison pronounces him the greatest performer in dramatic music then living, or that perhaps ever appeared on our stage, but our Governors did not appreciate the memory this celebrity would leave to King's Hospital; though he gave them a benefit night which fetched £40, they treated his performance as they had done that of the poor nameless acrobat, for in December, 1711, the Board resolved that the use of the hall for such purposes had given great offence, and that it should never again be employed for "Musick Meetings," or public diversions of any kind. But the loss from this source was partly compensated. There was then a usage that each newly co-opted alderman should give a feast to the Lord Mayor and his fellows in our boardroom, not in the Tholsel. Thomas Bell being Lord Mayor and chairman, it was ordered that the three late chosen aldermen and all their successors should in lieu of the banquet pay £10 to the Hospital, and this usage continued for many years.

At this time, too, the medical care of the School was placed upon a systematic basis, and the connexion with the K. and

Q. College of Physicians confirmed which lasted for generations, to the lasting honour of the College, whose generosity to our Hospital was beyond all praise. Their original charter bore nearly equal date with ours. Their royalty, like ours, comes from Charles II. For ten years past the Surgeon-General, Dr. Proby, had taken medical charge of the School gratuitously ; in 1705 he was obliged to discontinue for a time, and a special meeting of our Board was held, and very largely attended. Proby was called in, and the Lord Mayor conveyed to him the thanks of the Governors for his great charity in taking care of the sick and distempered children for all those years. He was thereupon elected a Governor, and took his seat then and there, promising to continue his good offices so far as possible. Dr. Minchin, who had acted in his absence, was also thanked, and a resolution passed to attend at the College of Physicians and ask that they might be pleased to allow one of their Fellows always, by turns, to afford their charitable advice to the children as occasion should require. In March, 1706, Dr. Grattan, the President, conveyed to the Board the decision of the College that they were so charitably disposed as to give their advice and assistance to the Hospital on all occasions gratis, and would take care that one of their members should every three months by turns constantly visit the School ; and they asked that three of the waste rooms should now be set apart as an Infirmary, and this was done. The names of Grattan and Minchin have been honorably represented in the medical profession of Dublin through many years, nearly reaching to our own times.

1706 witnessed a great movement in the making of Dublin which promised to be a signal aid to King's Hospital. The VI. Anne, c. 20, made Dublin for the first time a real Port. Reciting the miserable condition of the river estuary and consequent necessity of discharging the ships at Ringsend and carrying the cargoes up river through sandy shoals, this Act created a Ballast Office, which was in truth our first Port and Harbour Board ; its chief members were the Lord Mayor and aldermen. All ships were now obliged to take ballast from the estuary bed at a shilling per ton, with twopence per

K

ton besides as harbour dues, foreign vessels being charged at higher rates; and it was provided that the whole surplus revenue of the new board should be paid over towards the maintenance of the Blue Coat School. This apparently splendid subsidy, however, proved nugatory as such, for the operations of the Ballast Office throughout the century were so large and continuous in channelling the Liffey and constructing quays, that they not only never had a surplus, but were always heavily in debt. The provision, nevertheless, marks the high estimate in which our School was now publicly held, and its part in the life of the city, whose governors, as presently seen, gave the Hospital a considerable equivalent for the income that thus proved illusory. The proposed appropriation of the Port revenue to the city school was supported in an address by the City Assembly to Prince George of Denmark, the Queen's Consort, then High Admiral of Great Britain and Ireland, on the ground that the boys were instructed in navigation to qualify them for Her Majesty's sea service.[2]

What would our temperance reformers of to-day think of the governors who erected a brewery in King's Hospital to brew our own beer for our boys? We may plead in mitigation, however, that it was only small beer. There were even then nearly seventy brewers in Dublin; they had suffered like other trades through the political convulsions. In the fever of these, in 1689, Tyrconnell's troopers had impressed their horses, with such a paralysis to trade and excise that the Jacobite Government had to stop their own troopers by proclamation, and even now the small beer was dear. So our governors petitioned the Corporation, which was not then so strongly represented by "the Trade" as now, and, in January, 1707, the Assembly voted £100 to the Hospital for a brewhouse—" whereby the number of poor boys maintained therein may be encouraged in the frugal management of brewing their own drink."[3] Our governor, Alderman Hendrick, who lived close by, and from whom Hendrick Street is named, was commissioned to carry out the work. The

---

[2] Gilbert's *Calendar*, 6, 274.   [3] Gilbert's *Calendar*, 6, 36

quality of our brewings may be understood by experts from an entry in our minutes directing that 18 barrels of beer shall be brewed from 8 barrels of malt.

In 1707 Ezekiel Burridge, first rector of the new St. Paul's, died, and thereon ensued an unseemly quarrel, which affected our school routine for a time, and which throws curious light on the judicial system then in force. In May, 1708, there is an order of our Board directing Charles Carr, the chaplain, to preach every Friday morning and read prayers in the chapel, and in the afternoon to catechise the boys and read evening prayers, as provided by the original Order of 1675, and that for the future the boys should not continue to attend St. Paul's. This order they respited a few days after—"till the law suite between Mr. Carr and the Dean and Chapter of Christ Church be ended, provided it continue not more than six months;" and this respite was afterwards extended, for the suit continued through ten long years. Our books give no further hint of the subject of dispute, those of Christ Church scarce more, and no trace can be found either in the Public Records Office or the Irish Law Books. But a search has unearthed the story in Josiah Brown's reports of Cases in the English House of Lords, and shows it to be a first chapter of the fierce conflict which waged for sixteen years between the Dean and Chapter and Archbishop King.[1] Burridge died 4th August, 1707, and on the selfsame day the Dean and Chapter, in indecent haste, nominated Revd. William Williamson rector, acting on the right of nomination reserved to them by the Act of 1696; executed the Instrument of Induction on the following day, and before Burridge was buried; and certified their act to the Archbishop in September. On Sunday, 9th November, Williamson came to St. Paul's and read the morning prayers; but before he could read himself in according to law, our chaplain, Carr, shut the doors and excluded the congregation at evening service, and when Williamson proceeded again to officiate, Carr with both hands closed his eyes and mouth, and he was unable to read

[1] For more of this quarrel, see Dr. George Stoke's *Worthies of the Irish Church*, Chapter X.

himself in, a form then essential to perfect his title as rector, even if otherwise valid. This more than strong measure was manifestly dictated by the Archbishop in order to cast on Christ Church the burden of proving title, rather than forcing him to proceed against a rector *de facto* in possession, for the real objection to Williamson was that the Dean and Chapter had refused to present him for approval of the Archbishop as Ordinary of the Arch-Diocese. The Dean was then Dr. Welbore Ellis, Bishop of Kildare, so appointed in 1705. He was truly a fighting prelate. The contention of the Dean and Chapter was that, as the successors to the Abbey of the Holy Trinity, reconstituted by Henry VIII. as a cathedral, they still had the old abbatial right to a jurisdiction of their own, free from that of the Archbishop, and extending over all the prebendary churches of the cathedral, of which Old St. Michan's was one, and that this right was preserved when the parish was divided into three under the words of the statute, which gives them the patronage of all three in such manner as the right of presentation to the old parish of St. Michan's had previously existed, and not otherwise; or, as the lawyers expressed it, that their rights were *donative*, in their own free gift, and not *presentative* and subject to the approval of the Ordinary as all other parishes were. So, in 1708, they proceeded in the Irish Common Pleas by a feigned plaintiff against Carr for the prevention and exclusion of Williamson, and his personal acts of the 9th November. The Common Pleas decided on full argument in favour of Christ Church that the living was donative; but an appeal then lay from them to the Irish Queen's Bench, who, on bill of exceptions and writ of error, unanimously reversed the Common Pleas. This was in Hilary, 1709. From the Irish Queen's Bench there was a similar right of appeal to the Queen's Bench in England, which was taken in 1712, and they unanimously affirmed the Queen's Bench here, but Christ Church still went on. They took the case to the English Lords, where it was argued in 1717 at great length by great lawyers; Constantine Phipps, Lord Chancellor here when the litigation began, but who had returned to the English Bar when superseded on the accession of George I., was for Christ Church, and Raymond, the great lawyer and reporter, was counsel for Carr. The Lords unanimously affirmed the two Queen's Benches, and gave judgment for Carr, deciding that the Rectory was presentative, and that on the division into three parishes each became like all others in the city subject to the jurisdiction of the Metropolitan, the statute merely preserving the right of Christ Church to present, like other patrons. Three other contentions of the Dean and Chapter met a similar fate. On similar grounds they had denied the Archbishop's right to visit the Cathedral, and, locking the gates, compelled him to hold his visitation outside the west door. They also spurned his right to summon to his visitation the prebendaries of their cathedral stalls; obliged Theophilus Harrison, rector of old St. John's, to refuse to attend them and to bring an action against the Archbishop; they refused to admit the Archbishop's nephew, Archdeacon Dongat, to his *ex-officio* seat in the Chapter, unless he first swore canonical obedience to the Dean. All these causes, like Carr's, went each to the four above-named tribunals, and in all twelve hearings the Archbishop prevailed, having fifteen judgments in all against the single one against Carr on the original hearing in the Common Pleas.

Meanwhile the Archbishop, as upon a lapse, had presented Dr. Carr to St. Paul's to hold along with his Blue Coat Headmastership and chaplaincy, and it was thus he could not officiate on Sunday in our chapel—obliged to keep Williamson out and himself in, at St. Paul's Church. He had now become a notable, and was appointed also Chaplain to the House of Commons, for the Archbishop was a staunch friend. This Christ Church episode is more interesting to us from our relations in other things with the Dean Bishop Welbore Ellis; during Anne's reign the name of Dean Pierre or Peter Drelincourt very often appears in our records as a governor and benefactor. He gave the Hospital £700 charge on the estate of Sir William Ellis, a relative of the bishop. This estate proved insolvent, and our governors were involved in litigation with its representatives, of whom the bishop was one, to raise the charge, and it was only after several years that, in 1709, when the Christ Church suit was at its height, the bishop compromised our claim, paying himself £500 to the Board. Though a fierce litigant, he did not resent the action of the Hospital; his animus was against the Archbishop, for, a Jacobite himself, he hated the Archbishop, who was an arch-Williamite, and for a worse motive, because the Archbishop was bent on suppressing the abuses at Christ Church, many of which were flagrant, and which he has thus summed up:—" They live in opposition to all mankind except their lawyers, squander their earnings, have turned their Chapter House into a toy shop, their vaults into wine cellars, and allowed a room in the body of the church, formerly for a Grand Jury room, now for a robe room for the judges, and are greatly chagrined at my getting two or three churches built in the parishes belonging to them, which were formerly neglected, as several others still are: their Cathedral is in a pitiful condition, and they seem to have little regard to the good of the Church or the service of God. This has made me zealous to settle my jurisdiction over them, and the same makes them unwilling to come under it." These abuses could only plead prescription, for we have seen how toy shops and wine cellars had been denounced by Strafford and Primate Bramhall seventy years before; and yet Bishop Ellis merits a kindly word here, for, after his final defeat in the St. Paul's case, he joined our Board in 1715, though Carr was still our chaplain, gave us £50 in 1720 and £50 in 1729; and when made Bishop of Kildare and Dean, he had paid his Consecration Feasts, £30, which so many other bishops were then very chary of doing. He died in 1731, Bishop of Meath and a Privy Councillor, and is ancestor of the Agar Ellises, Viscounts Clifden. He came from Oxford, where his portrait still hangs, imported to Ireland like so many bishops then, as so furiously denounced by Swift; but he rests in Christ Church, headquarters of his lengthened wars.

Dean Drelincourt's £700 was munificent, for he was himself a refugee, the son of a notable French Protestant Minister. He came here in 1681, and was made chaplain to the great Duke of Ormond and Precentor of Christ Church. Struck by the warm welcome his compatriots received from the city, he preached a famous sermon before the Lord Lieutenant and Privy Council there, to return, as he said, the humble thanks of the French Protestants arrived in Dublin and graciously relieved ; and this sentiment was doubtless the motive of his gift to the City School. In 1691 he became Dean of Armagh, but still retained his connection with Christ Church and with our Board, loyally helping us to realise his gift. His correspondence with the governors, of whom he was an active one, exhibits the amiable personality which made him popular here and in Armagh. At the request of the governors, he sat for his portrait, which for several generations decorated our walls, but which has disappeared, we know not how. He died in 1722, Dean and Rector of Armagh, where his handsome monument in the cathedral preserves a worthy memory. His portrait was by Michael Mitchell, who painted many celebrities of the day, including that of George I. presented by that king to the city, but which was cut to pieces in 1719 by unknown vandals, presumably Jacobites, who forcibly broke into the City Hall of the Tholsel by night.[5]

In 1709 our chairman and Lord Mayor was Sir William Fownes, one of the worthies and makers of Dublin. Fownes's Street was laid out by him, as was Cope Street hard by, which is named from his son-in-law. A very interesting letter of Fownes' to Swift, who many years after consulted him on his project for Swift's Hospital, describes the condition of Dublin as regards the Insane, during the period of his mayorality, which is memorable for the presentation of the freedom by him of the city to "the Right Honourable Joseph Addison, Esquire, Chief Secretary of State to the Lord Lieutenant of this Kingdom." He had come with Lord Wharton on his first visit to Ireland, but his fame had preceded him. No other Secretary had till then been called "Chief," and he is perhaps the only one who has been publicly styled a Secretary of State. Amongst our benefactions at the

[5] Gilbert's *Calendar* 7, viii.

period were £400 by the will of Dr. Steevens, who also left £600 a year to found the Hospital called by his name, and which his sister, Madame Griselda Steevens, generously completed in the following reign; £100 left by Mr. John Salmon, a London merchant, and some similar bequests of the same amount; and amongst our nominators we find Sir Richard Pyne, Lord Chief Justice of Ireland, and the Countess of Donegall; she was a daughter of the Earl of Granard. There is also a legacy of £50 by Dr. Ezekiel Burridge, our old neighbour, first rector of St. Paul's alluded to above. It was a liberal bequest from a clergyman who was not rich. We find his namesake, Ezekiel Burridge, amongst the forty boys admitted to the School under the Toll Corne Subsidy, presently mentioned, on the request of his widow, and, having regard to this benefaction; it was his testimony as a witness to the value of the School, close by which he had officiated in the new parish church.

The success and popularity of the School had naturally led to an increase in the admissions, which, in 1713, had reached 110; this encouraged the governors to petition the city for such an annual allowance as would enable them to utilise the building constructed to receive 300 boys. There was a tax on all grain coming into the city then, for free fooders were not yet in evidence. This was known as the "Toll Corne." The Assembly thereupon ordered that £250 per annum, in case the Toll Corne should answer same, should be appropriated for the support of forty boys to be added to the number in the Hospital.[6] This, commencing from All Saints, 1712, proved one of our main sources of income for over eighty years. Some seventeen new boys were now admitted, but the full carrying out of the project was checked by the city schism in the last years of Queen Anne and the consequent interregnum to the mayoralty. About the same time two houses in Smithfield were devised to the Hospital by the will of Dr. Pooley, Bishop of Raphoe, and which we still hold at the present day. He was an old neighbour, when rector of the old undivided parish of St. Michan's, and as such had

[6] Gilbert's *Calendar*, 6, 479.

been a Prebendary of Christ Church. He was a Fellow of Trinity College, and was raised successively to the Bishoprics of Cloyne and Raphoe ; but he never forgot his old friends of Oxmantown, and showered gifts on his old St. Michan's, where he lies, and where his monument still records his large-hearted charities, of which a list is given in Harris's *Ware*. This Toll Corne subsidy was presumably granted owing to the failure of the Ballast Office grant as a source of income.

The Three Years War.

The history of England in the last four years of Queen Anne was reflected in Dublin, and affected even the Blue Coat School. Our minute book, which, save in James II.'s time, has given an unbroken record from the opening to 1713, shows an hiatus of fourteen months from September, 1713, to November, 1714. This is not neglect or mutilation, but the mute evidence of an interregnum when no meetings were held, due to the three years' conflict between the Irish Government and the Corporation, which itself reflected the conflict that then raged through the three Kingdoms. Thus the story has a place here. The flight of Bolingbroke, the impeachment of Harley, the attainder and exile of the Duke of Ormonde, were the outcome of the intrigues in the Tory ministry which Swift's genius kept in power through the preceding four years, when, conscious of the Queen's yearnings towards her stepbrother, some of them at least schemed to bring home the Chevalier of St. George as James III. on the next demise of the Crown. The Irish Government, under the second Duke of Ormonde, had certainly leanings that way ; but the aldermen of the Corporation, or their great majority, were Williamite or Hanoverian to the core. Even in 1712 they addressed the Queen after the Treaty of Utrecht, thanking her for supporting the succession of the Crown in the illustrious House of Hanover. By a very ancient usage our Mayors were elected annually at the Easter Assembly, to hold office from the Morrow of Michaelmas for the ensuing year. Essex's Rules of 1672, provided that the Lord Mayor, the Sheriffs, and the Treasurer should be elected by the Lord Mayor and aldermen of the city, that *no other person should have a vote*, and if any of these officers should not be approved by the Privy Council within ten days of presentation of their names, the aldermen should proceed to a new election. In Elizabeth's time, the expense of the mayoralty being onerous, a byelaw was made by the Corporation that each alderman should keep his turn for bearing the charge of the Mayoralty " according to his ancientry," that is, that the alderman next below the cushion as it was called, should serve. This byelaw was repealed in Oliver's time, but re-enacted in his son Henry's, in 1657; nevertheless this order of succession had frequently not been observed. In 1709, when the strong Whig, Lord Wharton, was Lord Lieutenant, Alderman Robert Constantine was senior alderman below the cushion. He was a very respectable gentleman, a druggist and apothecary, had been Sheriff in 1696, and for some fourteen years had been one of the most attentive of our governors ; in some years his name appears at every one of our meetings. At the Spring election of 1709 for the Mayoralty his name was put up with two others of our governors, Aldermen Forrest and Eccles. Forrest was elected, though not the senior. Constantine then relying on the rule, petitioned the Lord Lieutenant in Council to withold approval ; but the Council, regarding the rule of succession as " a sleepy and obsolete law," confirmed Forrest as Lord Mayor. At the Easter Assembly, 1710, Constantine was again similarly passed over, Alderman Eccles, his junior, being elected ; and again appealing to the Privy Council, he was refused permission to appear by Counsel, and Eccles' election was confirmed. But in Spring, 1711, things had changed ; the Tories had swept the elections in England in 1710, and the second Duke of Ormonde was now Lord Lieutenant. With him came Sir Constantine Phipps as Lord Chancellor. He had won high fame at the English Bar as counsel for Dr. Sacheverel at the historic state trial, and next year was honoured with the Irish Seals. He was High Church, High Tory, and Jacobite, and became the recognised leader of those principles here. The great majority of the gentry, nearly all the middle classes, and the upper artizans were predominantly Protestant and opposed to the Pretender. To all these Phipps became suspect; he added early to their suspicions by directing a *nolle prosequi* of the prosecution of a gentleman who had written a Memoir of the Chevalier of St. George, and by refusing to permit the decorating of the statue of King William in College Green, which had already become an annual festivity and a tribute to the pious and immortal memory, not unknown even in Queen Victoria's time, and even in that of Anne not always unprovocative of riot. For the Roman Catholic citizens and the mass of the mob were partial to Phipps and the Pretender; though even the mob had a good sprinkling of the orange weavers of St. Werburgh's and the Coombe. With the Chancellor, Vesey, Archbishop of Tuam, acted as Lord Justice. He had no reason to welcome the Pretender, for when James II. was here, he had to fly from Tuam for his life with an episcopal family of twelve children.

So when, at the Easter Assembly of 1711, the Lord Mayor and Aldermen for the third time superseded Constantine and elected Alderman Barlow, the Privy Council, on Constantine's petition, ordered the Lord Mayor and aldermen to answer, and directed both sides to appear by counsel before the full Council board. The answer is signed by fourteen aldermen, including Eccles, Lord Mayor. It claimed the right of election to be in them, which would, it said, be no election if they were compelled to choose the senior; and, traversing the immemorial usage alleged, it denied there was any irregularity in electing Alderman Barlow, unless, indeed, it added rather sarcastically, not electing the petitioner be one. The argument lasted two days. Forster, the Recorder, acting as counsel for the Corporation. The Privy Council affirmed the byelaw of ancientry and summarily disapproved Barlow.

Archbishop King, who sat at the hearing, writes to Swift, who was in London, an impartial account of the trial.[7] He

[7] 15th May, 1711. Scott's *Swift*, Vol. XV., 448.

says the case turned on the most slender point of the old byelaw; that as Archbishop of Dublin he thought he should support the city, and as the byelaw had been passed, not to coerce the electors, but to compel reluctant mayors to serve, and had frequently been disregarded, he warned his colleagues that the decision would beget ill blood, and that it was not the Duke of Ormonde's interest to clash with the city; but they said they didn't foresee any hurt to his grace, "and I pray God it may not." "You must know," he says, "this is made a party affair, as Constantine sets up for a high churchman, which I never heard of before; but whoever has a private quarrel and finds himself too weak, becomes a partizan, and makes his private a public quarrel."

The Privy Council thus drew first blood. But in the whole three years' war we discern through the mist a strong, skilful, and resourceful hand guiding the Corporation. This was Forster's, the Recorder. He had been made Solicitor-General by Lord Wharton in 1708, *vice* Sir Richard Levinge, who was a Tory, but displaced on the return of the Tories, when Sir Richard became Attorney-General. Forster keeps in the background in this conflict, but his knowledge and his spirit animated it throughout. Accepting the decision in favour of the byelaw, a full assembly was convened for the following day.[8]

All the aldermen and all the Commons were summoned, and the byelaw was formally repealed. The Privy Council two years afterwards alleged that this meeting was tumultuously ushered in with great noise and clamour, that there was a cry of "Popery, Popery," and "that the byelaw was repealed as Popish, though made in the reign of Queen Elizabeth." But the aldermen proceeded with all constitutional forms. To make Constantine again legally eligible they rescinded an order by which some time before he had been placed above the cushion "and to wear a scarlet gown"; then they proceeded to the second election, at which Constantine, Barlow, and Alderman Samuel Cooke were duly put in nomination; Barlow was re-elected Lord Mayor. In the

[8] See Eccles' *Statement*. Gilbert's *Calendar*, 7, 564.

above cited letter Archbishop King strongly deprecated the summary action of the city as provocative, and the Privy Council, angrily regarding it as such, and "a contempt of authority," again disapproved. The aldermen proceeded to a third election, this time nominating Constantine Cooke, and Ralph Gore; there were only three votes for Constantine, against 16 for Cooke, who was declared duly elected, but who in turn was duly disapproved by the Privy Council. A fourth election followed in August, when Constantine's name was dropped, and Alderman T. Quin, Samuel Walton, and John Page were put forward, Page being declared Lord Mayor with seventeen votes, but confirmation was again withheld. At a fifth election, also held in August, Alderman Gibbons was nominated with Quin and Walton, and receiving fifteen votes, was chosen, with the same fate, however, as his predecessors. But the aldermen were not daunted. At a sixth election they nominated Walton again, now with Gibbons and Benjamin Barton, and Walton was elected with thirteen votes. This was on the 31st August. The Privy Council once more declined to approve, and as Michaelmas was now in sight, when the existing Lord Mayor Eccles' tenure would cease, and no one yet appointed to succeed him, the Corporation, despairing of the Privy Council, addressed a petition to Queen Anne herself. It is a very able document —firm, dignified, and loyal. After reciting the Essex Rules vesting the election of the Lord Mayor and Sheriffs in the Lord Mayor and aldermen, *and in no one else*, it states that so careful has the city been in the election of its Lord Mayor that, since 1672 to within a few months past, no elected Lord Mayor was ever disapproved by the Privy Council, save when, in 1687, Tyrconnell, having superseded the ancient charters, refused approval in favour of Sir Thomas Hackett; "yet your petitioners," it proceeds, "have been so unfortunate as to have been obliged five several times since Easter to proceed to a new choice by reason the Council were pleased so often to disapprove the person elected, though no objection had been made to their sufficiency or loyalty, they being all educated in the Church of Ireland as by law established, and men who had always shown hearty affection towards Your Majesty's Government." Referring to the rule of seniority, the pretext for the original disapproval of Barlow, the petitioners set forth three precedents in 1672, 1674, and 1696, in which the byelaw had not been followed, and implore Her Majesty's generous interposition that the right of electing magistrates for the city may not be turned into a nomination by the Government and the Council. " Placing entire reliance in the Queen's justice and goodness," they repudiate any disrespect or opposition to the Government placed over them, and state their willingness to make any compliance " consistent with our right and freedom of election and the oaths we have taken to maintain the liberties of Your Majesty's most ancient and loyal city." This petition was forwarded to the Lord Lieutenant, Ormonde, by Eccles, the Lord Mayor, for transmission to the Queen. The Duke replied on 7th September, saying he had sent it into England. But Michaelmas was imminent, so, pending the Queen's decision, a seventh election was had, at which Alderman Pearson with Gibbons and Barton were nominated, and Pearson elected with thirteen votes, only to be disapproved like the six that went before him. Michaelmas was now at hand, and no new Lord Mayor.

The aldermen refused to be defeated. On the 27th September they proceeded to the eighth election. To emphasise their attitude, they again put forward Constantine along with Ralph Gore, who had already been nominated at the third election, and, with these, Alderman Robert Mason. There were twenty votes, of which two went for Constantine, and eighteen for Gore.

Michaelmas had come, and no Lord Mayor. On the 1st October the Corporation met and affirmed " the undoubted right of the Lord Mayor and Aldermen of the City of Dublin to elect to the Mayoralty such of the aldermen as they shall think most fit, without regard to seniority or juniority." For this resolution twenty voted ; there were only two voices *contra*. At last the Government caved in. Whether they had a hint from London, or as yet dared not contemplate anything so dreadful as a city without a head, they approved Alderman Gore, who became Lord Mayor from Michaelmas, 1711-1712. The year's campaign thus ended with a decisive victory for the Corporation.

The Privy Council, however, yielded with a bad grace. We have not involved the story with the case of the sheriffs, but should state that at five of the above elections the Council had disapproved the choice of the sheriffs along with the mayor; and at the sixth, while giving way as to the Mayoralty, they disapproved as Sheriff Daniel Falkiner, the banker, though without impeachment and chosen unanimously, and Walker, though chosen by sixteen votes to five, and a seventh election for the Shrievalty became necessary.

The war was renewed next year; this campaign was shorter than the last, but sharp. From the record of May, 1712, it would seem there had been some abortive meetings at Easter, for it recites—"former elections having been rejected." At this May assembly our old friend Constantine was again put forward with Barlow, who had been twice, and Cooke, who had been once disapproved, as we have seen, in the previous year; but he had only a single vote, and Barlow, with thirteen, was chosen Lord Mayor. With him were named Sheriffs Glegg and Somerville, who had both been disapproved as such in 1711. This election the Privy Council regarded as a further disrespect to the Government, and indignantly refused approval. But the aldermen stood to their guns. In July they again nominated Constantine with Cooke and Mason; again Constantine had only one vote. Cooke had fourteen, and was elected, with Bradshaw and Aldrich as Sheriffs.

The Privy Council at last approved of Cooke, who duly became Lord Mayor from Michaelmas, 1712 to 1713; but Aldrich was angrily disapproved for the Shrievalty. In their address to the Queen next year the Council say—"With the same spirit of obstinacy the aldermen had also certified one Aldrich for Sheriff, who had been twice before disapproved, and is a factious person and a dispenser of libels against the Government," but they omit to state that they had themselves first disapproved such a nominee as Thomas Somerville, against whom there was no objection, and who was a gentleman of substance, and very many others who were equally without reproach.

The laurels of this campaign were again with the Corporation, though their victory in the person of Samuel Cooke was, as the sequel proved, not so great as they had supposed; and possibly the Council in approving him knew what they were about.

The third campaign opened in April, 1713, at their Easter Assembly, Lord Mayor Cooke presiding. Poor Constantine was once more put in nomination, this time with Mason and John Stoyte, yet again he had one vote only. Stoyte carried seventeen. Stoyte's return with the Sheriffs is certified to the Privy Council with the signatures of nineteen aldermen, including Cooke, though his name appears only third. As Stoyte was the junior of the three, the Council, "therefore, and for other good reasons," conceived him unfit, and disapproved. There was a new Assembly in May, at which Lord Mayor Cooke appeared in a new character. He took from his pocket a piece of paper with the names of Sir William Fownes, Constantine, and Mason on it, and proposed them for election. Then the storm broke out; seventeen aldermen insisted on first putting the question whether any of the three should be elected. Fownes was objected to as having already served as Mayor in 1708, and Constantine as having been already eight times rejected by great majorities; and a formal vote was proposed whether Constantine should be "put in election." Cooke refused to put the question, and, declaring if they would not proceed to his three nominations he would allow no other choice, he rose to go. They implored him to remain; he refused. Then they told him if he wilfully withdrew they would proceed for the purpose for which they were duly summoned, and that they were almost unanimous for electing Alderman Pleasants for the ensuing year. The Lord Mayor withdrew nevertheless; seventeen aldermen remained. After waiting some hours in hope Cooke would return, they sent to him, expressing their extreme reluctance to proceed in his absence without absolute necessity. He replied that he would not come; so the seventeen thereupon elected Pleasants unanimously, and returned his name under their seventeen signatures. Of course the Privy Council disapproved. They advised the whole case to be argued before them. Then, after solemn debate on the 3rd and 4th September, they declared the election of Pleasants void, and directed a new election; and, on the 11th September, sent to Lord Mayor Cooke two resolutions affirming the right of the Lord Mayor to nominate three candidates, one of whom must be chosen, and that the proceeding in the Lord Mayor's absence was illegal and a breach of the Rules of 1672. The question what punishment was to be meted to the seventeen recusants was reserved; they seemed to forget that there was no Star Chamber now. The aldermen, still undaunted, called a new Assembly on the 21st September, and putting forward Constantine with Mason and Alderman Thomas Bolton, returned the latter as Lord Mayor by eighteen votes to two, he being the junior and one of the seventeen. With him they again named the "factious person," Aldrich, as Sheriff, and certified to the Privy Council on 24th September with the signatures of twenty-two aldermen, including Cooke, who signs second. The Privy Council were incensed; they directed that the seventeen recusants should be prosecuted, ordering an immediate new election, for Michaelmas was again at hand.

Cooke accordingly re-summoned the aldermen on the 25th, and offered them as candidates Constantine, Mason, and French; but the meeting refused to vote for any of them. Ormonde had now gone, and the Duke of Shrewsbury had just become Viceroy. The Privy Council some time before had sent over their statement of the case to the Government in London. It was not so successful as they had hoped. On the 27th September they received a letter from the Secretary of State, Lord Bolingbroke, suggesting as a compromise that the Lord Mayor should nominate a *new person* vice Sir William Fownes, whom the aldermen had rejected as a past Lord Mayor. Professing high satisfaction at this suggestion, the Council directed the aldermen to attend on Michaelmas Day itself, and, reading Bolingbroke's letter, invited them to act accordingly. They acceded to the plan as one which "would effectually quiet all their disorders," and forthwith assembled to carry it out. Sir Samuel Cooke, however, still in the Lord Mayor's chair, put forward again Constantine, Mason, and French, the three who had been rejected only four days before, alleging French to be a new person, in place of Fownes, in accordance with Bolingbroke's compromise. The aldermen regarded this as a mere pretence; they besought Cooke to be moderate, and stated their willingness to accept any other nominee whom they had not previously rejected; but Cooke persisted, and the meeting broke up, facing the catastrophe of Michaelmas come and Michaelmas gone and no Lord Mayor of Dublin.

On 1st October the Privy Council in deep chagrin sent their statement to the Queen. Petulant in tone, and partial as to facts, it sadly contrasts with the petition of the Corporation, which soon after followed it. It asserts the usages and law, but without adducing proof or precedent, and bitterly inveighs against the obstinacy of the aldermen. Yet it had high sanction, signed by the Lord Chancellor, Sir Constantine Phipps, and Vesey, Archbishop of Tuam; Sir Richard Cox, Lord Chief Justice; Sir Robert Doyne, Lord Chief Baron; the Earls of Inchiquin, Abercorn, and Kerry; the Bishops of Meath, Kildare, and Raphoe. With the statement they forwarded the opinions of some of the Judges and all the Crown Counsel in favour of the Lord Mayor's prerogative claim, and his right to continue in office till his successor was regularly appointed and approved. Sir Constantine Phipps wrote privately to Swift, asking his assistance with Harley and Bolingbroke, and appears to have had a reply which pleased him, for he writes again to Swift in October, thanking him effusively for "burning his fingers on his behalf;" but though Swift did then secure for the Chancellor's son a good office he was seeking, he writes the week after to Archdeacon Walls—" Your Mayor's squabble we regard as much here as if you sent me an account of your little son playing at cherry stones. I received the Lord Justice's representation sent to the Queen, and have said more on it than anyone else would, and I hope the new Lord Lieutenant will put an end to the dispute."

Still the aldermen stood staunch. They refused to recognise Cooke as Lord Mayor, and, as the Privy Council had declared his presence essential for every legal assembly and corporate act, they refused to exercise their corporate functions, to hold assemblies, to open the City Court at the Tholsel, or to have meetings of the Governors of the Blue Coat. Under counsel's advice the outgoing sheriffs refused to exercise office. These were Thomas Bradshaw and Edward Somerville. The Government ordered them still to act, and directed them both to be prosecuted. This was the interregnum. Thereupon the aldermen also addressed a petition to the Queen. Signally able, moderate, learned, and exhaustive, it was supported by proofs and precedents which seem irrefragable and conclusive. The Recorder and three aldermen were sent with it to London to argue the cause and negotiate with the Government. They went at their own expense, for they could not in the interregnum touch the city funds. They would appear to have made in their mission a considerable stay. The petition cites the royal charters of Dublin, of Henry III., Edward III., Henry IV., and Henry VI., giving choice of the Mayor to the citizens of Dublin. It sets forth a byelaw in the time of Richard III. providing that the *Jurees*, the old name for the aldermen, should, on each Holyrood Day, name one of themselves as Mayor for a year from Michaelmas, and the new Rules of 1672, enacting that the election of Lord Mayor and Sheriffs should be for ever thereafter only by the Lord Mayor and aldermen, eight being present. A result of a search through all the records for the trace of any rule giving the Lord Mayor alone the right to nominate three, of whom one must be chosen, showed that none such existed. By accumulated instances it is shewn that though the Lord Mayor in form always put forward these three names to the Assembly, this was always done after a conference with the aldermen, and that even then the right of the

Assembly to reject the seniors or to substitute a new name was repeatedly recognised. The petition shows further that Sir Samuel Cooke was himself a subscribing party to the order of October, 1711, which declares the undoubted right " of the Lord Mayor and aldermen " to elect to the Mayoralty such of the aldermen as they think fit, without regard to seniority; and several other orders of similar purport to which he is a signatory are also put in evidence.

Cooke's assumption to remain in office till his prerogative claims are acceded to is refuted with equal force. It is shown that the entries of elections always mentioned that the Mayor and Sheriffs are elected and approved to serve for one year only. A bye-law of 13 James I., is cited, enacting that no one should be continued Mayor two years successively, and though in the distraction of the rebellion of 1641, Smith was continued Mayor for four successive years, the entries showed he was duly elected at the close of each; whilst all the records proved a constant usage that the Mayor should hold office only to the morrow of Michaelmas, when his successor was sworn in, save when Michaelmas was on Saturday, and then he only held till the Monday following, the only case to the contrary being that of Hackett aforesaid, when Tyrconnell was Lord Deputy.

The extracts from the charters and rolls are attested with a precision which would do credit to our Court of Chancery to-day. Certificates are added: one, by eight ex-Lord Mayors, testifying that they always conferred with their brethren, the aldermen, and had their approbation for their three nominees, and that no Mayor within memory had ever held over after Michaelmas; another, by twelve aldermen below the cushion, testifying that the right of nominating the three was always in practice in the Lord Mayor and Aldermen, and not in the Lord Mayor alone. And there is a sworn deposition of Sir John Eccles, who served 1610-1611, to the same effect, in which he adds, that when at the close of his year, his successor, Ralph Gore, had not been approved on the Monday after Michaelmas, which had fallen on Saturday, he threw off his gown, laid aside rod, sword, and mace, and walked the streets to the Tholsel as a private man.

The petitioners, speaking throughout in most respectful and loyal language, protest they have no other view than a faithful discharge of their trust, and of their oaths, to maintain their rights and charters derived from the Crown, and under the royal prerogative, and they deeply deprecate the course by which "the city has been thrown into disorder and confusion, and its sessions, assemblies, and courts have remained ever since unattended."

If Cooke and the Privy Council were right, it is plain that the franchise of choosing the civic officers would be illusory, and this, with the power of perpetual disapproval in the Crown, would give the appointment of Mayor and Sheriffs to the Government of the day, whenever the Lord Mayor was subservient. But the appeals to the Crown were never actually decided. We know how, in the last year of Queen Anne, the disputes between Harley and Bolingbroke had become acute, and even Swift, dear friend of both, failed to reconcile them; this hastened the Queen's death, and when the year began to wane, on the 1st August, she died. Death was the *deus ex machina* that severed the knot which was strangling the municipal life of Dublin. The Jacobites were routed in London and Dublin alike, the Hanoverians ruled supreme. Whilst Harley was being impeached, Lord Chancellor Phipps retired to the Middle Temple, and resumed private practice at the Bar. All things were changed. At Michaelmas, 1714, the interregnum ceased, and James Barlow, the thrice rejected elect and original *casus belli*, was knighted and duly installed Lord Mayor of Dublin.

The war ended in conquest by the Corporation. Sir John Forster was made Lord Chief Justice of the Common Pleas, and John Rogerson, Sir John's son, Recorder, in his stead. To Forster the city voted £500 " as a mark of favour to their late worthy Recorder, who, by his abilities, vigilance, and steady adherence to the true interests of the city, was highly instrumental in preserving its liberties, to the neglect of his private concerns, and the considerable detriment of his private fortune," and his portrait, painted at the expense of the city, was ordered to be placed in the Tholsel. He had also a lease from the city of the lands and house at Donnycarney, Clontarf, where he resided. These passed later in the century to Lord Charlemont, on which he formed his beautiful demesne of Marino, and which are now in the possession of the Christian Brothers. The new House of Commons, in 1716, voted to him, and to the nineteen survivors of the twenty stalwarts, and to Somerville, the surviving sheriff, who had refused to continue in office, contrary to law, the Thanks of the House, for their great virtue in defending the rights of the city. £900 was voted in the Assembly to the Aldermen and Sheriffs to defray their costs of the late litigation before the Privy Council, the Queen's Bench, and in England. The disapproved Lord Mayors elect, Stoyte, Pleasants, and Bolton, were successively placed in the civic chair. Barkey, Quaile, Wilkinson, Forbes, Curtis and Dickson, followed as Lord Mayors in each successive year up to 1723, and Somerville had a special grant of £200. Sir Samuel Cooke was indicted before the Assembly for having betrayed the city, and acted as the instrument of arbitrary power. He defended himself ably, relying on the opinions of the Privy Council and Crown lawyers, but after an elaborate hearing, the sentence was that he "be disfranchised from all the franchises and liberties of the city, be henceforth rejected and taken as a foreigner, and removed from the place of alderman."

It may be thought unreasonable thus at length to wake the echoes of this long sleeping strife, and to call from oblivion these phantoms of our city worthies long ago forgotten, but to Blue Coat Hospitallers, the story is acutely interesting. To us the actors are not phantoms. These names that have shifted now before us like colours of the kaleidoscope, are all inscribed in living letters on the records of the meetings of our governors in those stirring years. The seventeen recusants—Sir John Eccles, Sir John Rogerson, Sir Ralph Gore, Sir James Barlow, Thos. Quin, Samuel Walton, John Page, Benjamin Barton, John Pearson, John

Stoyte, Thomas Bolton, Anthony Barkey, William Quaile, Thomas Wilkinson, George Forbes, Thos. Curtis, and William Dickson, who, with Thomas Pleasants, Matthew Pearson, and Robert Cheatham, made up the twenty stalwarts, all are living in our Minute Books to-day, as nominating children, apprenticing pupils, raising ways and means, managing our estate. Some of them attended almost every meeting, and the governors of to-day cannot but have a pride in corporate ancestors, so strong, so firm, and so brave. They are not wholly dead. Streets of Dublin still record the names of Rogerson, Fownes, Eccles, Pleasants, and the names of many of these sleeping combatants still survive in their posterity. Phipps is lineal ancestor of the Mulgraves and Normanbys, and Constantine, first Marquess of Normanby, Lord Lieutenant of Ireland in 1835. One wonders if that Christian name attracted the Chancellor towards his namesake, our so oft-rejected candidate. Vesey, Archbishop of Tuam and Lord Justice, is lineal ancestor of the Lords de Vesci. Somerville, the disapproved sheriff, is lineal ancestor of the Lords Athlumney. Benjamin Barton, the banker, the disapproved sheriff, is lineal ancestor of the Bartons of Pollacton, County Carlow. Daniel Falkiner, the banker, another of the disapproved, is great-great-great-granduncle of the present writer. Sir Samuel Cooke is ancestor by the female descent of one of the best country gentlemen of our day, Thomas Cooke-Trench, late of Millicent, Kildare, who carried the memory of his fighting forbear in his own gentle person and name, and many a family pedigree in Ireland would probably trace through others of these civic worthies of two centuries ago.

[Chairmen and Lord Mayors.

Our Chairmen and Lord Mayors in Queen Anne's reign were:—

1702	...	...	Samuel Walton.
1702-3	...	...	Thomas Bell.
1703-4	...	...	John Page.
1704-5	...	...	Francis Stoyte.
1705-6	...	...	Wm. Gibbons
1706-7	...	...	Benj. Burton
1707-8	...	...	John Pearson.
1708-9	...	...	Sir Wm. Fownes.
1709-10	...	...	Charles Forrest.
1710-11	...	...	John Eccles
1711-12	...	...	Sir Ralph Gore
1712-13	...	...	Sir Samuel Cooke.
1713-14	...	...	Interegnum.

The evolution of the City was somewhat stayed by the political contest of the three years war, but two of the most important events in the development of the City were inaugurated in this reign. The Constitution of the first Harbour Board, known as the Ballast Office, and the construction of the South Wall by Sir John Rogerson, which was continued by the City so as to enclose the gulf between Townsend street and Ringsend.

[1] The above narrative is drawn from the original records which are given in full in Gilbert's *Calendar*, Vol VI., and Appendix to Vol. VII.

CHAPTER VII.

TEMP. GEORGE I., 1714-1727

QUEEN ANNE died 1st August, 1714. The old regime had resumed here, as we have seen, with the new reign. The first act of the City Assembly was to present Archbishop King with the freedom of the city in a gold box, a distinction then only conferred on Lord Lieutenants or personages of highest rank or celebrity. The Archbishop was now the presiding member of the Government in the absence of the Duke of Shrewsbury, the new Lord Lieutenant. The meetings of our governors were resumed in November, under Sir James Barlow, Chairman and Lord Mayor; their first business was to complete the admission of forty new boys, as arranged with the Corporation. In the next few years their work is routine, and demands no special remark; but we note next year nominations of boys by the famous Earl of Galway, who was then the Lord Justice. This was Henry, Marquess de Ruvigny. He was one of the French Protestant exiles, and had come to England as representative of all the Protestant churches of France. He was a great soldier of William III, for whom he fought at the Battle of Aughrim, and by whom he was given an earldom in our peerage. In 1716, as we have already mentioned, our chaplain and schoolmaster, Charles Carr, became Lord Bishop of Killaloe, and Rev. Richard Gibbons was appointed in his place. In 1717 some important additions to our Board were made—Major-General Frederick Hamilton, who, dying a few years after, left the Hospital a legacy of £300; Forster, our late Recorder, who now rejoined as Lord Chief Justice of the Common Pleas. At the same time the Presidents of the College of Physicians were made *ex-officio* governors. But far the most important accession was that of Archbishop King himself at the special invitation of the governors, for he was perhaps the greatest governor the Blue Coat has had; and almost up to his death in 1729 he gave it a good share of his marvellous organizing power and generous liberality, which far outweighed the contentiousness, which made him some enemies, not the less because it was always directed against abuses, and in almost all cases prevailed. In 1718 he sent the Lord Mayor a cheque for £500 as a gift to the School. In the next year a bill was brought into the Commons by our Recorder, John Rogerson, who was M.P. for the city and Solicitor-General, for regulating the streets, and he was directed by the Government, of which the Archbishop was a leading member, to insert a clause for limiting and licensing the coaches and sedans of the city. The Archbishop was also then a leader in the Lords; more than half the peers who attended then were bishops. This bill, 6 Geo. I., c. 15, reciting the recent growth of the city, provided for licensing fifty more hackney coaches and forty more chairs, with an annual tax of £1 5s. 0d. each, to be applied to the support of the Blue Coat Hospital for six years. This increased its income by £180; and, thanking the Government, the Board increased the number of boys to 180, the highest mark they had hitherto reached. When, seven years after, this benefit had expired, it was renewed in another form. In 1727 the James's Street Workhouse was reconstructed by 1 Geo. II., c. 27, under commissioners who may be regarded as precursors of the South Dublin Union, and perhaps the most distinguished Poor Law Guardians on record; they included the chief magnates in Church and State, members of the Government of both Houses of Parliament, and the high civic dignitaries, Archbishop King being nearly first on the list. One of our statutory sources of income was the tax on the hackney coaches and chairs, which was now remodelled. The new license duties and annual tax were to be paid to the Commissioners, of which the revenue of one hundred and fifty coaches and one hundred and sixty chairs was allocated to the Workhouse, and that of fifty coaches and forty sedans to the Blue Coat School. This aid was continued to us for forty-four years, when it was taken away by 11 & 12 Geo. III., c. 11, and given to the Rotunda Hospital. Some of the accounts show more than £200 paid in a single year. The Archbishop was now Treasurer of the Erasmus Smith's Board, and his practical wisdom saw the policy, so often ignored in the history of beneficence, of making cognate charities work in alliance rather than in overlapping machinery. In 1723 he formed a Committee of King's Hospital to confer with a committee of the Erasmus Smith's board, and these, in July, in his own palace in St. Sepulchre's, agreed on a scheme of ten clauses by which the Erasmus Smith's board should contribute £300 towards the building of an infirmary in King's Hospital, which was sorely needed, the Hospital to receive from time to time any number of boys up to twenty nominated by the Erasmus Smith's board, to be maintained in all respects under the same regulations as the other boys on our foundation. For these the Erasmus Smith's board are to provide the necessary furniture and to pay quarterly a rateable proportion of the expenses of the School. They also undertake the apprenticing of their twenty pupils, and to pay £5 a year to our head master; the Lord Mayor and the Recorder for the time being are to be standing governors of the Erasmus Smith's school, four of whose members reciprocally are to be standing governors of the Blue Coat; and the Erasmus Smith's board undertake to apply to the ensuing session of Parliament for an Act to ratify the contract. This scheme was confirmed by our Board at their September meeting, and our seal affixed to the heads of the bill brought in under the Archbishop's auspices, and passed that session, during which he was an assiduous attendant in the Lords. This statutory alliance has now existed for more than 180 years, for it was fully recognised by the Municipal Corporations Act of 1840, and was never more faithfully carried out than in the late long years in which Vice-Chancellor Chatterton has presided at the Erasmus Smith's Board.

This Bill was passed in the session of 1723-24 as an Act for further application of the rents given by Erasmus

Smith for charitable purposes. The clauses affecting the Blue Coat will be found in Appendix B, It contains a clause empowering our governors to make building leases of their waste lands in Dublin for ninety-nine years ; our charter limited the term to forty-one. This valuable power, hidden away in the unnumbered sections of a local Act dealing with another charity, has been unnoticed in the indexes to the statutes and text books, and has been unnoticed by our governors for the past fifty years, during which they have believed it necessary to apply to Chancery or Charity Commissioners for leave to grant building leases. The only clue given in our minute books is an entry in 1724 of ten guineas paid to one John Dexter, " for his extraordinary trouble in London in soliciting a clause in a late Act of Parliament " to the above effect, without further indication of what statute it was.

Our records of this time include the names of many distinguished persons nominating boys :—The Duchess of Grafton, the Lord Lieutenant's wife, in 1722 ; she was wife of Charles Fitzroy, the second Duke, and grand-daughter of the Duke of Beaufort ; Lady Carteret, wife of the Lord Lieutenant in 1725 ; and Chief Justice Whitshed, Swift's prosecuting judge ; Presidents of the College of Physicians, in succession Doctors Grattan, Jammett, and Mitchell ; and several nominations by the vestries of the city churches, whose recommendations were always honoured by our governors.

Under the Erasmus Smith's alliance, the much needed Infirmary of our old Hospital was built. The energy and example of the Archbishop was visible everywhere. Alderman Quaile, who had been our Lord Mayor and Chairman in 1719, now, himself, expended £500 on the infirmary, and old Sir John Rogerson's legacy of £100 was added. The restoration of our chapel was also taken in hand, to which Dr. Daniel, the Dean of Armagh, contributed £50, and a charity sermon preached by Dr. Maule, Bishop of Cloyne, presumably at the Archbishop's instance, realised £60 towards this object. Hitherto there had been no supervision of the Hospital accounts ; and a drastic order, reciting that there was no method of charging the agent with his receipts of casual revenue, is made in the Archbishop's presence that one of the governors should be annually chosen as Treasurer, he to give his discharges for all contributions in support of the Hospital; all tradesmen's bills to be confirmed by a standing committee. An order also directs that the chaplain shall in future catechise the boys weekly, as provided by the charter; another that each of the 180 boys should have a Bible; and another that a sufficient number of the Archbishop of Tuam's (Dr. Edward Synge's) exposition of the Church Catechism should be bought for the boys; a list of all the benefactors of the School from the beginning, with a proper preamble, is directed to be made, and hung on tables in the Hall of the Hospital; and this was carried out and continued for years. An inventory of all goods and chattels in the house is to be made out and continued from time to time, and examined by the Committee periodically. Had this order been maintained, we should possess many memorials now, historic pictures, whole libraries of books, which have long since vanished. It was found there were now 188 boys, occupying twenty-nine rooms, with twenty-nine more for officers and servants, beside the Hall Chapel and schoolrooms, and other such buildings. Finally, this committee are directed to inspect all the laws of the house and the regulations affecting the officers and servants, and to report what further laws they recommend for the good government of the Hospital. The Archbishop was present at the election of an additional schoolmaster in 1725. Our chaplain, with our increased numbers, needed assistance. Mr. John Connell was elected. We can see the strong reforming hand in the minute which orders that the schoolmaster *in future* bring neither wife nor child to lodge or diet or to be a charge or incumbrance upon this house; that he apply himself wholly to the business of the School, and teach no other boys, either at home or abroad; and that he attend them constantly to church or chapel, so that they behave themselves reverently there, and orderly and decently at their meals. That " in future " in the above has a latent humour, suggesting how things had previously gone on, and it is more pointed by the fact that the Archbishop was a stern bachelor to the end. He last attended our Board in April, 1726, when he announced a benefaction of £500 from Lady Midleton, sent by her to himself: she was widow of Lord Chancellor Allen Broderick, first Lord Midleton. Oh, that Archbishop King had been with us for many a year before and after! His work at the Blue Coat, which was but a fringe of his vast official labour, might further illustrate the story of his life as told by Dr. George Stokes in the latest volume from his luminous pen, *Some Worthies of the Irish Church*, edited by Rev. H. Lawlor in 1900.

A fresh wreath has just been placed on his memory here. By the munificence of Lord Iveagh, the north choir aisle of St. Patrick's Cathedral had a few years since been restored and relighted by the removal of the darkening organ loft back towards the choir. Then the fine memorial to the late Dean Jellett was erected in the eastern window, and the old chapel of St. Peter, which formed this part of the aisle, was reconstituted. The side lights in the northern wall of this chapel are formed by two arches, each with two lancets. Those in the eastern arch are the memorial windows to Provost Salmon. The second lancet of the other arch, the collateral descendants of Archbishop King, Sir Charles Simeon King, of Corrard, and Sophia, his wife, have, at the invitation of Dean Bernard and the Chapter, this year filled with a beautiful memorial window to the memory of their noble ancestor. It shows St. Peter receiving the keys above, and addressing the multitude on the Day of Pentecost below. The inscription records the Archbishop's connection with the Cathedral as Chancellor and Dean. In the lancet close by, to the left, *posteri memores* of Archbishop Usher have similarly erected a memorial window to the great Primate, shewing above St. Peter named Cephas by Christ, and his release from prison below. On the opposite side of the choir aisle is Swift's fierce inscription over Schomberg's grave. In this illustrious company we recall the days when these, the two greatest Deans of St. Patrick's in the past, worked as contemporaries, and yet we are reminded how different were their methods, though both were masterful. This memorial has an interesting link with the Blue Coat, for Sir Charles King, who erected it, is son of Sir James Walker King, second baronet, who was once our Chaplain and Head Master, and grandson of Sir Abraham Bradley King, our long time Governor and twice our Chairman, as hereafter shewn. All four lancets illustrate scenes in St. Peter's life, and have been beautifully designed by C. L. Kempe, Esq., as conceived by Dean Bernard.

We have curious entries at this period illustrating the working of the New Penal Laws. One in 1721 records that judgment was had in the Common Pleas by default against Pierce Butler, a Papist, for £500, for taking upon him the guardianship of a minor, and the penalty was awarded to the Blue Coat. The Recorder is asked to give directions for enforcing it; next year Mr. Butler petitioned the governors for a remission, and a committee was appointed to treat with him for a settlement. They appear to have forgiven the penalty, for our accounts of casual revenue show nothing received on this. But a few years after, in 1729, we have record of a legacy of Henry Turner, Esq., " bequeathed for education of children in the Popish religion," and adjudged by the Court of Chancery to be for superstitious uses. One moiety is ordered to be paid to the Blue Coat Hospital, and the other to the Green Coat in Cork. Our half, £956, was duly paid.

The Archbishop sent us, under the Erasmus Smith alliance, four very eminent governors, one the most illustrious man of his day here—Jonathan Swift,—the Earl of Abercorn, Viscount Charlemont, and the Right Hon. Marmaduke Coghill. Lord Abercorn and Swift were old friends, though the intimacy had cooled. Twelve years before, when Swift was the idol of London society, courted by the Ministry for the political aid of his matchless pamphlets and pasquinades, by Dukes and Duchesses for his influence with Harley, the Prime Minister, by the wits of the town for his startling genius, Lord Abercorn had sought his advocacy for an object he had then much at heart. He was James Hamilton, eighth Earl of Abercorn, and was then seeking from the Court of France the Dukedom of Chatelherault, for which his kinsman the Duke of Hamilton was as eagerly competing. The claims were well balanced; both nobles were descended from the Earl of Arran, Regent of Scotland, on whom the Dukedom of Chatelherault was confirmed by Henry II. of France in 1548, in the time of the Franco-Scottish Alliance. The Abercorns were of the strict male line, the Duke claimed through an elder son; but the male line was broken when the Duke of Chatelherault left a daughter sole heir, and this, Lord Abercorn contended, gave him precedence under the patent and on the analogy of the Salique law. In March, 1712, Swift tells Stella that Lord Abercorn was wanting him to get him the Dukedom from the King of France; "his pretensions were very just; it's a great stir getting this Dukedom, but it's only to speak to the Secretary (Bolingbroke) and get the Duke of Ormonde to engage in it, and mention the case to Lord Treasurer (Harley) and this I shall do;" and so he did. But soon he was similarly courted by the rival claimant. The Duchess of Hamilton knitted him a pocket "with belt and buckles like a woman's" for a splendid gold snuffbox given him by Col. Hill, the famous Lady Masham's brother. Then Swift advised a compromise. It is most amusing to read how each side wooed him as if he were Prime Minister of Louis XIV. The Duke shortly after was killed, some said assassinated, in a duel with Lord Mohun, who was also killed; but the Duchess and the Duke's brother, Lord Selkirk, still pressed the claim. In 1713 Swift writes :—" Lord Abercorn was here teasing me about his French Duchy, and suspecting me of partiality to the Hamilton family in such a whimsical manner that Dr. Pratt (Provost of Trinity College), who was by, thought he was mad. Then comes in the Earl of Selkirk (the Duke's brother), whom I had never seen before. He is going to France to negociate their pretensions to the Duchy of Chatelherault. He teased me for two hours in spite of my teeth, and held my hand when I offered to stir; would have me engage the Ministry to favour him against Lord Abercorn, and convince them he had no pretensions ; and concluded he was sorry I was a greater friend to Abercorn than Hamilton. I had no patience, and used him with some plainness. Am not I gravely handled between a couple of puppies? The Ministers gave me leave to tell the Hamiltons they are to agree with Abercorn." Swift's mediation met the common fate of mediators ; he tells Stella " neither Abercorn or Selkirk will now speak with me, I have disobliged both sides." Strange enough, this *Cause Chatelherault* remained undecided till our day, when our princely Lord Lieutenant, the first Duke of Abercorn, brought it to a crisis in the regime of Napoleon III., when the French tribunal finally decided in favour of the Duke of Hamilton's claim.

Dr. Coghill was also an old friend of Swift's in the Queen Anne period. The *Journal to Stella* tells how " Dr. Coghill and I dined by invitation at Mrs. Vans' ". For, alas, even when writing these immortal love letters, Swift was visiting constantly at the Van Homrighs ; but he takes care never to mention poor Vanessa's name, suggesting the attraction to be her mother, Mrs. Van. Coghill was an eminent man, a Privy Councillor, M.P. for Dublin University, Chancellor of the Irish Exchequer, and Judge of the Prerogative Court. In this latter capacity lies his present chief claim to immortality. In a conjugal suit here he decided that " moderate chastisement with a switch " of a wife by her lord was within the male conjugal right. This was very good old Common Law, having been laid down by husband judges ; but Coghill was unmarried. He was, at the time of the decision, wooing a lady with some success, but when she heard of his judgment she cut him at once, and he died an old bachelor. Strange, too, that this legal question was only decided in our day. In the last case argued at the Bar by the Master of the Rolls, Sir Richard Collins, it was his duty to contend for the doctrine of moderate chastisement, but Lord Halsbury closured him peremptorily, and denounced the old dicta as the theories of a savage age. Coghill was son of Sir J. Coghill, Master in Chancery, and grand-uncle of the first of the Coghill baronets.

These new governors were all accessions to our Board. Swift was with us for twelve years, an assiduous attendant till his infirmities became acute. He at once joined Archbishop King's committees for the infirmary and the reform of our house and government. These included the restoration of our chapel, for the Archbishop was a wholesale restorer of churches, and to the Dean was specially entrusted the altar, the seats, and the pulpit. We shall have occasion again to recur to him as a governor.

Our Board had now become the fashion, and was joined by many of the highest in the land. The Primate, Hugh Boulter, who then virtually governed in Ireland, became a governor in 1726, and was a valuable member for many years. He does not seem to have attended any meeting at which Archbishop King was present. They were antipathetic both in politics and in Church affairs, Dr. King being wholly opposed to his exclusion of all Irishmen from dignities in Church and State, and his general anti-Irish and somewhat secular spirit. The Primate had been elevated to Armagh in 1724, though usage would have pointed rather to the Archbishop of Dublin. This was about the time of their memorable first interview, when Dr. King, remaining seated in his chair, received the Primate, saying, as he answered his salutation, " You see, Your Grace, I am too old to rise." About the same time we co-opted Sir Ralph Gore, Chancellor of the Exchequer, Lord Justice and a baronet. He had just presented to us a gift of £500 placed in his hands by his relative General Richard St. George, then the heir of the Kilkenny family of Woodsgift. St. George was cousin german of St. George Ashe, Bishop of Clogher, a bosom friend of Swift, and one of his brilliant coterie of punsters known as the Castilian Club in the early days of Queen Anne. Sir Ralph, who lived at Belleisle on Loch Erne, in his diocese, had married his daughter. Sir Ralph, as will be seen, had much to do with our after story.

George the First died in June, 1727. In April, John Rogerson, our Recorder, who had filled that office just for the term of the King's reign, as Forster had held it during

Queen Anne's reign, was now made Chief Justice of the King's Bench. For ten years he had sat at our Board with his father, old Sir John, till the death of the latter in 1724. For thirty-two years Sir John had been one of our best governors; he was a Dublin worthy, and must always be remembered as one of the chief makers of Dublin as it now exists.

In 1708 our first Ballast or Port and Docks Board as already mentioned had been formed, as the growing city required that the river channel should be so deepened and widened as to allow vessels to come up to the Custom House without discharging cargoes at Ringsend, to be carried in boats up the shallow estuary, which then stretched in the form of an irregular V from the apex at Essex Bridge to the open sea, over shoals, sands, and gravel. There was no South or North Wall. Sir John Rogerson had leases from the city of the southern coast land, and he offered the Ballast Board to construct a wall and quay from Lazy Hill to Ringsend, along the foreshore fronting the line of the present Brunswick Street, if the city would grant him the intervening land in fee, and the Ballast Board would allow him the use of the surplus sand and gravel from which they raised their revenue by ballasting the ships, and which he needed to raise the low shore behind his sea wall. This was agreed. This great work occupied many years, but Sir John lived just to see it completed. It not only formed our first South Wall, but the raising of the quays enabled the necessary deepening of the channel, and led to the construction of the North Wall on the opposite shore. Sir John's ground, however, left the shore to the west, where College Street stands, open to the tides, which menaced the new work, so the city took on itself the continuation of the wall here, and thus we understand how these southern quays are still respectively known as Sir John Rogerson's and the City Quay respectively. The hinter-lands now became a very valuable heritage, which descended to the new Lord Chief Justice. He proved one of the most eminent judges of his day. With the Recordership he held the Solicitor-

and Attorney-Generalship successively, and was a strong candidate for the dignity of Lord Chancellor just before he became Chief Justice. His daughter married Abraham Crichton, the first Lord Erne, whose successors still inherit the large property by Liffey side behind and beyond the quays that still hand down the Rogerson name. In the same year the Corporation undertook the construction of the North Wall on the opposite shore, on the line of the present Custom House and steamship quays. All the slob lands behind, and estuary of the Tolka to the Clontarf Road was now laid out in lots by the Assembly. An interesting map of the design and the city order appears in Sir John Gilbert's *Calendar* ; it shows a channel left for the Tolka on the line from Ballybough Bridge to the Clontarf Island still lying opposite the Clontarf Road, with the allotments as ordered by Thomas Bolton, Lord Mayor, and our Chairman in 1717. In these signal advances of Dublin the Blue Coat played a part ; for the city, in debt for Rogerson's South Wall, applied to our Board, and obtained from us a loan of £1,000 at six per cent.

Our Chairmen, Lord Mayors in George I.'s time, were :—

John Stoyte	1715-16
Thos. Bolton	1716-17
Anthony Barkey	1717-18
William Quaile	1718-19
Thomas Wilkinson	1719-20
George Forbes	1720-21
Thomas Curtis	1721-22
William Dickson	1722-23
John Porter	1723-24
John Reyson	1724-25
Joseph Kane	1725-26
William Empson	1726-27

CHAPTER VIII.

TEMP. GEORGE II. 1727-1744.

THE first act of the Board in George II.'s reign was to re-elect Chief Justice Rogerson : the assembly had chosen Francis Stoyte, who, like his predecessor, was a Lord Mayor's son, Recorder in his place.[1] The Lord Mayors of this period used to give a ball on each St. Stephen's Night, but in 1728 the Assembly made an order reciting that great inconveniences had ensued in late years from the custom, and directed that it should be discontinued, and that the Lord Mayor for the time being should pay over twenty guineas to the Blue Coat School in lieu of his feast ; the Lord Mayors were thus raised to the level of the Bishops. It is not stated what the *inconveniences* of these revelries were, but the Lord Mayors would seem to have made a good bargain by the composition, and the Blue Coat School certainly gained. In the same year, 1728, Richard Wesley, afterwards first Lord Mornington, and who had been some time a governor, transmitted to our Board a legacy of £500, left by the will of his relative, Garret Wesley of Dangan, in Meath, whose heir and executor he was and whose surname he took ; for his birth name was Richard Colley, representative of the Colleys of Castle Carbery. He was raised to the peerage as Lord Mornington in 1746, and then altered the surname to Wellesley. By his son Garrett he was grandfather of the great Marquess Wellesley and his greater brother, the great Iron Duke. He was one of our most assiduous governors for years, and his name gives us an historical association to which we gladly hold. In 1729 the Speaker of the House of Commons, the Right Hon. William Connolly of Castletown, sat on our Board, but he died in the

[1] Gilbert's *Calendar* 7, 425.

following year; and at the same time sat the Lord Chancellor, Thomas Wyndham, of whom a word presently. In 1730, after the death of Archbishop King, his successor, Dr. Hoadley, was co-opted a governor in his stead.

All this led to our recognition in other public quarters. The Royal College of Physicians, one of whose members had attended as our medical officer ever since their recognition of the School in 1701, now sent us in 1729 a fresh resolution stating that the President and Fellows, out of regard for the good and welfare of the Hospital, had transferred their attendance thereat for the future to Dr. Alexander McNaghten, as fully qualified for the charge, the President, Dr. Cope, assuring our Board that on the removal of Dr. McNaghten by death or otherwise the College would always take care that our house should be supplied with physicians as formerly. This was gratefully accepted; we thus obtained a permanent doctor who acted without salary.

The Parliament of the Blue Coat.

The patronage of some of our grandee governors at this time was not perhaps given without some ulterior object of their own. In 1729 was laid the foundation stone of the new Houses of Parliament, on the site of Chichester House, in College Green, Lord Chancellor Wyndham taking a leading part in the ceremony. Meanwhile the Houses had not where to lay their heads : there was no room at Castle or Four Courts. Lord Carteret being then Lord Lieutenant, the Government, at the end of 1728, applied to our Board to give the Houses place in the Hospital in the ensuing session. At our meeting in November Sir Ralph Gore obtained a Committee to consider the question, who reported forthwith, assigning as "most convenient for the use of Parliament" the whole ground and first floor of the Hospital and School, viz., the Great Hall, the Governors' room, with the Clerk's office, the Chaplain's apartments upstairs, with the two rooms on the same floor, the several rooms on the side of the passage leading from the hall to the garden, the Chapel and the Steward's apartments upstairs, with the three rooms opposite same. This appropriation the Committee concedes to be the " most proper, and which can best be spared with the least prejudice and inconvenience to this House." " In the meantime, the boys," they add, with delightful *naivete*, " may eate in the Stone Gallery," and that " the chaplain do read prayers in the school room up two paire stairs." He and the steward are to provide lodgings " near at hand." The report ends with a very wise direction that " all avenues " are to be made up, to prevent the boys interfering with the part of the Hospital granted to Parliament. The temptation to enter the House prematurely might be too strong even for boys with a better place to " cate " in than the Stone Gallery. This report, however, was adopted unanimously and at once. No wonder Sir Ralph Gore was chosen Speaker next year. The Hospital paid dearly for their complacent hospitality. So King's Hospital was the Parliament House of Ireland from 23rd September, 1729, to 15th April, 1730. The session was opened by Lord Carteret in person, who "arrayed in royal robes entered the House of Lords with the usual ceremonies of grandeur, and seated himself in the chair of State." His influence in this parliament was very great, for great was the interest he took in its proceedings. He attended again on 24th October, when Sir Ralph Gore presented himself on knee as newly chosen Speaker in the room of the Right Hon. William Connolly, who had just resigned from ill health. Thrice again he came in person, in December to receive the loyal addresses voting supplies to the Crown, and in April to give the royal assent to the bills before prorogation. But his keen sympathy in all that was for the material prosperity of Ireland, and which he transfused through the Houses, was the chief ground of his popularity. In the same year he forwarded to Holles, Duke of Newcastle, a memorial of the Dublin merchants complaining that under Acts of Chas. II. and Wm. III. importation into Ireland was penally forbidden of any merchandise from the English plantations in America, Africa, or Asia, and the consequent loss and inconvenience. Carteret indorses the memorial, stating " I have personally inquired into the particulars, and find that Ireland is under necessity of sending to foreign markets and trading with the French and other foreigners to procure commodities which they are prohibited from importing from British plantations." Verily we are not ashamed of this our Parliament of the Blue Coat. Reading the Journals one might think he had before him proposals of our Congested Districts Board or Sir Horace Plunkett, for they cast striking lights on social and material problems even now in evolution. The great measure of the session was that " for the encouragement, the better employment of the Poor, for more effectively draining and improving Bogs and unprofitable ground, and for expediting the carriage of goods from one part to another of the Kingdome." This became 3 Geo. II., c. 3. By this a Commission of the magnates of Ireland was constituted, with elastic powers, armed with a Developement Fund raised by taxes on carriages and chairs, plate, cards and dice. Then there are bills for cleansing the ports and harbours of Cork, Waterford, Limerick, Galway, Sligo, Wexford, and New Ross ; for establishing ballast boards in Belfast and Drogheda ; one to promote the finding of mines and minerals within the Kingdom, and one to enable the governors of the Workhouse in Dublin to employ the poor therein. We have the germ of Trades Union law in a bill to prevent unlawful combinations of workmen, artizans, and labourers, with beneficent provisions for the better payment of their wages. An early order directs our Recorder, Francis Stoyte, then sitting for Hillsborough, to attend the Lord Lieutenant with the heads of a bill to prevent the running of goods and encouragement of Fair Traders to be transmitted to London under Poyning's Act. Were these " runners " the forerunner of Mr. Chamberlains " dumpers," and the Fair Traders a shadow of Tariff Reform ? There are beneficent measures for Relief of Insolvent Debtors, for the extension and repair of churches, for enforcing residence of the clergy, and many local ones, as for the better lighting of Dublin and Cork, and for making the present coach road to Naas and Dublin. And the House could deal strongly with abuses. Aldermen Wilkinson and Bolton, both, alas ! governors of ours, are by statute made incapable of being made Justices of the Peace for taking extortionate fees in that capacity.

But our glory in this Parliament is the spirit of our own great governor, Swift, which it breathed. He was then in the fury of his marvellous war against the trade greed of England, and the anti-Irish policy of Primate Boulter. We can see his figure now animating the generosity of Carteret and the patriotism of the Houses. Their measures are at least an effort to reflect the *Short View of the State of Ireland* which he had thundered forth to greet Carteret's return to Ireland in 1727. This he had followed in 1729 with his historic letter to Archbishop King, and then with his *Modest Proposal* for fattening Irish Babes, our only available manufacture, for market, which is, perhaps, the most consummate sample of hideous-grotesque power the genius of satire has ever conceived. With much of his policy Carteret had a sympathy intense. They were now close, social, and literary friends. Swift dined *tete-a-tete* with the Viceroy repeatedly during this session. One clause in the great bill for encouraging industries would alone prove the presence of the spirit behind the scenes ; this was a project for lending money without interest to deserving tradesmen who had no capital, a plan long adopted by the Dean himself with self-denying success, and which, though now forgotten, was a main element in his unrivalled popularity with the people of Dublin. It is not actually embodied in the Act as passed, but may have been within the powers of the Commission in administering their Development Fund. When the Lord Lieutenant came in state to close the session in April in the Blue Coat, both Houses presented him with a cordial address, " for his constant care for the welfare and prosperity of the Nation, and especially for obtaining the King's assent to the Fund for improving tillage and trade." This referred to the remission of the hereditary Crown duties on wool and yarn, which, in assenting to the measure, the Viceroy announced he had obtained from the English Government. He replied to the address in person with characteristic grace. Shortly after he resigned the Viceroyalty. returning to England, where he became the first Earl Granville and a great statesman there. He was no partisan of Walpole, who was then supreme, and to whom Swift was a *bete noir*, and whose intimacy, there is too much reason to believe, was in part a cause of his resignation, which was deplored by all here. He was a universal favourite in the city. In 1726 the Corporation, in a loyal address to George II. specially thank his Majesty " for the great regard shown to this nation in sending Lord Carteret, whose just and prudent administration has rendered him highly acceptable to your subjects of this Kingdom." He was very friendly to the Blue Coat. Lady Carteret nominated several of our boys.

Our Blue Coat Parliament has been severely criticized for the very unconstitutional proposal made by Coghill as Chancellor of the Exchequer to vote the additional duties for a period of twenty-one years and thus so far leave the Government independent of the House for all that time. To the credit of the House the bill was rejected, but only by a majority of one, the votes being 51 to 50. It is most unlikely that Carteret had suggested such a measure; had he been more self-willed and ambitious his great talents would have raised him higher than he reached. The arbitrary policy was much more likely to have emanated from Primate Boulter, who ruled as an Undertaking Lord Justice in the absence of the Lord Lieutenant, and would have ruled despotically if he dared. Our Parliament was the " Longest " on record, the Blue Coat session being its second ; it lasted through the whole reign of George II., and this abuse led to the Octennial Act passed early in the following reign.

Pending the session, school went on in the Stone Gallery and garrets. The Board had reserved a joint right to their own room for their weekly meetings, and, perhaps attracted by the society of the Senate, the attendance of governors was above the average. But the boys seem to have been restive in their attic, if not classical, quarters, for several were discharged out of the house, "never to be admitted again," as being vagabonds and running away ! and William Rowland for being " a stubborne and incorrigible boy was straight sent to sea." We may excuse Parliament for its monopoly of the Blue Coat in view of their good work, but when the "avenues" were removed, and the boys came down, all things were in disastrous disarray. Every passage and lobby had been absorbed and trampled. Even the poor butler had been expelled to give an office to the House, and had a grant from the Board of £2 18s. 4d. for three quarters of a rent for a room outside. Parliament was prorogued by several adjournments to the autumn of 1731, for it then sat in alternate years, and when it met Lionel, Duke of Dorset, reigned in Carteret's stead. Our Board petitioned the Commons in November, 1731, for the expenses of rebuilding our dilapidated school, and there was a separate petition of our officers to be compensated for disturbance and eviction, but the result was only a scanty vote of £200 to the governors towards rebuilding by reason of alterations made for Parliament, £30 to Rev. Mr. Gibbons, our chaplain ; £20 to Alfred Howard, the agent ; and £20 to Thorne, the steward. This pittance was all we ever received for rent and the dilapidations, from which the old edifice never recovered. Carteret would have secured us better than that.

It should be mentioned, however, that in this session of 1731-32 a Merchant Seamen's Act was passed, by which all penalties were appropriated for the benefit of King's Hospital.

The return for our hospitality was ungracious as well as ungenerous. In the Lord Lieutenant's absence, Thomas Lord Chancellor Wyndham was head of the Government and President of the Privy Council, then all potent. From the Council came this letter to our steward :

"*Dublin Castle, 7th October,* 1732.
"Mr. Thorne,

"Their excellencies the Lords Justices have commanded me to signify to you their pleasure that you forthwith deliver to Mrs. Heath or her order the Chair, Cushion, and Footstool belonging to the Government which were placed in the House of Lords when it was held in the Blue Coat Hospital.

"I am your humble servant,
"Thos Tickell."

This letter is a prize among our archives, a fine autograph, and all in the strong hand of Tickell, the poet, eulogist, and elegist of Addison, who first brought him to Ireland many years before. He was now Secretary to the Privy Council, the intimate of Swift and Dr. Delany of Delville, Glasnevin, so continuing to his death in 1740. The sequel of the chair is told in a manuscript of Thorne indorsed on Tickell's letter, so graphic that we give it in full:—

"I received this letter Munday morning about 8 of the clock. I told Mrs. Heath that I could do nothing, but would waite on my Lord Mayor and give her his lordship's answer by 4 in the afternoon. She sent to me, and I sent her word that my Lord Mayor could give no order without a board of the governors, but at the next meeting he would lay the letter before them and then return an answer. Tuesday, about two o'clock afternoon, a person came to me from the Lord Chancellor ordering me to attend his Lordship at 4 of the clock, at the Bishop of Tuam's in Cavan (Kevin) Street. I first waited on my Lord Mayor, and acquainted him that I was sent for by the Lord Chancellor. His Lordship ordered me to acquaint His Excellency that he could give no order of himself, but if there were a necessity, he would call a board Wednesday morning. I went to my Lord Chancellor. When he came out to me, and Secretary Tickle (*sic*) in his company, he demanded me why I did not obey the Government's orders. I told him I was under the direction of the governors of the Blue Coat Hospital, and could not part with anything without their orders. I also told him I was just come from my Lord Mayor, and would have delivered my orders. His Excellency stopped me, and said my Lord Mayor was out of the question. Demanded of me who put the Thrown (*sic*) in my custody, and whether I would keep it, and said, 'Sir, I demand of you whether you will deliver it or not?' I answered I could not without orders from the governors. His Lordship replied with some warmth—'Sir, if you do not, I will have you turned out of your place to-morrow,' to which I made a bow. His Lordship returned to his company. I immediately went to my Lord Mayor, who dined at the 3 tunns in Essex Street. There were present Alderman Curtis, Alderman Porter, Alderman Hunt, 2 Shiriffs. My Lord Mayor with their approbation ordered me to send the Chair and Stool to the Castle, which I did by John Hodgin, Butler to the Hospital."

It is not hard to decide as to the relative dignity of the peremptory Lord Chancellor, who would not wait till Wednesday, and the poor servant, who was only doing his duty to his masters. This throne left in the fragments of our broken furniture would have been a splendid relic of our Parliament, for this was the chair in which Carteret had sat in state on his four visits to the Houses, under the canopy from which he gave the royal assent to the aids voted to the Crown in the old Norman French : *Le roy remercie ses bons sujets, accepte leur benevolence et ainsi le veult.* When in June, 1904, Lord Dudley inaugurated the completion of our buildings by the cupola, after one hundred and twenty years, our chairman, addressing His Excellency, lamented that we had not the throne wherein he might sit as a great predecessor had done ; it was added that we should have taken care that he should find in it no thorn to disturb him.

The Lord Mayor and our Chairman, under whom Thorne had hastened to take shelter, was Humfrey French, who had just commenced his Mayoralty. He is known as the good Lord Mayor (1732-33) ; his portrait is in the National Portrait Gallery. He was dining at the Three Tuns that October day probably to celebrate his inauguration, and did not care to begin with a quarrel with the Privy Council even for a throne ; but he was boomed by Swift next year, 1733, when candidate for the city, in a memorable broadside to the freemen recommending him as one who would vote patriotically, whilst his opponent, Alderman Macarell, who held an appointment under Government, would not dare to oppose anti-Irish measures. " He has shewn," says Swift, " more virtue, more activity, more skill in one year's government of the city than a hundred years can equal." This secured his election. Lord Chancellor Wyndham should have been gentler to Thorne, for he was himself one of our governors, and had been one of thirty-seven eagles gathered together at our Board of September, 1729, when Thorne was elected our Steward, vice John Kirkwood, deceased. Lord Mayor Page in the chair, and with him, beside Wyndham, sat Primate Boulter, Connolly, Speaker of the House, the Bishops of Meath and

Kildare, and a great tale of aldermen and sheriffs; and he was still a member of the Board. He afterwards acted on our Committee in 1737 to support our petition to Parliament for a grant to rebuild, and at his death he bequeathed £300 to the Hospital. Perhaps he felt he had been a little too severe in the case of the throne. He was ancestor of the Right Hon. George Wyndham, lately our brilliant Chief Secretary for Ireland. Secretary Tickell, too, should have been friendly; we had admitted a boy at his request in 1727.

In January, 1730, our Secretary, Bartholomew Wybrants, resigned, after a faithful service of thirty-six years. He was one of those clerks whose clerkly talent rises almost to genius, and by whom a vast part of the world's work is done, though they be unknown to the world. Every line of our first Minute Book, from our beginning in 1675 to 1731, is under his hand; for, though only appointed in 1694, he transcribed all the previous entries into the books, and after his resignation continued the entries for a twelvemonth. During his tenure with us he also acted as Clerk to the Commons in the Town Council. He merits a kind memory for his own sake, but a romantic domestic tragedy has connected him with the literature of Queen Anne's time, for the story is told by Sir Richard Steele in No. 172 of the *Tatler*, May, 1710. Wybrants belonged to a respectable family of Dutch extraction, which, like many others, was made free of Dublin city in Dutch William's reign. Steele uses the tragedy as an epilogue to an essay on the sad results of passion let loose between friends, and especially in married life, strikingly observing that there is *a sex in souls*. Wybrants' daughter was the wife of Mr. Eustace, a young gentleman of a good estate near Dublin. She was of a lively spirit, but somewhat high-tempered. The married couple and the lady's sister supped together in the spring of 1710, when a commonplace wrangle arose between the sisters. Eustace, intervening, took violent sides against his wife, who, vainly reminding him that their disputes were forgotten in half an hour, to close the quarrel retired to her bed. The husband followed, and, with a dagger he had brought with him, stabbed her in her sleep. Awaking, and thinking it was an attack on her husband by ruffians, for theirs was a lonely country house, she roused him to defend himself; he was feigning sleep, but he gave her a second wound in the dark. Then by the moonlight she saw that it was he. Horror disarmed her from further struggling, and, enraged anew at being discovered, he fixed his poniard in her bosom, and, believing he had dispatched her, sought to escape by the window. But when still alive she called on him not to hurt himself, as she was still alive; in an access of fury he jumped on the bed and wounded her all over with as much rage as if every blow was provoked by new aggravations. Then he fled; she died next day. Some weeks after, an officer of justice, attempting to arrest him, on his resistance fired at him, as did the criminal at the officer. Both balls took fatal effect. In Jones's *British Classics*, 1823, there is a sensational engraving by Corbould of this bedroom scene. Alfred Howard was chosen our Agent in Wybrants' stead.

Our poor chaplain, Richard Gibbons, did not long survive his extrusion from his quarters by Parliament, or even long enough to receive the pittance of £30 awarded him, for he died in December, 1731. Forty-nine governors, eagles gathered together *pro more*, met to elect his successor, the Primate, Lord Chancellor, Archbishop Hoadley, the Lord Chief Justice, Bishops of Meath and Kildare, Sir Ralph Gore, and Swift attending. They had before them the valuable report of a Committee as to the duties of the chaplain and schoolmaster, which recites the original order made when Mr. Colquit was appointed second chaplain in 1680, as set forth, *ante*, p. 88, also that of 7 May, 1708 (p. 131, *ante*), requiring the chaplain to preach and read prayers every Sunday, and to teach and expound the Church catechism every Sunday in the Chapel; the Committee report that the order as to preaching was once respited for six months on account of a law suit, when Rev. Mr. Carr was chaplain, but was never reversed, and they find that several of the above duties of the chaplain and schoolmaster have been for some years past wholly omitted, and are of opinion they ought to be revived.

This report is very noteworthy, not only as showing the strictly denominational nature of the Hospital, which obtained for it an exemption from the Educational Endowments Act of 1885, but because we trace in it the strong hand of the great Dean of St. Patrick's. The original, still in our archives, is signed by seven governors, of which "Jonath. Swift" stands second, immediately after Humfrey French, Lord Mayor. An order had been made a few months before that Testaments and Prayer Books should be supplied to every boy, and that in future no boy should be admitted without a Bible and Prayer Book provided by their friends at their first entrance.

The Grattans and the Blue Coat.

But we scarcely dare attribute this conflux of 49 governors solely to spiritual zeal. There was the great question of the appointment of chaplain and headmaster, for which there were several candidates. The Reverend Ralph Grattan was chosen. Small chance for any other, for he was a nephew and namesake of the speaker, Ralph Gore, one of the 49, as also nephew of another of them, Alderman Sir Richard Grattan, who, four years after, was our Chairman and Lord Mayor, whilst he and his uncle, Sir Richard, belonged to the clan Grattan, dear to Swift, who took a chief part, as we have seen, at the meeting that day. This clan was of his inner circle, he dubbed them "the Grattans, a set of men as generally acquainted and as much beloved, as any one family in the nation; nay, to such a degree, that some of the most considerable men in the church desired and thought it a favour to be adopted by them, and admitted Grattans." "Pray, my Lord," Swift asked Lord Carteret, "have you the honour to be acquainted with the Grattans?" Carteret replying that he had not that honour, "then, pray, my Lord, take care to obtain it, it is of great consequence, the Grattans can raise ten thousand men." The Grattans, properly so called, were then the seven sons of the Reverend Doctor Patrick Grattan, Senior Fellow of Trinity College, of whom Dr.

Delany (another Swiftian) says he had often heard the Bishop of Clogher (St. George Ashe, another Swiftian), declare that he kept hospitality beyond both the lords who lived on either side of him, though both were considered hospitable. The seven sons were :—1, Henry ; 2, Rev. William ; 3, James, M.D. ; 4, Rev. Robert ; 5, Rev. John ; 6, Sir Richard ; 7, Charles. Of these, Henry was father of James Grattan, Recorder of Dublin, and one of our governors, 1756-66 ; he was father of the great Henry, the patriot, who was born in the year after Swift's death. The Rev. William was a Fellow of Trinity, he married a sister of Sir Ralph Gore, and was father of our chaplain, Ralph, who held that office for forty-one years. Dr. James, the third brother, was an eminent physician, and President of the Royal College of Physicians, in which office we have seen him in 1706, promising, on behalf of the College, always to supply a Physician to our Hospital, on the wise condition that we should set apart rooms for an infirmary. The Rev. Robert was prebendary of Howth, in the Chapter of St. Patrick's, and as such, a colleague of Swift, and rector of St. Audoen's. The Rev. John was rector of Raheny, and became prebendary of Clonmethan, in the Chapter of St. Patrick's in 1720, doubtless, due to his friend, the great Dean. Sir Richard, our chairman in 1735-6, presented our petition to Parliament in 1735 ; he died during his mayoralty. The youngest brother, Charles, obtained a Fellowship in the Dublin University and applied for a royal dispensation from taking Holy Orders, which, failing to obtain within the prescribed period, his fellowship lapsed under the College statutes, and he came over to London to obtain from Queen Anne such an extension of time as would enable him to be ordained. Swift, then in his zenith of favour with ministers, took up the case. Writing to Stella, in March, 1714, he tells her :—" I spoke to all the ministers yesterday about it, but they say the Queen is angry, and thought it a trick to deceive her, and she is positive, and so the man must be ruined, for I cannot help him[2]." We know that Anne, like many weak people,

[2] *Journal to Stella*, 19th March, 1712-13.

was adamantine in some things, and, especially on things that related to the church. So Charles Grattan, failing his Fellowship, was forced to be content with the mastership of the Royal School of Enniskillen. This case seems first to have connected Swift with the Grattans, for he tells Stella that he had never seen Charles before. But the connection was lifelong. Dr. James, Robert, and John are all legatees in Swift's will, and Robert and John are executors. To Robert he leaves his gold corkscrew, his best beaver hat, and his strong box; the latter to go to Dr. James for life, "as having more use for it," for the Doctor was a landed proprietor. To John he gives "my silver box, in which the freedom of the City of Cork was presented to me, in which I desire said John to keep the tobacco he usually cheweth, called pigtail." Sir Richard left £100 to the Blue Coat, on condition that one of his executors should be chosen a governor, and, accordingly, the Rev. John was elected in 1742, thus giving us again two of "the Grattans" on our Board. The clan were chief members of the symposial set, which included their cousins, Dan and John Jackson, Dr. Sheridan, Dr. Delany, and the Dean himself. Their meets were often at Belcamp, St. Doulough's, where Dr. James lived, and where, perhaps, that gold corkscrew and the pigtail were not unknown. In the next generation the connection of the Grattans with King's Hospital was still maintained, when their nephew, James, became our Recorder, and a governor, but we must regret that his son, the great Henry Grattan, never joined the Board. His burning politics left him no sympathy for anything so narrow as a City School.

Belcamp belonged successively to two of our Grattan governors, for Dr. James left it to his brother, John, and he, in turn, devised it to his nephew, James, the Recorder. One of the revellers, rhyming upon it, says, that "when Swift and Dr. Delany were absent, Christmas appears at Belcamp like Lent."

Thorne was a faithful steward. In 1731 there were 160 boys in the School. Their uniforms were made by a contractor, one King, the governors supplying the cloth. The coats were of blue woollen frieze, and the cassocks they then wore of yellow, the Irish fabric Swift was so earnest to have introduced into England; the linings were of Irish linen. Thorne, observing the very large measure charged in King's accounts, suspected something was wrong, and, of his own motion, employed an old Blue Coat boy, Christopher Evans, who had gone into the trade, to measure three of the suits, which were found to contain seven and a half yards of blue, six yards of yellow cloth, and three of linen, as compared with nine yards of blue, seven and a half yards of yellow, and the linen in proportion, as charged in King's accounts. And Thorne thus calculated that in each of a series of years, the contractor had cheated the governors by eighty yards of blue, and eighty of yellow cloth, and some twenty-four of linen. Thorne's calculation was examined by the governors and found to be correct. King was found guilty of the fraud, with the governors further verdict that he intended to continue it. So King was ignominiously dethroned, and Christopher Evans, as the industrious apprentice, was chosen in his stead. But poor Thorne, too, did not long survive his extrusion by the Parliament of the Blue Coat. He died in 1738. He was a valuable officer, holding with his stewardship, the collectorship of the city tolls, and in the letter of Sir Williams Fownes to Swift, in 1732, containing an elaborate scheme for the founding of a Lunatic Asylum, which the Dean afterwards so warmly adopted, Thorne is suggested as the proper treasurer.

The state of our structure was now a burning question. In 1733 the Board started a rebuilding fund, to which Lord Mayor Nathaniel Kane gave £100, and they addressed their second petition to the House of Commons in the next session of 1735, setting forth our needs and showing that as their income was only sufficient for the maintenance of the school, if this were applied to rebuilding, this useful charity must cease for many years. They annex a plan, which, if executed in the plainest and least expensive manner, was computed to cost £6,000. The Commons appointed a Committee, whose report was presented by Stannard, the Recorder, then Member for Middleton, to the effect that the petitioners had proved their case, and the Hon. Arthur Hill, Member for Co. Down, and David Chuigneau, Member for Gowran, and both governors were directed to bring in a bill. This went into Committee; it provided an aid to the Hospital by a tax on oranges and lemons, but it added a clause for appointing new governors under the Act. To this the governors indignantly objected as an undue alteration of their old constitution, whereas " no mismanagement had been alleged against the present governors," and they resolved that the bill or petition be no further pursued. This was unfortunate, as the sequel proved, for their parliamentary hopes were never again so near bearing even such fruit as these oranges and lemons would have yielded. So, failing Parliament, the governors sought for voluntary contributions, but it would need years to reach £6,000 by these; the ruin was now waxing perilous, and a renewed petition to the next session of 1737 was resolved on. The drafting Committee met at the Parliament House itself to prepare it, headed by Sir James Somerville, our chairman. It described the building as in so ruinous a condition as to absolutely need restoration, and asked £6,000 as before, which, if supplied out of the Hospital funds, would disable the charity for years. The petition, presented by Somerville and his colleague, Alderman Pearson, the members for the city, was referred to a Committee of the House, who were given special powers of examining witnesses and calling for records. Meanwhile in December the peril became desperate, and a Minute records " that the Middle Isle (aisle) of the Hospital is in so dangerous a condition, that to preserve the lives of 138 boys and 8 nurses, which will, in all probability, be destroyed with its fall, which they apprehend will be very soon by the assistance of the high winds this winter, it is ordered that said boys and nurses be immediately removed to less dangerous parts of the Hospital, and in case there be not sufficient room to contain them, the governors' room be fitted up to put the rest in."

Thereupon, perhaps, the strongest committee we ever have had was selected to support the petition before Parliament. The Primate Boulter, Archbishop Hoadley of Dublin, L. C. Justice Rogerson, Bishop Price of Meath, and Dr. Cobb of Kildare, and eleven members of the Commons, the Speaker, Henry Boyle (Cork), Somerville (Lord Mayor), and Ald. Eason (Dublin City), Stannard, Recorder (Middleton), Hon. Arthur Hill (Down), Richard Wesley (Trim), Luke Gardiner (Thomastown), Ald. Chuigneau (Gowran), Ald. Dawson (Portarlington), Ald. Falkiner (Baltinglass), M. Coghill (Dublin University), and Robt. Ross (Newry). Armed with the terrors of the "Middle Isle," it might be thought such voices as these must prevail for at least £6,000, but the petition seems never to have emerged from the Select Committee. This may have been because the Commons were offended at the rejection by our governors of their lemon bill of the previous session, or more probably because they were then engaged in finding money to complete their own Parliament House, which, for several years, remained incomplete after the Houses had actually sat there. And yet our supporters were amongst the strongest men in the Commons. Henry Boyle, who had succeeded Sir R. Gore as Speaker, ruled the country for many years, as one of the Undertaking Lords Justices, now the friend, now the enemy, of the handsome Primate Stone, and was ultimately raised to the Earldom of Shannon. Coghill was Chancellor of the Exchequer, two were afterwards, peers, Arthur Hill as Viscount Dungannon, Richard Wesley, first Viscount Mornington, and Luke Gardiner's son was afterwards Lord Mountjoy. Sir James Somerville, one of the most respected citizens, came to us as Master of St. Anne's Guild; he was ancestor of the Lords Athlumney. They might have secured us £6,000. This failure deterred the Board from appealing to Parliament for a generation to come. The condition of the buildings during this decade had a calamitous effect on the discipline of the School, as the fierce quaint entries too often show. In 1732, Adam Darling is discharged as a runaway vagabond, and John Mead is ordered " to be publicly whipped by all the boys of this house out of the gate thereof, and never more admitted therein." He was an E. Smith boy, and Coghill the treasurer, is ordered to have notice. In 1735, James Maddox is sent to the workhouse " for stealing wine out of the Rev. Ralph Grattan's chambers, and enticing John Davis and Wm. Brown to do the same, for which said Davis and Brown are ordered to be severely lashed in the hall in the presence of all the boys." This wine story seems to imply that our chaplain shared in the convivial nature of his clan, as commemorated in Dr. Sheridan's couplet :—

" The time, O ye Grattans, was happily spent
When Bacchus went with me wherever I went."

Yet the Total Abstinence Societies could scarce have inflicted more terrible penalties for this unlicensed sharing with a Grattan cellar. In October, 1737, we read, " Wm Jones, Sr., being a vicious, incorrigible boy, he be sent to the Plantations the first opportunity." In February, 1738, " Whereas, several vicious, incorrigible boys have of late been detected picking locks, thieving, getting drunk, mitching and running away : Geo. Runy and Peter Lynch now run away, and guilty of the above facts, to be expelled, and never more admitted. Arthur Lockhart and Wm. Harrison to be immediately lashed out of the house by the boys, and, if their parents agree, to be sent to the Plantations." Six less guilty are " to be publickly lashed in such manner as the steward pleases, and the governors, will, according to their behaviour, consider how to dispose of them." It is to be pleaded for these delinquents that this was the time when " The Middle Isle " was in danger of falling on them, and when they would have been safer in the Stone Gallery, whither they were sent by the Blue Coat Parliament, and the poor runaways might also have pleaded an incident worthy of a page of Dickens in *Dotheboys Hall.* In 1735 the governors held an inquiry over Hugh Smith, the butler, on a complaint by the boys, that he habitually cut off from the share of bread allotted to each, a small piece which he put into his own pocket. His defence before the Board is delightful and ingenious, his assize of bread was that he might have a stock with which to reward the boys, whom he, the butler, considered the most deserving. The Board gravely ordered " that it was none of his business to distinguish the merits of any boy by depriving others of the due the governors were pleased to allow them, and, being reprimanded, he remains in the service on his good behaviour for the future."

The voluntary building fund was continued, and much money was collected, but it never was enough to restore on the thorough scale, and so it was virtually wasted in patch-work and temporary repairs, for the defects were radical and ever decadent, till of necessity they must be replaced by the new Hospital. Thus, £500 left us by John Holroyd, Master of Trinity Guild, and £400 left by the Bishop of Clogher, in 1742 (both were governors) were spent on buildings doomed soon to come down. Once success was in sight. In July, 1742, the Right Hon. Luke Gardiner, who had himself subscribed £50, brought a message from the Primate Boulter, directing the governors when they had fixed on a complete plan, to proceed and build. We know what this meant, for, if Boulter was an autocrat, he was munificent, and left a fortune to maintain poor parishes, but this message was one of the last acts of his life, for he died in the following September, succeeded in the Primacy or Government of Ireland by the equally masterful Archbishop, George Stone.

Our Chairman and Lord Mayor in 1739, was Daniel Falkiner, of Abbotstown, Co. Dublin. He was a governor for thirty-three years, 1726-1759. A partner in Burton and Falkiner's banks, he was for many years a chief member of the Ballast Office, engaged through the century in forming the modern port of Dublin. As member for Baltinglass, he had a principal share in supporting our petition to the Commons in 1735 and 1737. His great grandson, Frederick Falkiner, of Abbotstown, Colonel of the 100th regiment, created a baronet in 1812, as member for Co. Dublin, voted against the Union. In this year, 1739, Lord Chancellor

Jocelyn became a governor; he was afterwards Lord Newport, and father of the first Lord Roden, and at the same period we have boys nominated by James, twentieth Earl of Kildare.

During the thirties there was considerable trouble in collecting the £30 Consecration Fees from several of the Bishops. This was, perhaps, because the chief defaulter was Dr. Hoadley, who is returned in arrear in all the ten years from 1730, he having succeeded William King in the See of Dublin in 1729, and we have no record that he ever paid. In this context it is pleasant to see on our printed boards of benefactors, the name of George Berkeley, the great Bishop of Cloyne. That he would hold back would be inconceivable, for his heart was as large as his intellect. "He is an absolute philosopher with regard to titles, wealth and power," writes Swift to Lord Carteret as early as 1724, and our annals are enriched even by this slight connection of our School with one of the very noblest and greatest of his day.

In the early thirties Swift continued to attend our Board, but only occasionally, for his health was on an increasing decline. Our archives contain two original letters of his, which, having never been hitherto published, we feel justified now in printing *in extenso*; they exemplify his passion for patronage, which was one of the most amiable traits of his complex character. The first is addressed to Nathaniel Kane, then Lord Mayor and Chairman of our Board. It runs, "Sir, I have so ill a state of health that I cannot safely attend at the Blue Coat Board this evening. I must, therefore, intreat you to recommend Isaac Bullock, a hopeful honest boy, to be admitted into the Hospital at my request to my Lord Mayor and the Board, wherein you will much oblige, your most obedient servant, Jonath. Swift, Deanery House, February 7th, 1734. The boy was recommended to me by the Lady Elizabeth Brownlow from her own knowledge." This lady was the wife of William Brownlow, M.P. for County Armagh, and thus the ancestress of the Lords Lurgan. She had been Lady Elizabeth Hamilton, sister of Swift's friend, Lord Abercorn. We find her "hopeful honest boy," Isaac Bullock, was admitted at the meeting of governors on the 4th July following, the Dean being personally present. The second letter is addressed to Sir James Somerville, then our Lord Mayor and Chairman, ancestor of the Lords Athlumney, and is as follows :—" My Lord, my ill health will not permit me to attend your Lordship and the Board at the Blue Coat Hospital to-morrow, I, therefore, desire your Lordship to recommend to the Board Edward Riley. His father was of this city, and dyed in the service of the present Earl of Orrery, after having lived fifteen years with the late and present Earl. The Earl of Orrery has a great deal of merit with this kingdom, having lived some years in it, although he be a Peer of England, and born there. I have not for several years recommended one boy to this Hospital, nor would have done this if I could have refused any command to so excellent a person as his Lordship. I am, with great respect, my Lord, your Lordship's most obedient and most humble servant, Jonath. Swift. Deanery House, July 7th, 1737." We find Edward Riley admitted in the following October, but the Dean was still unable to attend. His last recorded presence as a governor was on February 4th in this year, 1737. Much of his power was still displayed at intervals, but that his memory was then partially at fault, is shown in this very letter, when he says he had not recommended a boy for several years, for an entry in our books of the previous December, shows the admission of James Fulton, at the request of the Dean of St. Patrick's. Lord Orrery had been flattering him for several years when the glamour of his name might reflect some light on the Earl's own literary pretensions, but who, when the lion was dead, repaid the friendship he had won by his banal " Remarks," whose offensive sneers the living lion would have silenced with a growl. Orrery had learned from Pope how to "damn with faint praise."

But even in these years the Dean did not confine himself as a governor to the patronage of boys. In 1734 he is one of the strong committee to examine the proposals of Mr.

George Vaughan to take twenty of our boys as apprentices to the linen trade. It is easy to conceive the interest Swift would take in a subject so affecting our home manufactures. In 1736 he is one of the standing committee " to inspect and direct the dyet of the children of this house." Finally, in 1737, he was placed on the committee to prepare the petition to Parliament for the rebuilding of the Hospital, though it is probable he never was able to attend it.

In 1734, Mr. Vaughan's proposal for twenty-four linen apprentices was referred to a Committee of Governors, including, with Swift and many of our Aldermen, the Primate, Dr. Boulter, Archbishop Hoadley, the new Bishop of Meath, Dr. Arthur Price, whom we had just elected a governor, Chief Justice Rogerson, Dr. Marmaduke Coghill, and Arthur Hill, on whose report seven boys were sent to Buncrana, in the north, to Mr. Vaughan. This experiment, which covered ten years was not a success, the master and the apprentices continually were quarrelling. The truth was that, the indentures being for seven years, the boys could earn good wages elsewhere long before their apprenticeship expired, and they often settled the question by running away. They complained, too, of their treatment, and that they were not paid the wages stipulated in their indentures. Several teams of our boys were sent up, but the experience as to all was similar. At last, Mr. Vaughan, in 1744, called on our governors to settle the disputes, sending forward this list:—

Marm. Matthews	
Thos. Walsh	
Henry Hoffman	
Cor. Malone	Ran away before their seven years expired.
Theo. West	
Pat Tyrrell	
Wm. Atkinson	
Richard Lenhouse	6th April, 1739, desired to be discharged for new cloaths.
Hen. Allen	
Jas. Halpin	Discharged by consent of all parties.
Arthur Maginiz	
Tim. Hagan	Desired to be discharged for £3 each.
Arthur Motley	
Thos. Dixon	
Henry Jackson	Still with Mr. Vaughan.

The dispute ended by the cancelling of all the indentures, Mr. Vaughan paying £19 to the boys who had not run away, and retaining his only faithful Henry Jackson in the capacity of clerk.

The failure of our treaty with Vaughan was deplorable, not only because of the opening it offered our boys in the great linen trade of the north, which was even then of imperial magnitude, but, in it Vaughan made a fortune, which, in 1753, he bequeathed in trust to seven of the then Bishops of the northern province, the Chief Judges, and other magnates, £2,000 a year to be applied to found a great Industrial School of 300 boys and 200 girls, to be called "Vaughan's Charity" for instruction in the several branches of the linen manufacture and other cognate industries. This was incorporated by statute in 1775, and is now represented by the Tubrid School in County Fermanagh, still maintained out of Vaughan's estates. It is more than probable, had our alliance continued, we, too, should have had some share in "Vaughan's Charity."

CHAPTER IX.

TEMP. GEORGE II., 1743-1760.

CHARLES LUCAS AND THE BLUE COAT.

AN entry in our Minute Book, 13th August, 1742, tells " that Mr. Charles Lucas, one of the Members of the Commons of the city for the Corporation of Barber Surgeons, appeared this day at the Board, and informed the governors that in perusing the charter of this Hospital he found it was granted by King Charles II. to the Lord Mayor, Sheriffs, Commons, and Citizens of Dublin, and as one of these he apprehended he was a governor of the Hospital, and desired to know why he was excluded. He was answered that this Board always received addresses in writing, which, when presented, they would answer properly, meantime he was ordered to withdraw." This was the foreblast of a storm which shook civic Dublin for eighteen years, and seriously affected our school, as its government depended on the constitution of the Municipal body; and this movement was itself a vibration of the great Liberal uprising that stirred these kingdoms in the middle of the eighteenth century—Lucas was its stormy petrel here. He was an Ishmaelite, with a decided dash of Esau's generosity, even when his hand was against everyone. Called by Lord Townsend afterwards the Wilkes of Ireland, he was undoubtedly a precursor of Henry Grattan and the so-called Free Parliament of 1782. A skilled apothecary, he began his agitations in 1741 by a pamphlet, "Pharmacomastic," in which he lashed the heads of his craft, to their great wrath, but thus secured the representation of his guild in the city Commons. There, in alliance with James Digges

La Touche, of the great banker family, he organized an opposition Committee of the Commons, in April, 1742, against the oligarchy of the Lord Mayor and the Board of Aldermen, and the Commons assembly indorsed his proposed " Regulations for the better management of the business of this city." These first claimed only a larger control over the city finances for the general committees on which some members of the Commons sat ; but in the August Assembly the assault was enlarged and a committee appointed to inspect the charters, the Acts of Assembly, and such papers as relate to the government of the city and of the Blue Coat Hospital ; and it was following up this that Lucas came in person to our Board. The real attack was upon the city magnates. To understand this we must bear in mind the constitution of the city as then existing under the Essex rules of 1672. The Lord Mayor, the Aldermen, and the Common Council were the corporate body. The Lord Mayor and twenty-four Aldermen sat apart as the upper house. The Commons were the two sheriffs, the sheriffs' peers, that is, those who had served or been nominated as sheriffs, of whom there were always an average of ten to twenty, and ninety-six members elected by the twenty-five city guilds, who themselves were elected by the freemen. The constitution was fancifully compared to that of King, Lords, and Commons. The upper house exclusively appointed the Lord Mayor, the Sheriffs, and Treasurer ; the Recorder, the city Chaplain, and the Town Clerk, and all other officers were chosen by the Common Council in the quarterly assemblies. The Rules did not prescribe from what area of the citizens the upper house should elect either Lord Mayor or Aldermen, but by long usage they always chose the former from amongst the Aldermen, and the Aldermen by co-opting a sheriff's peer, who himself had been originally chosen by themselves ; and thus it was said : " Once a sheriff, sure to be an alderman ; once an alderman, sure to be Lord Mayor." The Aldermen were *ex officio* the justices of the peace of the city. As the Lord Mayor was chief man in the city ; was clothed in scarlet with the collar of SS. ; controlled the city militia ; was called My Lord, and his wife My Lady ; and lived in the Mansion House, the prerogatives of the upper house became the object of popular attack, of which Lucas now made himself the voice, with the claim that all the city officers should be chosen by the whole body of the citizens, as represented by the whole Corporation in the city assemblies.

But the Blue Coat was selected for frontal attack. As our charter was then only seventy years old, its records were modern, and it was more difficult for the upper house to plead for their privileges a prescriptive usage which might presume a legal origin, than where the records were ancient and obscure. Throughout this year and 1743 the conflict was waged with signal ability on both sides. At the October Assembly, 1742, the Commons sent to the Lord Mayor the report of their committee setting forth their whole case. This was answered by the Lord Mayor and Aldermen in January, 1743, and the Commons rejoined in the following July, neither side conceding anything. These protocols occupy sixty pages of the ninth volume of Gilbert's *City Records*, and also are found in the *Haliday Pamphlets*, 1749. They are replete with learning and research. The case of the Commons, condensed, was that the great City Charter of Henry III. confirms to " the citizens of Dublin and their heirs that they may for ever elect a Mayor annually out of their own body, a discreet and proper person for the government of our City of Dublin, when elected to be presented to us or our Lords Justices in Ireland ;" that the assembly rolls in Queen Elizabeth's reign dealing with the city offices are expressly made " by the authority of the assembly, according to the antient and laudable orders of this city." Then that the Charter of Charles I. in its preamble runs :—" Whereas we are informed that the Mayor, bailiffs, commons, and citizens from time to time, and time immemorial, by long and ancient usage, have chosen within said city of the worthiest and discreetest men twenty-four citizens to be aldermen of the city." And setting forth a voluminous list of precedents showing the election and removals of specific officers to be in the name of the assembly, they rely on the rolls in which all Mayors, aldermen, and sheriffs are entered as chosen by the assembly at large. The answer relies on the uninterrupted usage of modern years; it sets aside the apparent evidence of the assembly rolls by showing these prove too much, as the entries run in the same form during all the years in which the Commons indubitably took no part in the elections, the names being merely sent forward from the upper house and always adopted by the assembly as mere matter of form. The strongest fact is the negative one that the records show no single instance of a joint appointment, nor could the Commons suggest the mode in which it was conducted; above all, in the face of the fact that the upper house had sat apart within all legal memory. They meet the language of the charters by showing the elections could never have been by the citizens at large, and that the only proveable immemorial usage is that now existing, which must be assumed as of legal origin. They rely on the Essex Rules, 1672, acquiesced in ever since as concluding the question of electing Lord Mayors, and though this did not deal with the election of aldermen, which was obscure up to 1711, the usage ever since always acquiesced in was sufficient evidence of the usage before; they justified the existing system as always securing for the government of the city the most independent and wealthy men, who could afford their time to public service; they had only a pittance of £4 a year to each alderman, and the Lord Mayor only a few hundreds, far below the expenses of his office, which engrossed all his time; whilst on the other hand, the citizens were saved the turmoil and expense of continuous popular elections.

The truth, perhaps, is that our Corporation, like most other bodies long exercising power, had evolved some of their functions rather than usurped them, the general body of citizens being quite ready to leave public duties to the few who undertake them, till all practical authority would insensibly become centred in these.

The Lucas Committee then limited their attack to what

they regarded as the two weakest points of the defence, the constitution of the Blue Coat and co-option of aldermen by themselves. As to the former, their case was that whilst the Charter was to the Lord Mayor, Sheriffs, and Commons generally, the Act of Assembly, 1675, did indeed give power to the upper house to manage the affairs of the Hospital and carry on the work, calling to their assistance such other sub-governors nominated in the assembly of 1673 as they thought proper, but that this gave no power to elect as sub-governors persons who were not members of the Corporation, at their own discretion and irrespective of the Commons. To this the aldermen replied that the Blue Coat was a distinct Corporation, of which the Lord Mayor and aldermen only were members, together with the Recorder, the Sheriffs, and Sheriffs' Peers, and a great number of gentlemen of most eminent station and worth. Whilst the contest raged in August, 1743, the Commons sent to the upper house a proposal for a conference between the Houses, the Recorder to preside as Moderator. The Lord Mayor at once replied that at the next quarter Assembly the proposals would be considered, but the Assembly still in session forthwith attended at the upper house, and, being admitted, demanded a conference without further delay. Eaton Stannard, the Recorder who was popular with both sides, counselled peace and unanimity and dispatch of public business, but the Commons insisted on instant discussion, one, presumably Lucas, claiming the right of all members to offer their sentiments; whereupon Lord Mayor Aldrich, declaring that this was no conference, ordered the Commons to withdraw. " Gentlemen, then I desire that you will go out of the room." The Commons withdrew in a rage; and in September a message from the Lord Mayor categorically denied all the rights they claimed.

Then it was agreed by both sides to leave all matters in dispute to Stannard, the Recorder, who, in October, gave in writing a very learned and judicial opinion, holding as to the Blue Coat that the Acts of Assembly of 1675 constituted a lawful Bye-law vesting the government of the Hospital in the persons mentioned therein, and that the general words of the Charter were thereby restrained ; and as to the election of aldermen, whilst giving due weight to the antient city charters and the entries on the rolls, yet the existing usage, which might presumably have been by Bye-law, or still more by antient prescription, was too strong to be overturned now, and that the election of aldermen is in the Lord Mayor and the Board of Aldermen.

But the Lucas opposition still refused to yield. They took the opinion of the most eminent counsel of the day. The Attorney-General, Sir George Caulfield, was in effect against them. As to the Blue Coat, his opinion coincided with Stannard's ; as to the aldermen, he advised that the usage at least threw the burden of proof on the Commons, who had no evidence to offer of joint election of the Houses. The Prime Sergeant, Anthony Malone, now leading the Bar, and rising to the highest eminence as a statesman, would offer no opinion as to the Blue Coat in the absence of full information. As to the aldermen's prerogative, he thought the Commons must have had some original share in their elections, but as they had so long neglected to assert their rights, he deprecated litigation as possibly leading to a withdrawal by the Crown of the City Charters ; if, however, they were bent on judicial decision, their course was by an information in the King's Bench on a *Quo Warranto* against any alderman chosen by co-option only. Mr. Sergeant Marshall also declined to give any opinion as to the Blue Coat on the facts before him ; as to the aldermen, he thought the long existing usage would be sufficient to presume a Bye-law, though whether such would be lawful needed further consideration. Mr. Vandeleur and Mr. Bradstreet, afterwards our Recorder, gave opinions favourable to the Commons. Reading these opinions, we recall Oliver Goldsmith's Chinese philosopher, who, visiting Westminster Hall with a litigant friend then expecting judgment in a suit which had lingered for years, asked " Why do you hope now, after such long delays ? " " My lawyer tells me I have Salkeld and Ventris strong in my favour, and that there are no less than fifteen cases in point."

"O," said the Chinese, "are these two of your judges?" "Pardon me, these are two lawyers who gave these opinions some hundred years ago; those which make for me are for my lawyer to cite, those which look another way are to be cited by the lawyer for my antagonist. I have Salkeld and Ventris for me; he has Coke and Hales for him; and he that has most opinions is most likely to carry his cause."

In 1744 La Touche and Lucas filed a *Quo Warranto* information in the King's Bench against George Ribton, a co-opted alderman, challenging the right of the aldermen to elect irrespective of the Commons. On full argument the King's Bench dismissed the information, "there not having appeared any grounds for the same," and in 1746 the Corporation voted £200 to cover the charges of the defence.

But with the insuppressibility of a true agitator Lucas warred on. Following up his *Divilina Libera* with his *Complaints of Dublin*, he for five years fulminated pamphlets, broadsides, letters to the citizens, to the Lord Mayor, to the Government, which made him the hero of the populace; but in 1748 he became candidate for the city in Parliament, opposing La Touche, his old colleague in agitation, which caused an angry split, and he was thrown out at this election. He was now flying at higher game than Lord Mayors, launching violent assaults on the Irish Government and the constitution of Parliament, for which he now first raised the claim of national independence. Some of the bitterest of his broadsheets he addressed to Lord Harrington, who came here as Lord Lieutenant in 1747, and who at first treated him civilly; but calling personally to enforce his "great Charter of Dublin," Lord Harrington became angry, turned him out of the Castle, and sent forward his vehement addresses to Parliament. In October, 1749, he was summoned before the House of Commons, who thereupon declared him an enemy of his country, and ordered him to Newgate. Then he fled as an outlaw, and the Corporation, taking their cue from the Commons, summoned him in his absence to answer for his addresses to the citizens of Dublin and specially his " Dedication to the King as scandalously reflecting on the Viceroy, tending to justify the several horrid and bloody rebellions which have been raised within this kingdom, and to traduce and vilify the magistracy of this honourable city;" and in January, 1750, failing to appear, he was adjudged disfranchised from all liberties of the city, and to be henceforth reputed as a *Foreigner*.

When candidate for the city he had poured forth twenty-four broadsides, violent, vehement, striking ubiquitously, styled "Addresses to the Citizens,"[1] and numbered like the *Drapier's Letters*, but it is curious that his final onslaught before his outlawry was upon the Blue Coat, in form " a narrative of the Hospital in Oxmantown Green." Reciting the acts of the founders, whose piety he warmly praises, he prints in many pages, all the original contributions, and calls Lord Ossory's letter of 1678 which led to these " the laying of the first stone of the good and great design." He then indicts the governors, first for laying aside the primary intention of an Hospital for the Dublin poor as well as a School. He then bitterly renews the charge of illegally excluding the Commons from the Government, the co-option of governors not members of the corporation is denounced as open to criminal prosecution under a statute of Henry VII. which forbade under penalties the intrusion of strangers in city affairs. But the gravamen of his charge is that the nominations of the boys are not given exclusively to the poor lads of the city, but at the caprice of the governors to the sons of their followers or to strangers. This was, of course, an appeal to the electors, but not content with generic indictment, he founds a charge of specific corruption against two governors, Alderman Nathaniel Kane and Sir Samuel Cooke, the one for taking leases of the Hospital estate, the other for farming the City Toll Corne granted to the Hospital. He further, by innuendo, suggests that Kane had bought, in trust, the Island Bridge Mills for the city water supply, at a gross overvalue from Mr. Darby, the owner, so as to secure a large

[1] Halliday's *Pamphlets*, 1749.

debt which Darby owed him. And he calls on the citizens to discharge "these perfidious trustees, these usurping governors," by electing him as the only means, because, having found agitation in the Assembly and appeals to the Law Courts without avail, the sole redress must be in the Legislature.

But he had now overshot his mark. Kane, who was then elderly and an invalid, in a temperate letter asked Lucas to state distinctly if the innuendo of corruption in the purchase of the mills meant him, that he might disprove it in a Court of Law. Everyone knew that Kane was aimed at, but the then practice in libel cases required strict proof of the innuendo. Here Lucas acted meanly indeed. In a scoffing letter he refused to answer the straight question, evasively suggesting that 'if the cap fitted" and so forth, and with serio comic insolence regretting to hear of the Alderman's illness, he gravely offered to send him a medical cure. Then Kane publicly addressed the city. His letter is dignified and even pathetic. Through the long years, he said, in which he had served the city, he had hitherto lived without stain or reproach; he recounted the whole affair of the Island Bridge Mills. The charge that he was a creditor of the vendor is indignantly disclaimed as entirely baseless, the course of the treaty is disclosed with certifying letters from Mr. Darby of Leap, and of all that were parties to the treaty, and the good faith of the purchase is proved. He admits he had taken a lease of some Hospital houses in Oxmantown, but that on learning it was unlawful to hold them, he had long since offered to surrender, but that his offer was declined, as the leases were unprofitable. It is strange that seven years exhaustive search should have disclosed so little to warrant Lucas' calumnies, and there is no doubt that the virulence and failure of these were a chief cause in his condemnation in the Castle and the Tholsel.

But in the Parliamentary biennial session, 1752 and 1753, an opposition, headed by Speaker Henry Boyle, Prime Sergeant Malone, and Carter, Master of the Rolls, was, for the first time formed against the Castle, and the undertaking Lords Justices, then represented by the Primate, George Stone. They successfully asserted the independence of the Irish Commons as to money bills, with a vehemence surpassing that of Lucas himself, for which they had so recently outlawed him, and they were now named the Patriots. Their spirit electrified the masses, and penetrated even to the court of aldermen, in which an opposition section was now formed. In the Parliamentary session, 1755-56, Adderley, an independent member, took up the city case, and two bills were brought in for a drastic change in the Corporation. No longer striking at Lord Mayor and Aldermen only, they asked for a radical reform of the Common Council. Their grievance was that in the election of the ninety-six members by the guilds, the merchants or Trinity Guild chose thirty-one, leaving the twenty-four other guilds only sixty-five between them, whilst the merchants were nearly all city magnates, many of the aldermen belonging to it. The bills now provided to divide the city into thirteen wards, each of which was to choose its own aldermen and councillors, thus opening all the offices directly or indirectly to popular vote. The promoters fully relied on the support of the Patriots, but the fire of their patriotism had now been drowned in the sweet baths of promotion and pension. Speaker Boyle, now Lord Shannon, with £2,000 a year, Carter, now Secretary of State, with £1,000 a year added to his salary as Master of the Rolls, and Malone, now Chancellor of the Exchequer, counselled the promoters to postpone the bills. The Duke of Devonshire, L.L., gave the same advice, but they persevered, and then ensued a high comedy. The bills were allowed to pass without opposition, and even with acclaim, but the postponers and opponents were laughing in their sleeves, for they well knew that the Privy Council would decline to forward the Bills to London under Poyning's Act. So these became abortions, and the people, finding they had imagined a vain thing, raged against the Patriots, and took their revenge in riots, which alarmed and re-united the Aldermen. Thomas Mead, who had strongly supported the Bills, was chosen Lord Mayor, and in the next session the Bills were dropped.

But in 1756, James Grattan had become Recorder and a governor on the death of Thomas Morgan, who had succeeded Eaton Stannard six years before. He was an able man, moderately conservative, and never adopted the tribunic rôle of his son, the patriot, Henry. Failing at the city election in 1758, when he was beaten by Dunn, one of the dissentient aldermen, who had resigned in order to oppose him, he now set himself to bring back peace to the city, and drew a moderate Bill which the Corporation by a majority sent to the House by petition. The populace opposed it with counter blasts, but it was coached through the House by Sir Charles Burton, then city member, and our chairman in 1752, and it passed with slight modifications as 33 Geo. II., c. 16. The old constitution and old members of the Corporation were retained, but the Assembly were so far to share in the choice of the mayoralty, that of three aldermen's names submitted to them, they should select one; if they vetoed all three, new names were to be submitted, and so till they selected someone, failing which, the aldermen could elect the Lord Mayor, lest the city should be left without a head. So as to the Sheriff, the Assembly, and not the aldermen, were to select eight names, from which the aldermen were to choose the two sheriffs of the year. As to the aldermen, the Upper House were to send to the Assembly the names of four sheriff's peers, from which the Assembly were to select, to the vacated seat. Further, the Guilds were to choose their representation in the Commons directly without any *conge d'elire* to the Upper House. The Blue Coat remained untouched.

Though the populace without still raged and rioted, this compromise brought peace and held its ground till the Corporation Act of 1840, and is thus a standing tribute to the constructive ability of Recorder Grattan.

In his long exile Lucas applied his talents to medical subjects with marked ability, though he occasionally launched broadsides from across Channel, the last of which

From the Statue by Edward Smyth,
Executed for Royal Exchange, and now
in the City Hall of Dublin.

[To face page 199.

was a pungent indictment of the placated patriots in 1759. But on the death of George II. next year, he personally went to the young King in London, was kindly received, and returned to Dublin with the royal recommendations. A *nolle prosequi* was entered by the Crown, he was now a general favourite, for he had borne misfortune well, and was elected for Dublin in the new Parliament of 1761. He had obtained a mandamus from the King's Bench to reverse his disfranchisement of 1750, which the Corporation did not defend, being also advised that their action had been of doubtful legality. He held his seat for the city to his death in 1771, and though he continued his campaigns against the constitution of Parliament, he did not actively renew his war on the Corporation or the Blue Coat.

The last echo of this Lucas feud sounds something like a joke. In 1766, the Commons sent to the Upper House a petition to grant Charles Lucas, from the city funds, a life annuity of £365, as a reward for his merit and public services, but the Lord Mayor and Aldermen, judging it inexpedient to give any countenance to the petition, " as the circumstances of the present juncture are of too much notoriety to leave room to doubt the motive of such an application," unanimously and indignantly rejected the proposal.

Yet, on the whole, we must deem that Lucas merited the posthumous honour by which his statue, one of the best in the city, now stands one of the chief ornaments of the City Hall. It was the work of a great Irish sculptor, Edward Smyth, whose name deserves to be better remembered, and is a splendid protrait in marble. It was executed for the Royal Exchange, the founding of which was carried through Parliament chiefly by Lucas's driving force, and alone would give him a claim to public gratitude. This statue, with the Exchange itself, passed to the Corporation when they made their headquarters there. Smyth, who was the sculptor of the fine figures on the Bank of Ireland, the Four Courts, and the King's Inns, is so far connected with the Blue Coat, that he was the pupil of Vierpyl, the Italian Statuary, hereafter noticed as charged with the ornamental stone work of the present King's Hospital.

But this city storm was not an ill wind that blew nobody good. In the years from 1743 to 1751, when it was blowing, no less than eight of the aldermen nominated as Lord Mayors, excused themselves from accepting office, presumably in terror of the turmoil and the costs of litigation. Their excuses were accepted, but only on the condition in each case of a fine of twenty guineas to be given to the Blue Coat, and a hogshead of claret each to the existing and the incoming Lord Mayor. Thus one hundred and sixty guineas gilds our memory of Charles Lucas.

These agitations did not damp the exuberant loyalty of our city magnates. In December, 1744, they addressed the King, congratulating him on his return from his great victory at Dettingen, " in defence of the liberties of Europe." Next year, upon the threat of Prince Charles Stuart's invasion of Scotland, they again addressed him " with the resolution of hazarding our lives and fortunes in support of your Majesty's undoubted rights against this horrid enterprize." They offered a reward of £6,000 for the capture of the Pretender, though it is hard to say where the reward could have been found if claimed, for when the Lord Lieutenant, the Duke of Devonshire, issued a commission of array, requiring the city to raise three regiments of militia and one of horse, and in response the city voted £1,100 towards the expenses of accoutrements, they were obliged to borrow the money. Twenty-four of our Blue boys appear to have been enrolled in these forces. We have some accounts submitted to our governors in 1746, headed " Expended on the Boys Malitia (*sic*) which include ' Wilkinson's mounting 100 guns, pikes, and halberts, embroidering twenty-four caps, a charge for orange colours, gold lace for hats, and four drums.' "

Then, after Culloden, they felicitate the King on the Duke of Cumberland's victory, " and the defeat of the French designs to bring in the Pretender and to overthrow the Protestant Succession." We may imagine with what joy our Blue boys beat their six drums, and waved their embroidered caps on that memorable occasion. In this year, 1744, is the last entry in our books of Swift's name. It is pathetic, though merely the admission of a boy nominated by him, for he was now in his last sad stage summed in Dr. Johnson's line :—" And Swift expires a driveller and a show."

As the loyal addresses of the city emanated from the Court of Aldermen, and were composed by the Recorder, all concerned being governors of the Blue Coat, we may mention that no less than eighteen [2] were presented to George II. On his accession in 1727 ; on the birth of the Prince of Wales (George III.) in 1738 ; on the taking of Porto Bello in 1740 ; then the three already specified, in connection with Charles Stuart ; on the Peace of Aix la Chapelle in 1748, and on the King's return to England in 1750 ; in 1756 on the threat of French invasion ; on the taking of Cape Breton in 1758 ; on Hawke's victory at Quiberon, and Wolfe's at Quebec in 1759, and on the majority of the Prince of Wales, George III., in the same year. The other addresses were on the occasion of the births or marriages of the royal Princes or Princesses, the King's children and grandchildren, who were often the annual gifts to the nation. But besides these the city addressed Pitt at the close of the *annus mirabilis*, 1759, with the freedom of Dublin in a gold box and like honours were conferred on Hawke " for his great service in defeating the French Fleet at Quiberon, under Marshall Conflans, whose known destination was a descent on Ireland." Like honour, too, was given to Sir John Elliott for the final dispersion of the French Armada, under Thurot, after his descent on Carrickfergus. Thus we are conscious of the spirit of Chatham at the great epoch in the evolution of the Empire animating the life of Dublin, and awake even in the Boardroom of our School.

In 1753, Sir Charles Burton being Lord Mayor, the great sculptor, Roubiliac, was invited to estimate for an equestrian statue of George II., but his charge of £2,100 being thought

[2] They are printed at length in the 7, 8, 9, and 10 Vols. of Gilbert's *Calendar*.

too high, Van Nost, who then worked in Dublin, attended a Committee at the Tholsel, and undertook the statue for £1,000, exclusive of pedestal and quarterings. At the end of three years he conveyed it by deed to the Corporation for ever, in that burning year, 1756, and it was then erected where it stands in the centre of St. Stephen's Green. The pedestal and quarterings, of Ardbraccan stone, cost £730, making a total expense of £1,730.

George II. died 25 October, 1760. Our Chairmen during the reign were the Lord Mayors following :—

1727- 8	Sir Nat. Whitwell.	1744- 5	John Walker.
28- 9	Henry Burrowes.	45- 6	Daniel Cooke.
29-30	Sir Peter Verdoen.	46- 7	William Walker.
30- 1	Nat. Pearson.	47- 8	Sir Geo. Ribton, Bart.
31- 2	Joseph Nuttal.	48- 9	Sir Robert Ross.
32- 3	Humphrey French.	49-50	John Adamson.
33- 4	Thomas How.	50- 1	Thomas Taylor.
34- 5	Nat. Kane.	51- 2	John Cooke.
35- 6	Sir Richard Grattan.	52- 3	Sir Chas. Burton, Bart.
36- 7	Sir John Somerville.	53- 4	Andrew Murray.
37- 8	William Walker.	54- 5	Hans Bailie.
38- 9	John Macarell.	55- 6	Percival Hunt.
39-40	Daniel Falkiner.	56- 7	John Fookes
40- 1	Sir Samuel Coote.	57- 8	Thomas Mead.
41- 2	William Aldrich.	58- 9	Philip Crampton.
42- 3	Gilbert King.	59-60	John Tew.
43- 4	David Few.		

Sir Samuel Cooke was the son of the Sir Samuel of Queen Anne's time ; Sir George Ribton was ancestor of the Woodbrook family, Co. Dublin; he was the objective of Lucas's attack, he was created a baronet in 1759 ; Sir Robert Rosse was M.P. for Newry, and grandfather of the hero of Bladensburgh ; Philip Crampton's name was honourably continued in the following generation in the persons of his great nephews, the very eminent physician, Sir Philip, and by the distinguished judge of the Queen's Bench.

CHAPTER X.

TEMP. GEORGE III., 1760-1784, *TO THE OPENING OF THE NEW HOSPITAL.*

IN the earlier years of George III. the School was in a transitional state, and the ordinary records are obscure. The governors having spent many thousands on a new Infirmary, and in partial reparations, now found that the whole building was threatening to fall about their ears, and that a thorough reconstruction on a new site was essential. So far back as 1753 the Corporation had granted them the old artillery yard which ran westward to the Royal Barracks from the rere of the old site in an askew strip to the south of the Bowling Green, but this was practically useless in presence of the adjoining decay. But in 1769 Sir Thomas Blackhall, whose name is ever to be held in honour at the Blue Coat, was Lord Mayor, and took upon him the burden which now had fallen on the Board. The members for the City were then the young Marquis of Kildare and our old friend Charles Lucas. In November, Kildare having obtained a Committee on the petition of the Lord Mayor and governors, brought up their report recommending the prayer for a building grant, which the House merely directed to lie on the table for perusal of members, but in the next Session 1771, he vigorously renewed the claim. Kildare had entered the House whilst a minor, and had now only just reached twenty-one, but he was a most loyal and active representative of Dublin. Son of the first Duke of Leinster, his mother was the beautiful Lady Emily Lennox, daughter of the Duke of Richmond, and Lord Edward Fitzgerald was his younger brother. He was a prime favourite in the city.

A few years before he had presented the Lord Mayor and City with a State Coach or berlin, and in the House we find him moving for grants to improve the Harbour, and in aid of the Grand Canal, in which the City was then deeply concerned.

In 1771 he moved the further report of the Blue Coat Committee. It sets forth that the Committee had examined in the most solemn manner Mr. James Goddard—he was then the Registrar of the Blue Coat and Clerk of the City Commons; that there were then 170 boys in the school, that it was only now kept together by patchwork, and it was absolutely necessary to rebuild it, for which £12,789 would be necessary. Thereupon the matter was referred by the House to the Committee of Supply, which was then regarded as almost an equivalent to a grant.

Whilst the subject was thus before Parliament, the City Assembly in October, 1771, in anticipation of a grant, conveyed to the governors the whole remaining space of the Bowling Green in Oxmantown, for the purpose of building a new Hospital, which, they affirmed, would not only be necessary and useful to the School, but would tend much to the improvement of that part of the old City Estate, for they, at the same time, ordered that all the residue of the Oxmantown Green should be laid out in building lots, so as to be no longer unserviceable and waste, but an ornament "to your honour's estate."[1] Thus the whole site of the present Blue Coat was acquired, comprising the old practising grounds of the City Militia, and the old Bowling Green, as laid out a century before, whilst its bounds on the west are the Royal Barracks, the gift of the City to the great Duke of Ormonde just after the Restoration. The surveys for these adjacent lots were entrusted to Ivory, the Architect selected for the new building.

The Committee of Supplies, in 1771, having many other irons in the fire, made no present grant, but, under the full hope of one, the governors proceeded with their plans, and on the 16th June, 1773, the first stone was laid, with great

[1] Gilbert's *Calendar*, Vol. XII., p. 156.

ceremonial, by the Lord Lieutenant, Lord Harcourt. He was a descendant of Sir Simon, Queen Anne's Attorney-General, and Swift's friend, and ancestor of the late Sir William Harcourt the brilliant Knight of Malwood.

The following notice of the pageant appears in *Faulkner's Journal* of the day :—

Wednesday last, when His Excellency, Lord Harcourt, arrived at the Blue Coat School, he was received by all the officers of that house, who showed His Excellency several of the apartments, which were in a most ruinous condition, from whence his lordship, attended by the Lord Mayor and other governors, went through one of the Courts which was lined with two rows of the children, very clean and neatly dressed, who made a most pleasing appearance, and sang psalms in a most harmonious manner. His Excellency passed down through a guard of the army into Oxmantown Green, and laid the foundation stone with a silver trowel, with the Lord Lieutenants arms engraved thereon, with the following inscription :—" This stone was laid by H.E. Simon Harcourt on Wednesday, 16th June, 1773, in the thirteenth year of the reign of H. M. George III. Right Hon. Richard French, Lord Mayor; James Sheil, James Jones, High Sheriffs; Thomas Ivory, Architect."

This description is most probably by George Faulkner himself, who was present as one of the governors. The *Dublin Journal*'s notice of the pageant tells that His Excellency, attended by the Lord Mayor, His Grace the Archbishop of Dublin (Dr. Craddock), several Privy Councillors, and many aldermen, went in grand procession to the Hospital, and that after the ceremony all proceeded to the Tholsel, where a most elegant dinner was provided by the governors for His Excellency, which was served up with the greatest decency and propriety.

A notable Governor at this time was George Faulkner, mentioned above, He lives to-day in the reflected glory of a satellite of the great Dean, whose Boswell he was in Swift's later years, since when in 1730 his *Journal* introduced him, and he became Swift's printer. But he did the Blue Coat a good service, and thus has a niche in these annals. Swift personally bullied him, and treated him with hauteur, writing to him as "Mr. Faulkner," not even adding "Dear Sir," but, like many great men, he liked toadies, and protected them against all comers. In pleasant letters [2] he introduced him to Pope, to Lord Bolingbroke, Lord Howth, to the Archbishop of Cashel, Dr. Bolton, and Barber, Lord Mayor of London, and, though sulkily, allowed him even to purloin and publish his manuscripts in Dublin, where there was no copyright, though he could himself have published in London, where there was. Dr. Josiah Hort, Bishop of Kilmore, afterwards Archbishop of Cashel, had sent Swift a satire on the game of Quadrille, in which Sergeant Bettesworth, the Dean's foe, was pilloried, requesting him "to peruse the loose feathers, and send the kite to the Faulconer and set it a flying?" all which the Dean did. Bettesworth moved in the House that this was a breach of privilege: [3] Faulkner was indicted, imprisoned in Newgate, and as Swift tells Dr. Hort, confined to a dungeon with common thieves and others with infectious disease. But all this made Faulkner's fortune. Henceforth he was a Dublin celebrity, he paid the gaoler's fees, £25, with his pirated copies of Swift's works, and the author ended by calling him the prince of printers. He was somewhat fantastic, a little one-legged man, very vain, but with a large head, and a great deal of ability. When Swift was gone he was taken up by Lord Chesterfield, when Lord Lieutenant, and made his confidant in Dublin affairs. Chesterfield calls himself the only Lieutenant Faulkner ever absolutely governed. He continued for life the great repository of Swiftiana, telling the stories, showing the bust by Roubiliac, now in Trinity College, to all the many who visited him in his shop in Parliament Street. His edition, in twenty volumes, 1759-1770, is the first great collection of Swift's Works, and the basis of all that have followed, and thus "Peter Paragraph," by which name he was laughed at in Dublin, has been a substantial benefactor to literature.

In 1767 he was elected High Sheriff, but his health was now failing, and in a grateful letter to the Lord Mayor he

[2] Swift's *Epistolary Correspondence*, 1735.
[3] Letter, Swift to Bishop of Kilmore, 12th May, 1738.

asked to be excused. The fines on refusals, by usage, were given to the Blue Coat ; these at this time were fixed at ten guineas only, but Faulkner now particularly requested that it should in his case be one hundred, as had been paid 161 years before, and this was graciously accepted. The liberality proved most valuable, not only did it create a precedent, but encouraged the city to raise the fine, a few years later to £200.⁴ In 1772 five sheriffs successively declined, Luke Stock, Joseph Lynam, Harcourt Lightburne, Benjamin Ball, and Robert Rickey, and their five hundred guineas were assigned "towards rebuilding the Blue Coat Hospital." Thereupon the Assembly in July raised the fine to £200, and two more sheriffs declining, George Sutton and Thomas Green, raised the fund from this source that year to £925. In 1774 there were again four refusals, David La Touche, Alderman Kirkpatrick, James Lane, and George Maquay, thus bringing in £800 more. These gentlemen were all governors, and found this a convenient form of contributing to the building fund, which then so sorely needed such aid. Faulkner remained on the Board to the last ; he died in 1775.

Inspired by the prestige of the Harcourt Ceremonial, the Lord Mayor and Corporation renewed their petition to Parliament in the new Session of 1773 ; they now stated the new grant from the city of the site, and that the plans would cost £16,000, whilst the failure to rebuild would be a fatal loss " to the public in general, and to the Protestant Religion in particular." Unfortunately, just as the subject was to come before the House, it lost the powerful support of Lord Kildare ; his father died in November, and he succeeded to the Upper House as second Duke of Leinster. The city addressed him then in an affectionate farewell entrusted to Sir Thomas Blackhall and three others and the Recorder. After condolence in the loss of his father, they return to His Grace their most sincere and grateful acknowledgments " for your very faithful and vigilant discharge of the important duty of one of our representatives in Parliament,

⁴ Gilbert's *Calendar*, Vol. 12.

assuring Your Grace that the very affectionate concern you have manifested, not only in that capacity, but on every other occasion, for the true interest and advantage of this Metropolis have made an impression on our minds which time can never efface."

Lucas was now dead. Dr. Clement, who succeeded him in the city, took up the cause in the House; but there was merely a repetition of the tale of the previous session. The case of the petitioners was declared proved and deserving of the aid of Parliament, and it was again referred to the Committee of Supplies; yet no supply was granted, and the subject once more fell through.

But the governors still persevered in hope, and raised several thousands in private subscriptions. Thomas Ivory was one of the constellation of famous architects in that Augustan age of Dublin building. He was Master of Drawing to the Royal Dublin Society for many years, where Sir Martin Archer Shee, afterwards President of the Royal Academy in London and friend of Reynolds and Romney, was one of his pupils. Another fine work of Ivory's is Newcomen House, opposite the Castle gates, now the Municipal Building of the Corporation, erected on the site of the mansion of the Earls of Cork, and still known as Cork Hill.

Ivory's designs for the new Blue Coat are splendid, their fault being that they were too ambitious and costly. So much of them as have been carried out have cost more than £20,000. To finish them as planned would have entailed at least £10,000 more. In 1776 the governors presented the original plans to George III. in a handsome morocco volume inscribed—"with all humility, by Your Majesty's dutiful and loyal subjects and servants the governors." These remained in the King's Library, until George IV. made a gift of the Library to the British Museum. There they were lately found by our present governor, Mr. F. E. Ball. They are a very fine specimen of the Dublin art of that day, and are still regarded by experts in London as of exceptional excellence, both artistic and technical. There are twelve

Front Facade of present Hospital.
As originally designed by T. Ivory.
(From plans in British Museum.)

drawings, that of the front elevation and façade being more than three feet by nearly two. This has been substantially carried out as the building now stands, save that the centre rises, not to a dome, but to a lofty spire, highly enriched, in which Ivory took as his model that of St. Martin-in-the-Field, which though very ornamental, yet, being Gothic, is hardly in harmony with the general Italian conception. But in the rere the plans show a great quadrangle, whose sides run north and south from the Chapel and the Schoolroom respectively in arched stone cloisters, over which, in a single storey, is a great range of sleeping rooms for the boys, and this arrangement is partly continued on the western side, opposite the main building, to a very fine dining hall in the centre, from which branch some fourteen offices on each side—dairy, laundry, storerooms. All this intended quadrangle was abandoned. Then the interior of the Chapel as designed is gracefully ornate; there are double Corinthian pilasters between each of the windows on the south wall, and over these a classic cornice beneath an arabesque frieze all round the church; nearly all the above that was decorative had, alas, to be given up for lack of funds.

Associated with Ivory in the artistic work as executed was Simon Vierpyl, an Italian statuary, to whom we may fairly attribute much of the elegance seen in the finished façade. He had been imported by Lord Charlemont for the purposes of the beautiful mansions in Rutland Square and at Marino, which he was then constructing, and especially for the Italian casino in the grounds at Clontarf. Charlemont and his travelling companion, Edward Murphy, had found Vierpyl in Rome, where he executed for Murphy a commission for which he should be better remembered in Dublin to-day. This was to copy in terra cotta some seventy busts of the Roman emperors and empresses in the museums of the Capitol and Vatican. Some of these as executed are of very high excellence, for Vierpyl spent several laborious years over the work. Murphy, having no adequate show place for them, left them by will to Lord Charlemont, whose library in Charlemont House, Palace Row, they decorated for many years. His grandson, the late Earl, in 1868 presented them to the Royal Irish Academy, where some sixty of them, still complete, may be seen. Asked by Murphy in Dublin to say what he considered their real value, Vierpyl writes at length, shewing they are unique, as the first and only collection ever made by a single artist, and, having regard to the time and toil spent, he says that if a monarch engaged him to model the series again, he would not take less than £500 a year for ever.[5] Vierpyl was naturalized in Dublin, and became a member of the City Commons; he received the special thanks of the Ballast or Harbour Board for his services in connection with the Poolbeg Lighthouse. The front of St. Thomas's Church in Marlborough Street was executed by him from a design of Palladio in Venice. He lived and died in Bachelor's Walk.[6] Edward Smyth, the sculptor, as already mentioned, was a pupil of his, who, as an original artist, surpassed his master.

Our new building progressed intermittently; means did not permit of a contract with a single contractor at an estimated cost, so a Building Committee, with Sir Thomas Blackhall chairman, employed the tradesmen directly, paying them when and as best they could. The stone work was assigned to Vierpyl; the others were chiefly members of old and long known Dublin freemen families. Semple was bricklayer; Thorpe, plasterer; Cranfield, carver; the extensive woodwork was done by Chambers. Blackhall personally superintended everything in all the long years, collecting subscriptions and expending them. The Assembly at the same time undertook the surrounding building lots as planned by Ivory; these showed the broad thoroughfare through the Green from Queen Street to the front of the New School, three-fourths of which included the north side of the Old School site. It appears that what is called a great "gulph hole" existed here then. Was this the ancient Scald Brother Hole of Stanihurst? The city entrusted the execution of these improvements to Blackhall, and when,

[5] 15th August, 1774, *Charlemont Papers*, Historical Manuscripts, p. 323.
[6] Whitelaw's *History of Dublin*, Vol. II., p. 1186.

shortly after, the street was named, it deservedly became Blackhall Street. So, too, when the road from Stoney Batter to the Liffey was completed in front of the new Blue Coat gates, it was called Blackhall Place, and thus our worthy's name is still written on the site to record his devotion of more than thirty years. He became a governor in 1761, when sheriff, and was made an alderman in 1763.

On the Building Committee Blackhall was well assisted by Mr. Benjamin Ball, who, on declining the shrievalty in 1772, paid his hundred guineas fine, and thus, being a sheriff's peer, became a governor ; he was kinsman of the founders of the eminent banking firm, and was ancestor of the late Lord Chancellor Ball, through whose son, Mr. F. Elrington Ball, his name is worthily represented on the Board of the Blue Coat still. But funds were still lacking, and relief was again sought in Parliament in the Session of 1777. Sir Samuel Bradstreet, who had succeeded James Grattan as Recorder in 1766, and also as Member for the city, now urged our petition, but with no happier result than that it was again ordered to lie on the table for perusal.

There was now nothing for it but to cut down the plans, and Blackhall and his committee were in 1779 directed to confer with the architect for a reduction of the offices, which meant a surrender of the fine cloistered quadrangle on which Ivory was then engaged; but the direction to Ivory " to contract rather than increase the expense of these " seems to have mortified him sorely, for next year he resigned when the work was only half finished, though fortunately not till after his fine conception of the main building had been secured. The governors appointed in his place one of their own number, Mr. John Wilson, who was contractor of the city works, and whom they had also made registrar and agent ; he will be mentioned hereafter. Over the mantelpiece in the Boardroom now hangs an oil painting presented to the governors some fifty years after, in 1835, by Mr. Ball, the son of the Benjamin Ball just noticed, but the execution of which we can fix as in this year, 1779, for it evidently represents this conference with Ivory for the reduction of his plans. It is an excellent picture by Jonathan Trotter, who attained some eminence as a portrait painter; he had studied in Rome. There are nine figures, all having the character of good likenesses; nearly all of them can be identified. At the extreme right stands Trotter himself, palette in hand, talking to Benjamin Ball, a handsome gentleman clothed in black like a bishop; at the farthest left stands Wilson, just appointed registrar, but not yet architect, for in the centre is an oval table; at its head is seated, green-coated, well-looking, a gentleman who points to the open plans, and is anxiously questioning Vierpyl, who sits opposite in his working white jacket, and who seems nonplussed and not quite pleased with the examination. Between them, in the centre, is Ivory, in maroon coat, attentively listening to Vierpyl and the chairman; beside the latter is seated a gentleman in scarlet doublet, half turning his face as if to speak to Wilson; either he or the man in green we assume to be Blackhall, but as both are at the head of the table we cannot decide. Two other figures standing between these and Wilson are said to represent Alderman Trulock and Alderman Tucker, who were both on the Building Committee.

The Boardroom where this picture hangs is the only part of the house completely finished as Ivory planned it, save, perhaps, the front façade and the two Italian corridors, with their arched niches on the ground and first stories. It is a very fine example of the best work of the period, thirty-four feet long by twenty-one and fourteen feet high, with a rich Corinthian cornice and a coved ceiling laced with graceful traceries. The three windows face the west and the square of the Royal Barracks, known as the Palatine, with the bright green playground between. This room has been long the subject of recurrent architectural praise in Dublin. Beneath Trotter's painting is the fine chimney-piece presented for the room by Mr. George Ensor in 1780; it is of white Carrara marble, of which much had been imported at this time by Vierpyl, and of which there are Ionic pillars at each side; the panels below the sill are of ruddy Sienna marble. It seems to have incurred some damage in carriage, for a contemporaneous entry directs Vierpyl to repair it, and fix it up in the Boardroom as soon as possible.

The great school room and the dining hall were finished; in the latter the quaint and somewhat imposing Royal Arms of Charles II., gilt and emblazoned, and now taken from the old building, were erected over the central fireplace as they are to be seen to-day.

But the Chapel was still unfinished; the dormitories, the offices, the kitchen, were only half complete; and in the old crumbling building the old chapel was of necessity used as a schoolroom, so far a sanctuary from the menacing walls; so, in the Session 1781, a final and vehement effort was made for a grant from Parliament. At the same time the Lord Lieutenant, Lord Carlisle, Mr. Secretary Eden, and Lord Harcourt were urgently besought, but without much result. The new petition was committed to Sir Samuel Bradstreet and Dr. Clement, the city members. It was the most persuasive appeal yet made.[7] It detailed how in 1689 the ancient edifice had been turned into a barrack, and having been restored at great expense to the citizens, had had the honour to be the Parliament House during the erection of the present one, but from age and these changes and alterations it was now necessarily taken down; that the governors had begun their new Hospital on a plan for 300 boys, relying on the beneficence of the legislature "who had given bountifully to everything that can promote the prosperity of the kingdom," and flattered themselves with the modest presumption that the Parliament whose generous grants had reached the remotest parts of the land would not now overlook this useful charity at home, which had flourished so many years and now needed the fostering care of the legislature to complete it.

And yet this *ad captandum* appeal was doomed like its predecessors only to lie on the table. It is not easy now to guess the true causes of this ill success, for, as hinted in this

[7] *Com. Journal*, 1781, 218.

petition, the House was then lavishing money on all sorts of projects, not only through the island, but in Dublin, continuing the policy by which, when defeated in the claims to pass money bills without even the formal consent of the Crown, they revenged themselves by voting as they pleased all the surplus of the Hereditary Revenue of Ireland, the balance of which only, after providing for the annual votes, was payable into the Exchequer. The *Commons Journal* shows, for instance, that in the three years 1779-81 £10,000 was voted to the Dublin Society, £19,000 to the Foundling Hospital, £14,000 to the Incorporated Society, £6,000 to the House of Industry, £3,500 to the Hibernian School, and £3,000 to Swift's Hospital. But new favourites make old ones unfashionable.

The work after Ivory's resignation, which was absolutely necessary to permit of transferring the boys to their new quarters, cost £6,000. This was executed under Wilson over a period of three years, and for almost the whole the Hospital remained indebted to the tradesmen. At long last, at Christmas, 1783, the Committee reported to the Board that the accommodations were so far completed for the reception of the boys and servants that these were now received into the new Hospital, " and most comfortably provided for." We may hope that the inmates themselves concurred in this comfortable judgment. Many subsequent entries make this somewhat doubtful.

CHAPTER XI.

TEMP. GEORGE III. 1784-1800.

THE School resumed in the new buildings in the opening of 1784. It might have been thought that the fine Renaissance palace which it exteriorly seemed to be, would now have attracted the public support necessary to complete it and extend its operations. Such hopes failed, owing to the very events which might have seemed likely to secure them: the new Independent Parliament, with the consequent vast increase in the notables and nobles resident in Dublin. For the expanded arena into which the public life of Ireland had now entered diverted men's gaze from things so local as a city school. In the first half of its stormy career, this legislature was engaged with questions of imperial moment, which were closely involved with those of Great Britain, such as John Foster's great Act for the Protection of Corn in 1784, with his refusal to protect Irish manufactures, which latter raised vehement riots in the city; the discussion of William Pitt's offers of a commercial union with Ireland, and its final ill-starred rejection because Ireland refused to adhere to the British colonial tariff; then the Irish demand to vote for the Regency, when George III. was ill, in complete independence of the Parliament or Ministry in London; and many other assertions of Ireland's unrestricted autonomy. The last decade was passed in the fever of the scarcely veiled rebellion, which overtly broke out in 1798, fomented all through by the United Irishmen, ever since, assuming control of the Volunteer movement, they leagued with France for the establishment of a Republic on the principles and lines of the regicide revolution.

All through these conflicts, from first to last, rose the voice of Grattan, now in superlative eloquence, oftener, still, in rhapsodic rhetoric, and this, with the clash of parliamentary debate, so filled the public ear, as to leave small entry for the appeal or the claims of a Municipal School Board. Our Minutes, which, in the previous hundred years, are studded with the names of distinguished statesmen and courtiers, show, in the last sixteen years of the century, the attendance of only three Privy Councillors, the Archbishop of Dublin, Dr. Fowler, who was present only once, the Archbishop of Cashel, Dr. Agar Ellis, who was present once in 1786, and twice in the next year, when he was Viscount Somerton, and the Right Hon. David La Touche, who appears once in 1786, and only twice the year after. There are no other governors at the meetings outside the Corporation members, except the Bishop of Cloyne, Dr. Bennett, the Bishop of Kildare, Dr. George Lewis Jones, elected in 1790, and Archdeacon Fowler of Dublin, all whose visits are few and far between, and Baron George, who, however, atoned for many absentees; the Primate, Lord Rokeby, was elected, indeed, but we cannot find that he ever attended.

The City Hall itself was drawn into the current of public events. The enthusiasm, kindled by the Volunteer movement was everywhere contagious for a time; in those stirring years riots in Dublin were rife and continuous, and the agitations outside, doubtless, penetrated the Tholsel, and tended to disintegrate the solid Williamite phalanx with whom the Blue Coat had been so long a primary concern. We have an ominous entry, 20 October, 1789, when James Napper Tandy appears as a governor, a stormy petrel on an inland lake. What he came for then we do not know, but the routine details of that day had little to engage his troublous spirit, and this was his first and only apparition. It was just at the close of his earlier period as a tribune of the people, when, treading in the steps of Charles Lucas, he made war on the civic authorities; he was now about to embark on the seas of conspiracy and high treason, whereon he tossed to the end, seeking with Wolfe Tone to overthrow the British empire by a French invasion, even though this might have made Ireland an appanage of France.

We now find the attendances, even of our aldermen, are meagre. Save when an appointment was in the wind, often there was not a quorum. Boons to the Blue Coat had hitherto often originated in the City Assembly ; now its appeals are coldly received or rejected, and even the old grants are reluctantly maintained, and this was not for want of funds, for the city was freely spending in other directions. The weakening of sympathy at the centre tended to weaken the old attraction to our Board of great personages outside, whose presence had always attracted in turn that of the citizen governors, who were glad to sit in conference with them, and their abstention now increased the disposition of many of the Corporators to stay away.

Whatever the combination of causes may have been, we are forced to conclude that in these years of the Grattan Parliament, the public interest in the Blue Coat had reached its nadir with a corresponding decline within.

Just before the re-opening in 1784, the Rev. Hamilton Morgan resigned. He had succeeded Ralph Grattan as chaplain and headmaster in the sixties, and the first act of the governors now was to appoint his son, Mr. Allen Morgan, in his stead. They were both University gentlemen, but both lacked the qualities that go to make a great head of a public school; yet their successive tenure of office covers nearly seventy years. The father had never taken his duties very seriously; he was an easy-going gentleman, who had married young, and came to the Blue Coat as a mere means of living, but he had interest outside ; he had been a school fellow of Foster, the Chancellor of the Exchequer, and, through the Duke of Leinster, was now appointed in the rectory of Dunlavin. As his son, Allen, in after years, devolved his teaching duties on others, and assumed to be chaplain only, with much ill consequences, as hereafter seen, we note here that when elected in January, 1784, he was called before the Board, Lord Mayor Thomas Green in the chair, and the duties of chaplain and headmaster, as defined by Swift, were read to him. He promised, if elected, to comply with them, and on this basis was approved by the Archbishop of Dublin, Dr. Fowler, as provided by the charter.

Then followed the consecration of the chapel by the Archbishop; it was opened for Divine Service on Trinity Sunday, 1784, in the presence of a large assemblage, convened by public notice in *Faulkner's Journal*. The painting of " The Resurrection " by Waldron, just then executed, was placed where it hangs now behind the Communion Table.

Seeking extraneous aid, the governors, in 1785, elected the Primate, Lord Rokeby, and sent a deputation of the Lord Mayor, Sir Thomas Blackhall, and others, to wait on his Grace. He was a man of great administrative power, of large fortune, and of noble munificence. Created Lord Rokeby in 1777, from his romantic estate on the Greta in Yorkshire, the scene of Sir Walter Scott's *Rokeby*, he is, perhaps, better remembered in our day as Primate Robinson, and by the splendid charities which long bore his name. Though we count him upon our roll of worthies, he would seem to have been unable to take an active interest in the Hospital, engrossed by the great institutions he founded in Armagh, and the building of churches all over the province.[1] Of him, Grattan said, " he has the first episcopal dignity in this realm; it is his right, he takes it by virtue of the commanding benevolence of his mind, in right of a superior and exalted nature."

In 1785, Denis George became Recorder and a Governor. On the death, in 1784, of Sir Samuel Bradstreet, who had been with us for eighteen years, Dudley Hussey succeeded him. George continued an able and faithful friend of the Blue Coat till far into the new century. In 1795 he was promoted to be a baron of the Exchequer, but was then re-elected on the Board, as the Recorders were upon it, only *ex-officio*. It was he, who, with our Lord Mayor Chairman, Henry Gore Sankey, inaugurated the building of the new Recorder's and City Court in Green Street. On 14 June,

[1] Right Hon. J. T. Ball's *Reformed Church of Ireland*, p. 221.

1792, they went in State together from the Tholsel. Sankey who is styled in the newspaper account, "a bright freemason," then practically exercised the craft of the order. Clothed in its apron and insignia, he laid the first stone with his silver trowel, and, of course, the ceremony ended in a banquet. Whitmore Davis was the architect. On his promotion George was succeeded as Recorder by William Walker, who held the office and sat on the Board for twenty-seven years to 1822, when he was followed by Sir Jonas Greene.

There has been little change since in the original aspect of the chapel. In 1787 the organ gallery, with seats for the choir boys, was erected by Sir Thomas Blackhall's committee. The other boys' seats ran in rows below, as now, but these, instead of facing the Communion Table and Pulpit ran parallel to the side walls and central aisle, with high partitions between each tier, thus fairly screening the sitters from the chaplain's ken, and enabling them to while away sermon time with elaborate carvings on the panels in front of them. This alluring arrangement continued to some twenty years ago, when a special fund was raised for repairing the chapel, mainly aided by an inaugurating ceremonial, when Archbishop Lord Plunket preached an eloquent sermon based on Nehemiah's restoration of the Temple. The old partitions were then found inscribed with the initials of generations of Blue boys and hieroglyphics, many and enigmatic as the inscriptions on an Egyptian column. But high plain panels were hideous, and the boys might have pleaded the expediency of some wood carving upon them. The walls now bear some tablets in memory of some of our worthies of the past. The latest of these is a handsome brass, by Mayer of Munich, in memory of John Hatchell, one of our best governors for forty years; it records his bequest of £500 to the Hospital, appropriated by his executor, Mr. Louis Perrin Hatchell, also a governor, to the completion at long last of the Cupola. This was dedicated last year by Archbishop Peacocke of Dublin.

The governors now found themselves exposed to the proverb of the men who began to build but were not able to finish. Not only were the buildings not finished, but the builders were unpaid for those that were to the amount of some £4,000, and there were no funds in hand to meet this. To Chambers, the carpenter and joiner, alone, £1,600 was due, for which the Board could only give him debentures on the Hospital itself at six per cent, and several hundreds each were owing to the quarries, the masons, bricklayers, iron masters, carvers, and painters. These they could only keep at bay by paying heavy interest. Even in 1787 they were forced to give five per cent debentures to all, until in 1790 we read that the builders are now very importunate, and the governors resolved to pay the most pressing out of their capital lent to the city at four per cent, and thus to save something by reduction of interest. Even Ricky's bill for the boys' clothing in 1783, could only be met by half yearly interest extending over years.

In this distress which lasted more or less to the end of the century and after, the governors resorted to many devices which were not attended with much success. They drew up a petition to the king, with one to the Duke of Rutland, the Lord Lieutenant, earnestly seeking the royal bounty. Nothing appears to have come of this. The Duke was indeed most popular, and took a generous interest in the Dublin charities, but for the reason above mentioned, the tide of favour at this epoch had passed to other objects of government bounty. Bartholomew Mosse's Rotunda Hospital seems now to have absorbed the sympathy of the wealthy and the great. The Duke visited it in state, and in his honour, the gardens lately laid out behind it were now named Rutland Square, with Granby Row, from the Duke's second title, for its western side. Palatial houses were now being erected all round; the place became the centre of fashionable Dublin, and the Rotunda the spoiled child of ladies of high degree; large grants were voted to it by Parliament, and a tax on carriages and sedans, once granted to our Blue Coat, but taken from it, was now transferred to the Lying-in Hospital. Had he lived, the Duke would probably have helped us, but he died in Dublin whilst Lord Lieutenant in 1787, at the early age of thirty-three, to the universal sorrow, for he was beloved and beneficent, as his noble grandson, who so long represented the House of Manners, has been in our day.

Then the Board attacked the governors of Erasmus Smith, their old objective, claiming as a right a large contribution to the new building in view of their twenty nominations to the School.[2] The E. Smith governors on our Board are directed to " to support our claim with firmness," and again to attend at their own next meeting, and " make a demand of a sum of money due to this charity towards the rebuilding of this Hospital," but we had not then on our side the treasurer of E. Smith's, who, so often before and after, has helped the Blue Coat in emergencies, and for the then present we asked in vain. We might have yearned for the days of Archbishop King. Nothing could be hoped for from the Corporation now; they were, themselves, obliged to retrench, and by an Act of Economy resolved on withdrawing from the Hospital the Toll Corn annuity of £250, granted in Queen Anne's time, of which £750 was in arrear in 1784, and it was only by strong pressure they were persuaded to suspend this order from time to time.

All that the Blue Coat could ever extract from the Grattan Parliament were some fines imposed on market jurors for non-attendance, by 27 Geo. III., c. 46 (1787), and penalties inflicted by the Dublin Presentment Act of 1793. The fines were heavy, but the magistrates were slow to inflict them, and they did not add much to the Hospital revenue.

A project for Charity Sermons in aid now adopted, had a fair success. Dr. Craddock, the Dean of St. Patrick's, complying with the request of the governors, preached in our new chapel on Sunday, 29 May, 1785, to a large congregation. He had a good name in Dublin, for a few years before, when his Deanery House, which had been Swift's, went on fire, regardless of all other possessions, his only thought was for the portrait of his great predecessor, by

[2] 8th December, 1784, 3rd December, 1789.

Bindon, presented by the Chapter in 1738, and, perhaps, the best of his extant likenesses. Dean Craddock himself carried it from the flames into the street, and saved it, to be still a chief treasure in the home of the Dean of St. Patrick's.

Shortly after, the governors approached Kirwan, the greatest pulpit orator of the day—some have said that he has never been equalled. His Charity Sermons were irresistible; thrilled with emotion, ladies would tear off their bracelets and jewels and fling them on the plate, and men's gold watches have been placed there too. One of these sermons alone resulted in a collection of £1,400. Though his oratory did not stand the test of printing and time as those of some great pulpit orators have done, it is doubtful if any surpassed him in living power. Educated for the priesthood by the Jesuits at St. Omer, he conformed to the Established Church in Ireland, but was never promoted beyond the Deanery of Killala.[3] Yet, his eloquence was the theme of wonder outside church-going people. Grattan, in the acme of his own fame, exclaimed of him :—" He came to interrupt the repose of the pulpit. The curse of Swift was upon him, to have been an Irishman, and a man of genius, and to have used it for the good of his country."

Kirwan cordially accepted the invitation of our governors, and promised to preach on the first Sunday in May, 1785, for the benefit of the charity. All the due arrangements were made, and the Rev. Dr. Law is thanked for giving his parish church for the purpose. We have no direct record of the result, but the accounts for this year show an entry :—" Collection, Charity Sermon, £145," from which great contribution to a single offertory, in those days, we may fairly assume that Kirwan's sermon still lives in the stones of the edifice it aided to raise.

Another entry near these suggests the activity of the Dublin coiners then :—" Bad silver in chapel, £5 13s. 9d."

Such precarious help, however, could never have enabled the Hospital to stem this period of depression and public apathy. But if public authorities withheld direct aid, the

[3] Ball's *Reformed Church in Ireland*, p. 226.

VERY REV. WALTER BLAKE KIRWAN,
Dean of Killala.

From Engraving by Dr. Ward.] [From Painting by Hugh Hamilton.

(See List of Illustrations, page vii.)

legislation of the Grattan Parliament in the early eighties, indirectly almost supplied an equivalent. Of John Foster's measure, giving a protection duty against foreign corn, with a large bounty on Irish grain exported to England, Mr. Lecky says :—" It is one of the capital facts of Irish history. In a few years it changed the face of the land, and made Ireland to a great extent an arable instead of a pastoral country."[4]

If re-enacted it might have that result again.

This, coupled with the bounties lavishly though strangely voted for the inland carriage of corn from the rural districts to the Irish towns and ports, enhanced the rental of the Hospital estates amazingly. Our Nodstown, yielding £182 rent in the twenty-one preceding years, was, in 1785, re-let at £527. So the tithes of Mullingar, previously leased at £135 yearly, were, in 1791, re-let at a rent of £210, and 188 acres of Kilcotty, in Wexford, were, in 1795, let for twenty-one years at £1 8s. per acre. This had been devised to the Hospital by the will of Mr. George Kavanagh many years before, but only this year came into its possession. This good estate has since been lost, apparently through negligence and the Statute of Limitations. And in 1793 the site of the old Hospital, extending along the entire south of Blackhall Street, was leased to Thos. Wildridge for ninety-nine years, at a rent of £100, with a covenant to build dwelling-houses from end to end. When twelve of these had been erected he failed, and was allowed to let the western end for stores. At the end of the term, in 1893, the street fell, with the Hospital, into a sad state of dilapidation, but has now been very profitably restored by the present governors.

Thus strengthened, the governors undertook some of the sadly unfinished work. In 1792, the infirmary, so essential for the School then, was built as it now stands. But instead of husbanding their revenue to pay off their discreditable debts, and to complete the sad omissions of original plans, they spent their money in repeatedly raising the salaries of indifferent or worthless officers, and giving them pensions.

[4] *Ireland in the 18th Century*, Vol. II., 386.

Sir Thomas Blackhall, who had been the chief corner-stone of the new building, and had attended every meeting for five years after its opening, guarding all its interests, was unable to be present after 1789, though he lived to 1796, and others of the original projectors were dropping off ; and so we find some, even of the new work, already falling into ruin, for it could not be expected that unpaid tradesmen would not have scamped much of their work.5 The laundry and wash-houses are found in 1795 being " very ruinous," and are allowed to remain so for more than two years, and so we read of the porter's lodge and entrances to the chapel, whilst the bowling green and all the curtilage round, and in front, are left with half finished walls, and without gates, at the mercy of trespassers from without and truants from within. And yet we note £37 yearly added to Mr. Allen Morgan's salary in 1795, following an entry in 1794, of Doyle, a tradesman's bond for £350 with three and a half years interest due ; in 1795 the bond is taken up and a new one issued at 6 per cent., and in 1796 two new debentures of £100 each, at the same interest, are handed to Dixon, the shoemaker, for the boys shoes.

And at this time the poor boys seem to have fared but poorly; unable freely to use the playground, which was used for grazing, because the low walls were tempting, they petitioned the governors for leave to go to the Phœnix Park in 1790. This fair requset was flatly refused, so an entry two years after causes no surprise ; it orders " that the worst of the boys that quit the house without leave, be punished by confinement for some hours in the coal vault, and deprived

[5] But the main building is sound and solid. A short time since a tradesman engaged at some repairs, turned to Rev. Mr. Richards, our head master, who was regarding his work—"Look at those," said he, pointing to the fine cut stone in the façade, " the men that raised those knew what they were at, *they* knew how to build. Look here, I have a new house that I pay £29 a year for, and when I'm at my dinner, I can hear the meat fryin' on the fryin'-pan in the kitchen next door, and the doors shut. That's what they're buildin' now." "But," said Mr. Richards, "was it not a pity the old Governors had not enough money to complete the original design ?" "Original design ? Sure when the King came and looked at the place—'Why,' says his Majesty, 'that's more like a Palace than a House of *Pain*.'" He did not specify the monarch who had this notion of a school

of shoes and stockings for three days, and go to bed supperless for three nights." This rather savage minute is somewhat softened by another of the same day, instructing a committee to take steps " to give the bowling green to the Blue Boys," and yet this was only effected in two years more, when the walls were partially raised, and the windows were latticed, and at last on 20 May, 1794, the old bowling green of Oxmantown was opened for the boys to play at all hours, and so it remains to this day.

And yet in these years the Hospital enjoyed some valuable private gifts; one deserves special mention. A boy, named Hemming, had been trained in the Hospital in the fifties. He entered the army or navy and saved money. In 1795, the governors are informed that Captain Hemming had left, by his will, £300 to his old school, with £2,000 more subject to a life estate. The immediate gift was applied to the infirmary, the reversionary £2,000 only fell in 1838, and this was the subject of heated discussion with the governors some years afterwards, for having been invested as capital in the name of Mr. Mallet and two other governors, when it was needed for current expenses by the Board, Mallet angrily refused to sign the transfers, and was only forced to do so by an injunction bill in Chancery, as to which he gave indignant evidence before the Endowed Schools Commission in 1858. Hemming's sister was housekeeper to the Hospital when the first legacy fell in, and the governors gratefully superannuated her at full salary shortly afterwards. No one should challenge that act of grace.

Of the governors who loyally wrought for the School like Blackhall to the end, Alderman Sutton should be named. For the immediate needs at the opening he advanced £750, and in 1794 he presented the Board with £200, for which their thanks were ordered to be printed in the *Dublin Journal*, and the nomination of two boys so long as he was a member was conferred upon him; a course which was often pursued from the beginning towards our benefactors; it has long fallen into disuse, but the usage might well be restored at the present day. Sutton had proposed, when the new building opened, that all the charities of Dublin should be asked for aid, on the plea that the new palace, if filled, would indirectly lighten the burden of them all, but this appeal did not prove fruitful. Towards the close of the century, the governors, of whom he still was one, became more earnest. Archbishop Fowler came there in 1797. Some twelve hundred pounds came in for six sheriffs' fines. The old Dublin Rope Walk was now walled off and sold, the ruined laundry was restored, and the building debts were largely reduced, and in the very last days of the old century we have an order to remove the cattle from the bowling green.

In 1791, on Alderman Sutton's proposal, the Board directed that "a large Northumberland Mahogany Table to accommodate 24 persons, and covered with green cloth, be provided for the Boardroom, also 24 chairs covered with fine black leather, and a two armed chair, of the same material, for the Lord Mayor." This was done with a direction to give "The Old Armchair," to our Surgeon Whiteway, Swift's pupil. The table, armchair, and 22 of the chairs are still in our boardroom. They are good specimens of the sound Dublin work of the eighteenth century, and this incident is noted here as these *ladder* chairs have reached in our time a high value in the luxury market of London.

In the period comprised in this chapter there were many changes in the Blue Coat staff. John Whiteway, who had been surgeon in the old school, carried down the connection with Swift; he was the son of Martha Whiteway, the Dean's cousin, and his amanuensis and guarding companion in his failing years, and to the Dean's gratitude he owed his profession. He fills a long paragraph in Swift's will, which directs that he is to be brought up as a surgeon, and places £100 in his mother's hands towards this end, to be paid out of the arrear of his church livings." £5 is added for buying "such physical and chirurgical books as Dr. Grattan shall think fit for him." He was a very effective member of our staff, and took a leading part in the building and management of the infirmary. Dying in 1797, he was succeeded for two years by Surgeon Philip Woodroofe, on whose death in

1799, Surgeon William Leake was appointed, also a valuable officer, who served the school for the more than thirty years that followed. Dr. Archer was replaced as physician by Dr. Harvey, in the first year of the new school in 1784, and on his resignation, ten years after, Dr. Bryan was elected, and continued to be physician into the new century. All these medical officers were members of our Board. Harcourt Lightburne, who had succeeded Thomas White as steward, on the opening of the new building, died in 1792, and in his place Alderman Edmund Beasley was appointed, one of the worst appointments the governors ever made; it might have fairly been called a flagrant job. Sheriff and alderman in 1775, he had been himself a governor some seventeen years. He was elected steward at first on strict conditions that it was to be only for a year, and during pleasure, and that he was to resign his seat on the Board whenever asked, but not only was he retained as steward, with his maintenance and much-needed room in the Hospital, but his salary was increased. This would have been well if he had not been useless, but though his duties were confined to the stewardship or household management, he was unable to perform them; for when, two years after, Mr. Hart became registrar and agent, he was obliged to take Beasley's work in addition to his own, gratuitously, with the assistance of the butler, still leaving Beasley his salary and maintenance and rooms. Meanwhile the Board voted him an increase, first of £15, and then £25 a year. This abuse is severely exposed by the Educational Commissioners in 1808; they condemn the appointment of a governor as an official, and further find that when Mr. Beasley at length formally resigned, he was still retained in his apartments, with his full salary of £135 as pension. This final job is not noticed in our Minute book; perhaps the governors were ashamed of it.

Then John Wilson, who had been registrar and agent since 1779, died in 1794. His position in the city as once a sheriff's peer and town surveyor, and his succession to Ivory, as architect of the Hospital, gave him an authority with the Board, of which he was himself a member. Some £6,000 of the new building cost were expended under him, and withal he undertook the duty of lecturing the Board in this period of depression. They probably deserved his strictures, for the letter which he had printed and circulated, was itself an act of insubordination, which governors, if efficient, should never have tolerated, or placed, as they did, in their archives. But we give it here in full, not merely as an internal evidence of the low estate of the Hospital at this time, but for the irony which this gentleman's own sequel imparts to it.

To the Governors of the Blue-Coat Hofpital.

My Lords and Gentlemen,

BOUND as I am by the ties of duty, and Affection for the Welfare of this Hofpital, I cannot but lament the Decreafe of Benefactions and Legacies to the Charity; I have been told, to my great Mortification, that, different Charitable Perfons, who had bequeathed Sums of Money, have of late altered their Wills, and given the Preference to other Charities, thinking ours undeferving.

Reflection ftaggered me: I blufhed, confcious of the Public's difcerning eye! I looked into myfelf, and inftantly, every other Perfon concerned in the Government of this Charity came into my View. I could not (even with a Partiality in their favour), pronounce their acquittal ; nor fhall I condemn any one, but fhall remind the Governors, that better and wifer Rules and Orders were never framed, than were fupported in this Hofpital for many years; if they had been adhered to to this Day, I fhould not have this unpleafant Story to relate.

We had nearly ftruck on this Rock, but I hope a revival of our good old Laws, will recover the Veffel and bring her fafe into Port again. I have often admired and read over and over again the old Books, and as often regretted our departing from the strict Obfervance of the Laws that made us admired, and under which we profpered.

I have not the leaft enmity to Mortal, nor do I wifh for Innovation, but that every Perfon in Office fhould keep his own particular Station: becaufe, I am fully convinced he will find enough to do in his own Department.

I am encouraged to thefe few Remarks, by the gleam of favourable Attention fhewn laft Affembly, to the Hofpital; and I harbour the ftrongest hopes, that the Gentlemen have given an earneft, that they mean to be the Protectors of fo great and fo laudable a Charity.

It is hoped the Governors will accept of this as it is meant—

merely to do good. It is the overflowing of a Heart that can have no other meaning,--but to act the part Providence has assigned to him, who is, and always was, my Lords and Gentlemen,

Your faithful humble Servant,
JOHN WILSON,

B.C.H.
April 4th, 1792.

When, two years after, the writer died, his own accounts showed no less than £1,300 due to the Hospital which were lost for ever, for when the governors appealed to his sureties, and proceeded to put their bonds in suit, the demand was boldly repudiated. The governors were dared to go to trial, and on the advice of eminent counsel abandoned the claim. Their own remissness in allowing their officer to do as he pleased, would probably have proved an unanswerable plea on the equitable principles of suretyship.

There is an entry of Wilson's in his own hand, as registrar, which gives another touch of his quality : " August, 1791. The assistant housekeeper was admonished for not treating Mr. Wilson with the respect due to him as a governor and agent, by telling him she did not care a pin for him." He was succeeded in 1794 by Mr. Robert Hart, who held office for thirty-five years, and of whom we shall have more to say.

Yet Wilson had been elected at a great meeting in 1779 by fifty-one governors, including twenty-one aldermen, with the Earl of Roden, Sir Lucius O'Brien, and Provost John Hely Hutchinson, none of whom ever attended before or after. He then succeeded Thos. Hawkshaw, whose accounts had been found by Wilson also defective to the amount of £800 : he followed the precedent effectively.

[Chairmen and Lord Mayors.

Our Chairmen and Lord Mayors from First George III. to the Union were:—

1760-61	Sir Patrick Hamilton.	1780-1781	Kilner Swettenham.
61- 2	Sir Timothy Allen.	81- 2	John Darragh.
62- 3	Charles Russell.	82- 3	Nathaniel Warren.
63- 4	William Forbes.	83- 4	Thomas Green.
64- 5	Benjamin Geale.	84- 5	James Horan.
65- 6	Sir James Taylor.	85- 6	James Shiel.
66- 7	Edward Sankey.	86- 7	George Alcock.
67- 8	Francis Fetherston.	87- 8	William Alexander.
68- 9	Benjamin Barton.	88- 9	John Rose.
69-70	Sir Thomas Blackhall.	89- 90	John Exshaw.
70- 1	George Reynolds.	90- 1	Henry Howison.
71- 2	F. Booker, W. Forbes.	91- 2	Henry S. Sankey.
72- 3	Richard French.	92- 3	John Carleton.
73- 4	Willoughby Lightburne.	93- 4	William James.
74- 5	Henry Hart.	94- 5	Richard Moncrieff.
75- 6	Thomas Emerson.	95- 6	Sir Wm. Worthington.
76- 7	Henry Beadan.	96- 7	Samuel Reed.
77- 8	William Dunne.	97- 8	Thomas Fleming.
78- 9	Sir Anthony King.	98- 9	Thomas Andrews.
79-80	James Hamilton.	99-1800	J. Sutton & J. Exshaw.

CHAPTER XII.

THE EVOLUTION OF DUBLIN IN THE EIGHTEENTH CENTURY.

THE decline of King's Hospital as the exclusive favourite it had been in its first hundred years was doubtless due to the growth of the city through the eighteenth century, in the last three-quarters of which the erection of great public buildings and stately mansions was phenomenal. Side by side with these the city was expanding into new quarters, streets, squares, always cieating new interests in which the Blue Coat governors as the municipal authority were deeply concerned, both as public and as private persons; and, as each advance suggested another, grants from Parliament and the city estate were constantly sought at the expense of the monopoly which the Blue Coat had once almost enjoyed. The development may be seen in a general way by comparing Brooking's Map, 1728, when it began, with Roque's, 1765, when it was in full operation; good copies of these appear in the seventh and eleventh volumes of Gilbert's *Calendar*. But to conceive this evolution duly, one must follow each great step in the order of dates, thus seeing to what each led on; and as such a review has not, perhaps, hitherto been made in any of the Dublin histories, it is attempted here, so that we may thus compare the city at the time of the Union with the Dublin of the Restoration, as sketched above in Chapter I.

We begin with the noble library of Trinity College, which, though commenced when Anne was Queen, was only completed in 1732. This changed the whole aspect of the quarter; facing Nassau Street, still called by Brooking

St. Patrick's Well Lane, where all to the west of unfinished Dawson Street were still the Minchen Fields; it may be styled the Renaissance in Dublin, for few Renaissance works surpass it anywhere. Its forgotten designer was found by Dr. Stubbs to be Mr. De Burgh, of Old Court, Kildare.[1] It gave the keynote to all that followed. Next comes the Parliament Palaces; begun in 1729, when Lord Carteret probably laid the first stone, it received the Houses in 1731, but was only completed eight years after, still leaving both the wings for another generation. The original conception has been credited by many as due to Cassels, but the practical architects were, undubitably, first Sir E. Lovett Pearce, and then Arthur Dobbs. This great work, of course, revolutionized old College Green. Then, in 1741, rose Tyrone House, the mansion of the Beresfords, built for the first Earl of Tyrone on the space behind Marlborough Street, then known as Marlborough Green, where the eastward city had ended, save for a group of houses on the strand at Mabbot's Corner. This led to the making of streets adjacent. Tyrone, Mecklenburgh, Cumberland Streets were built in the great era of George II., though modern decadence has fallen on these, scarce arrested by the conversion of the mansion into the Schools of the Commissioners of National Education. The designer was probably Cassels, for he was the architect of Leinster House, which was finished in 1745 for James, the twentieth Earl of Kildare, just then created Viscount Leinster in England, and some years after Duke, and Marquess of Kildare. In the same year, 1745, Trinity College, whose library had probably led to the selection of the site of Leinster House, erected the present Dining Hall; whilst round Leinster House began to rise Leinster Street, Kildare Street, Molesworth Street, though Merrion Square behind was still open and swampy. These extensions gave an impulse to building round St. Stephen's Green, where few good houses had hitherto existed. Van Nost's statue of George II. was erected in the centre in 1759. In the north,

[1] Stubbs, *Trinity College*, p. 176.

Dublin ended at Great Britain Street in the middle of the century, but, in 1751, Dr. Bartholomew Mosse obtained for the Corporation the site of his Lying-in Hospital, which he transferred from South George's Street, and this induced very striking sequels. It was finished, with its beautiful Rotunda, in 1757. Cassels was the architect. Behind lay the gardens, and beyond open fields to Phibsborough village, with the Barley fields, on the space now filled by Frederick Street, Hardwicke Street, and Gardiner's Row. The new gardens, as they were called, were enclosed by stone walls, and it was only in 1784, when the Duke of Rutland visited the Hospital, that these were taken down and replaced by railings and the place named Rutland Square, with Granby Row to the west in honour of the Lord Lieutenant. But the Hospital fronted to Drogheda Street, running then as far as the Abbey Streets, where it was stopped by the back houses of the Bachelor's Walk, which then extended far down the present Eden Quay. But when Lionel, Duke of Dorset, was secondly Lord Lieutenant, 1750-1753, the northern end facing the Rotunda, as far as Henry and Earl Streets, known as the Mall, was widened out and planted at the sides, and was now named Sackville Street in honour of the Viceroy, as the road from Bolton Street northward was named Dorset Street; the residue from the site of Nelson's Pillar to Abbey Street was still Drogheda Street. All this led to the forming of St. Thomas' Parish, including the new district of Tyrone House and St. Thomas' Church, with its handsome Greek front by Ivory in the centre.

Next year, 1759, Trinity College, inspired no doubt by the grand vicinity of the Houses of Parliament, erected the present fine front facing College Green, and at the same time the Provost's House close by. The designer of this was the Earl of Burlington and Ross, who adapted it from the mansion in Piccadilly, then built for General Wade. It is in all respects worthy of its position as the home of the Presidents of the University, who in brilliant succession have owned it, having as a private residence few rivals anywhere.

But a new and potent impulse to the development was given

by the Wide Streets Commissioners, whose functions under repeated statutes continued well into the nineteenth century. Their first Act was passed in 1757 to improve the connection of north and south by a straight street from Essex Bridge to the Castle. For, at foot of Cork Hill, on the site of Old Dame Gate, two carriages could not drive abreast. In widening Dame Street here, the Commissioners, unfortunately, were content to give it the breadth as it now appears from Cork Hill to the Lower Castle Yard. They found their mistake when, in 1780, they were empowered to enlarge Dame Street from thence to College Green. Essex Bridge had been rebuilt at a great cost in 1753, but at the southern end a narrow causeway only reached to Essex Street, and the entrances to the old Custom House there, meeting a network of ancient lanes and houses by Isoult Tower, blocking the access to Cork Hill. The titles and tenures of these were ancient and complex, and it was not till 1769 that Parliament Street was fully opened. This at once led on to the conception of the Royal Exchange, promoted by the merchants to thwart the exactions of unfair tonnage tolls imposed on the up-river craft. Thomas Cooley was the architect of this splendid building, now the City Hall, but the city, as already mentioned, owes it to Charles Lucas, who forced it through Parliament when he was city member, obtaining a grant of £13,000; and his fine statue by Edward Smyth is still justly a chief ornament in the great central hall, standing not far from that of his friend George III. by Van Nost. The first stone of the Exchange was laid by Lord Townshend, when Lord Lieutenant, in 1769; it was finished in 1779, and it ought to stand for ever, for it is founded upon the rock which stretches thence and under the Liffey, long known as Stand Fast Dick. And now Parliament Street and the Exchange at the one end, with the Parliament Houses and the new College front at the other, necessitated the widening throughout of Dame Street.

[2] *Ante* Chapter IX.

This was commenced in 1780, and went on for nearly twenty years. The Rotunda Gardens were now being girdled with costly mansions. In the sixties Lord Charlemont erected that from which the north side of the square was called Palace Row. He was himself a great connoisseur, and is said to have designed this mansion himself; but we know about the same time he was engaged in beautifying his country house at Clontarf. For the Casino in the grounds his architect was the famous Sir Richard Chambers, the designer of Somerset House on the Thames, who had been his intimate friend and correspondent for many years,[3] consulting him on all his elaborate ornamentations, and to whom we may attribute much at least of Charlemont House. No expense was spared upon it, and it was marked *first* amongst the noble houses of the city. Nearly at the same time Powerscourt House was built, 1771-74, for Richard Wingfield, third Viscount Powerscourt; its architect was Robert Mack, and it was once accounted third in beauty of these homes. For many late years it has been occupied by the mercantile house of Messrs. Ferrier and Pollock.

Next comes the Hibernian Marine School, far to the south-east, at the further end of Sir John Rogerson's Quay, which was opened in 1773, under very high auspices, for the training of the children of seamen of the navy and the merchant service. It had large grants from Parliament, the edifice costing £6,600, and was a formidable rival to the Blue Coat Hospital, as the navigation school there gave one of its chief claims to the favour of the mercantile classes. Our Thomas Ivory was architect. But it was built far to the east to connect it with the deep seaport then still at Ringsend, and thus could not take class as a city ornament. It has long been occupied by the timber stores of Sir Richard Martin & Company.

Immediately after Ivory was engaged upon our new Blue Coat Hospital, which took ten years to complete, 1773-83, as detailed above in Chapter X.

In 1777 Trinity College began their great Theatre or

[3] See *Charlemont Papers*, Historical Manuscripts.

Examination Hall between the library and their west quadrangle, known as Parliament Square. It was built by a Mr. Meyers, who Dr. Stubbs probably thought was the designer, for he does not name the architect; but, in 1779, Sir Richard Chambers[4] writes Lord Charlemont that, two years before, he was requested to make designs for considerable additions to the buildings in Trinity College, but that the vast work with which he was engaged on Somerset House, which, he says, was then on the anvil, prevented his coming over to Ireland to complete them; and he was thus only able to give a general disposition of what he intended, from which, however, he adds, "the buildings are now being executed," and he may therefore claim the chief share of any merit there may be in the general intention. There is very high merit in the general design, and Sir Richard's claim should be the more gratefully recognised because the façade of the College chapel, erected some years after at the opposite side of the quadrangle, is a replica of the theatre front.

Leinster House naturally led to the enclosure of Merrion Square. The fine mansions around were begun in 1780 by our benefactor William Robert, the second Duke, and occupied some twenty-two years in building. The need for these, both here and in Rutland Square and St. Stephen's Green, was vastly enhanced by the reconstitution of Parliament in 1782, and artists from England and the Continent came to co-operate with our native talent, which was then rich. The graceful work of Angelica Kaufman and of several Italians is still beautiful on the ceilings and walls of many of the houses of our gentry, and even of some that have since degenerated into tenements, as in Henrietta Street. Meanwhile Essex Bridge had remained, as it had been for more than a hundred years, the only link between north and south to seaward. But the spread of the city on both sides eastward now made a new connexion inevitable. The restoration of Essex Bridge in 1752 was followed by projects in Parliament in that and the next year for a new bridge and a new Custom House. Thereupon the old conflict

[4] *Charlemont Papers*, Historical Manuscripts, p. 349, 20th May, 1779.

with vested interests, the foes of reform, which had raged round Essex Bridge itself in 1676, was now renewed; the city was in arms; both Houses in the City Assembly called on Parliament to reject the proposal as *disastrous*. We may smile at this opposition now; but, when we remember the vast interests of mercantile and even of working men that had gathered round the old Custom House, and see in the old pictures the vessels that thronged the river up to the bridge, and recall how even the new expansions had increased the value of the old Ferry franchises, we can see how revolutionary the project was, and feel no surprise that the bills then fell through.

But in 1760 Aston's Quay was restored. The city lease of the Restoration times to Lord Anglesea, of the slobs then fronting Fleet Street, had been assigned to Major Henry Aston generations before; he had reclaimed them, and formed a rough quay with poor buildings behind that had fallen to ruin, and the city this year renewed the grant to his grandson on the terms of his rebuilding and restoring the quay. Encouraged by this, the project for the new bridge close by came again before Parliament, but, vehemently opposed by the city, was again thrown out. The need, notwithstanding, grew yearly more imperative; docks had been constructed far down the river by the Harbour Board, the space at the old Custom House was now quite inadequate, and at last, in 1780, the first stone of the new Custom House, which is the glory of Dublin, was laid. This masterpiece of James Gandon's took many years to complete, but the foundation stone had sealed the fate of opposition to the bridge; for, though this was only finished in 1794, it then took the name of the Earl of Carlisle, Lord Lieutenant 1780-82. It was to change our centre of gravity for ever.

The very prospect of it imparted new impetus. In 1791 £100,000 was assigned by statute to the Wide Street Commissioners. A fourth of this was devoted towards forming the pride of our causeways by erasing the east of Bachelor's Walk and Drogheda Street to Henry Street, so that Sackville Street should open as now from the river to the

Rotunda; £25,000 was allocated to connect this line by Cavendish Row with the Great Northern Road, which the Act recites had been then completed by broadening Dorset Street towards Drumcondra. Then Frederick Street was cut through the Barley Fields, purchased for the purpose from Lord Mountjoy, whose estate thus began to form an important part of the city—Gardiner's Row leading to the line of the Gardiner Streets; and so a new parish became essential. In 1796 St. George's Parish was created by statute, within limits which even then comprised parts of the ancient St. Michan's, which had reached from the Park to the sea. Lord Mountjoy gave the site for the church and churchyard, which originally occupied the slope over Great Britain Street, but Mountjoy Square, designed just as the new century began, when finished, with its offshoot streets, compelled the transfer of the parish church to its present site in Temple Street. With the balance of the £100,000, under the Act of 1791, the Commissioners are directed to complete Dame Street. The Act recites that the Commissioners had already taken down and rebuilt the southern side of new Dame Street, from the Lower Castle Yard to Trinity Street, and that they were then about to take down and rebuild the north side from Anglesea to Eustace Streets; and then provides that all future houses from Trinity Street to Church Lane, and from Eustace to Parliament Streets, shall be built by their owners to range in uniform style with the rest, to form a grand passage from His Majesty's Castle to the Parliament House and College Green. To connect these with the new bridge was now essential, and Westmoreland Street, so called from the Viceroy of 1790-95, was now laid out. The beautiful eastern wing of the Parliament House had lately been completed by Gandon; and, before the century ended, the continuous line was now complete, south to north, from St. Stephen's Green to the Great Northern Road.

In all this while the Law Courts in Christ Church Place had become wholly inadequate, both in site and size, but their replacement needed many years, and it was only in 1796 the new Courts were opened on Inns Quay. The original splendid design was by Cooley, who, beginning so far back as 1776, only lived to complete the western wing, and the great work passed into the hands of James Gandon. The new Recorder's Court, transferred from the Tholsel, was opened in 1797.

So stood the evolution of our capital at the time of the Union. It had to force its way not only through financial difficulties and structural obstructions, but in the face of keen oppositions at many stages.[5] Even Parliament Street was fiercely resented; and, when the Commissioners, having purchased the houses, proceeded to remove them, the inhabitants refused to stir, and were only expelled when in a single night the roofs were removed, and the terrified inmates rushed elsewhere. But Dublin had now won a place amongst the beautiful cities of Europe, though

Tantae molis erat Dublinam condere gentem.

[5] Whitelaw's Vol. II., p. 1078.

CHAPTER XIII.

TEMP. GEORGE III. 1800-1820.

It might have been hoped that the Act of Union would have restored to the Blue Coat its relative status in the city at least, and attracted to the Board, as of old, many of the best men in the country, but this was not so, for a time at least.

When the new century opened the number in the school was 110, but now, once more our story reflected the current of public events, and darkened for a while. For the Corporation, alarmed at the loss to the city sure to follow the cessation of Parliament, and the flight of notables to London, began to shrink from maintaining their usual subsidies to the City School. In sending at the end of 1801 the Toll Corn annuity of £250, regularly paid for eighty years, they voted it expressly for a single year only, and, with deep regret, the Governors resolved to limit the number to 100. Richard Manders, grandsire of the family so long afterwards esteemed members of Dublin society, was then our Chairman and Lord Mayor; with him sat the Archbishop of Dublin, Lord Somerton, he was the Hon. Charles Agar, grandson of our old friend, Welbore Ellis, Bishop of Meath, whose daughter had married the first Lord Clifden; he was raised, in 1806, to the Earldom of Normanton, and is another of our many governors who have recruited the House of Lords. Manders did his best to stem the decline. In 1802 an appeal to the Board of Erasmus Smith was met by a gift of £1,000, and the Right Hon. David Latouche, ancestor of the families of Marlay and Belleview, joined our Board. A strong Committee was directed to collect subscriptions, and two proposals were made to elect the city members *ex-officio* governors, and that all future governors should pay £300 on his appointment ; both projects proved abortive, for the members were off to London, and the number of those able and willing to pay so much for such an honour, were shrivelling too.

Next year, when Jacob Poole was Lord Mayor and Chairman, the Corporation were again petitioned to require all High Sheriffs on appointment to contribute a fixed fine in support of the School, and though this was favourably answered, it brought no immediate revenue. So, again, in 1805, the governors felt bound to reduce the number to 100 boys as vacancies arose, but they forwarded at the same time a petition to the Imperial Parliament, urging " the great advantage that must result to the State from educating a number of youths in the pure and loyal principles of the Protestant religion, thereby attaching them, by every principle of gratitude, to the city and to the Government." This they sent to the Right Hon. John Foster, " that friend of the city, the Chancellor of the Exchequer," asking his advice as to the best manner of presenting the petition. Foster replies in his courteous style from London in June, most willing to help, but advising that the session is now too far advanced for money applications, and that the recommendation of the Lord Lieutenant would be essential. We now know how the then Lord Lieutenant, Lord Hardwick, was bowed down by the draughts, many blameless, some baseless, some base, made on the Government in connection with the passing of the Act of Union, and how little hope there was of his recommending money for a simple charity. We had this year on our Board the Archbishop of Cashel, the Hon. Charles Brodrick, a great grandson of our friend, Queen Anne's Chancellor, first Lord Middleton, and direct ancestor of the late distinguished Secretary for War. The Archbishop was an active governor, and proved very useful shortly after, when our estate of Nodstown, which was in the vicinity of his palace at Cashel, became a subject of anxious care.

A short entry in 1805 gives another slight echo of the

history of the time; it is that of the admission of Charles Vaughan, son of Charles, "elected by the Board at large in consideration of his father having been murdered in the rebellion (Robert Emmet's in 1803), and the inability of his mother to support him."

In 1807 three events happened of moment to us:— (1). The Napoleon wars, now at their height, had immensely stimulated the growing of home wheat, and the value of land went up by bounds. Our Tipperary estate of Nodstown had been let in 1785, at a rent of £527, for a term of twenty-one years now expiring, and the advertisements of the governors for new lettings were met by no less than fifteen tenders, offering from £2 to £2 10s. per acre. New surveys were ordered, which disclosed that many acres had been filched by encroachments, but more than 600 good arable acres remained; and, in 1810, a new lease was executed to Francis O'Kearney at £1,459 a year, or a net increase of £930 on the old rental. This should have set us up, so long, at least, as war rents lasted; but, on hearing of the tenders, the City Assembly, by a majority, resolved to withdraw their casual contributions: the Toll Corn annuity of £250, the sheriffs' and other fines, averaging in all more than £800 a year, and thus almost to neutralize the Nodstown increment. (2). But at this time the Educational Commission, under the Act of 1806, was sitting in Dublin; they had extensive powers, not only of enquiry, but of making recommendations to the Lord Lieutenant. Their report on our Hospital, already mentioned, contains a very able and exhaustive survey of its history for the twelve years to the end of 1808. The commissioners highly commend the School and its public utility; they find the average income in the twelve years to have been upwards of £3,000 yearly, and suggest that the withdrawal of the Corporation grants must seriously affect the number of pupils maintained, even in view of the prospective increment from Nodstown, the number then having, as presently explained, again risen to 130. They acknowledge the artistic beauty of the building, but deplore the ambition of the plans, by which, after an expenditure of £21,000, the Hospital was not only left incomplete, but with a debt of £4,000, loading the revenue with £750 a year, which they strongly recommend should be paid off with all speed, as the dormitories, though designed for 300 boys, now scarce sufficed for 120. The report has minute tables of the sources of revenue, and of the dietary then in use. This to us very serviceable report is signed by six commissioners, the Primate, Dr. William Newcomen, Provost Hall, of Dublin University, Dean Verschoyle of St. Patrick's, Rev. James Whitelaw, the very worthy historian of Dublin, William Disney, and Richard Lovell Edgeworth, the eminent father of a more eminent daughter. He was a great practical educationist, and one of the most accomplished Irish gentlemen of his time.

In commenting on the Beasley case, the Commissioners commend the governors for consolidating again the offices of steward and registrar, on Beasley's resignation, in Mr. Robert Hart. Whitelaw, in his *History of Dublin*,[1] says of Hart : " that from the period of Mr. Beasley's superannuation to his death, he had performed the important duties of steward gratuitously, and with that integrity, ability, and solicitude for the interest of the institution with which he has uniformly discharged every trust reposed in him by the governors," and he congratulates him " on the increase of his salary, on the union of offices, to £250." This eulogy was well deserved at the time, and for some years after. Yet, it was, perhaps, unfortunate, as it may have induced the governors to leave Mr. Hart, as they did, an almost uncontrolled management of all the business affairs of the Hospital, and now offers a painful contrast to the serious reflections upon that management in later years, made in the reports of the Education Commissioners of 1858.

Whitelaw attributes the abuses, which had been permitted, to what he calls the never failing consequences of government by great numbers of unaccountable governors. There were then seventy-five governors in all, and, no doubt, there

[1] Vol. I., 575.

is a tendency when a Board is large, to leave to officials routine administration, on which, however, results chiefly depend, and themselves to attend only in full array when an appointment is to be made. This, our annals prove, they always did; the system leads to canvassing, and the choice of officials by favour. All through we find a not very edifying relationship of the person selected, to some influential member of the Board, not always those most zealous for the welfare of the institutions. But on the whole Whitelaw's judgment on our governors is favourable. The interior economy, he says, is excellent; the officers discharge their duties from the purest motives, and the general conduct of the boys is good, and he concludes with the anxious wish that funds should be found, not only to restore the former numbers, but to enlarge them so far as the plan of the buildings will admit. (3). And in 1807 the Board had an accession, the most effective and beneficent since that of Archbishop King. Lord Chief Justice Downes had succeeded to the King's Bench, on the murder, in Thomas Street, of Lord Kilwarden in Emmet's rebellion. He was now, like Dr. King, treasurer of the Erasmus Smith Board, and followed his steps in the wise policy of making the cognate charities work in unison. In February, 1807, he personally informed our governors that, as treasurer of the Erasmus Smith Board, he was entitled, as a personal perquisite, to a poundage of one fortieth on its revenues, which he now contemplated applying to the support of such additional pupils in the Hospital as this would meet, these to be nominated as the Erasmus Smith Board should appoint. The governors thereon sent a Committee to wait on the Chief Justice, gratefully accepting his public-spirited proposal, and adding the single condition that the boys on this new foundation should be "the offspring of Protestants."

In April the Chief Justice sent a final resolution to the effect that his poundage fees would then support seven new boys, and afford a reserve for their apprenticeships, in addition to the twenty already on the Erasmus Smith foundation, under Archbishop King's statute of George I., and he further proposed to add ten new boys on that foundation, making thirty-seven in all, the sons of Protestants, all to be maintained in like manner as the rest of the pupils. They stipulated only that all the new nominations should be made by the treasurer for the time being "until further order," and that all their own future treasurers should be chosen, subject to this application of the poundage fees, this order to be read at all future elections to that office. This treaty, of course, was gratefully ratified, and seventeen boys were forthwith added to our rolls.

Thus encouraged, the governors suspended the order to reduce, which had not yet taken effect, and so the number stood, in 1808, at 130. Under these influences the Corporation suspended their withdrawal of the casual grants, and made 130 the nominal limit.

But the Chief Justice did not stop here. In the end of 1808 he told our governors that on personally visiting the Hospital he saw many things in many places which needed amendment, and obtained a Committee of Inspection, he himself being first on the list, the Lord Mayor, Frederick Darley, being chairman. Their visits revealed the many bald defects, for the building, as we know, had never been finished, and premature decay had already set in. The pillars, half erected, meant to sustain Ivory's great steeple or cupola, stood gaunt against the sky as if they had been shattered in a hurricane. Many of the necessary rere offices had never been even begun, and most of them were incomplete, so the whole matter was committed for report to Mr. Francis Johnston, the architect of the Board of Works, and the most eminent Irish Architect of his day. His duty was prolonged, for he was to estimate the cost of everything necessary to put the whole building and offices in thorough repair, "and fit and commodious for the purposes for which they were designed," and it was not till March, 1810, that the Chief Justice was enabled to lay before the governors the resolution of his own Board, based on Mr. Johnston's estimates. It was found that the completion of the cupola would alone cost £4,000, and that other subjects of the original plans, now recommended by Johnston, were beyond any presently procurable means, but that the actually necessary works could be effected for about £3,000. These comprised the reparation of the chapel, the adaptation of the chaplain's room into a dormitory for forty boys, a laundry, and sanitary arrangements not usually thought of so early in the century, for these included a great arched sewer to the Liffey, and ventilation in all the dormitory windows, the enclosure of the Hospital front within railings as they now exist, and the taking down of the cupola shafts, and removal of the turrets on the wings, which Johnston reported even then were tottering. This £3,000 the Chief Justice, as treasurer, now offered on behalf of his Board, on the sole condition that it should be spent by a Committee of our governors, and confined to the above utilitarian objects. This committee he nominated himself. There were the Lord Mayor, *ex-officio*, the Lord Chief Justice, the Dean of St. Patrick's, Dr. Verschoyle, Dr. Hall, Provost of Trinity College, Right Hon. Sackville Hamilton, Mr. Walker, the Recorder, and the Hon. John Pomeroy. This most handsome offer was accepted by our governors with effusive gratitude, and ratified in the Spring of 1810, Sir Wm. Stamer, Bart., being then Lord Mayor and Chairman. All these improvements were carried out, save that the poor cupola, ruled out of court as non-essential, was not taken down, nor were the turrets; their completion had been anxiously considered in three successive years since the beginning of the century, but always deferred for want of means, and even now the hope survived that some benefactor might still arise; and so the stark shafts were left to stand up against the the sky in Palmyrean desolation, chronic ruins, which, though pronounced by Johnston to be even then in danger of falling, lived through the storms of 1839 and 1903, till replaced by the new cupola inaugurated by Lord Dudley in June, 1904. But though Ivory's great steeple never pierced the sky, it has affected architectural Dublin, for when Francis Johnston, a few years after, was building St. George's church, he modelled his handsome spire on this ideal.

In the two following years the energy of the Chief Justice was felt everywhere. The Beasleys, husband and wife, were dispossessed and pensioned off, and Mr. Dalton, the second schoolmaster, given their rooms, with a large increase of his salary, to £200 a year, in view of the increased number of the boys, but on the terms of the entire devotion of his time, and of his giving up private tuitions. Mr. Hart had justice done him in regard of his having discharged Beasley's duties gratis for several years, and of his now permanently taking the double duty. All the rooms were overhauled, a drying yard added behind the infirmary, and the master's garden, as existing now; the dormitories were refurnished with proper bedsteads, and arrangements made for sending invalid boys to country or seaside; the handsome Board room was re-decorated and carpeted. Fifteen and then twenty guineas a year were voted for premiums and medals to deserving pupils, these to be conferred by the governors in person, and nearly all these things are noticed as done at the instance of the Chief Justice, whom we find usually accompanied by Baron George. In 1811 he added thirteen more boys, thus raising those on the Erasmus Smith foundation to a total of fifty, and under this impulse the governors added seven on that of the city. Our chairmen in these years, 1811 and 1812, were Nathaniel Hone and W. H. Archer, who worthily supported the Lord Chief Justice. In 1809, Dr. Bryan, who had been our physician for fifteen years, resigned, and Dr. Lestrange replaced him, and on his resignation in 1811, Dr. William Harty, an admirable appointment, undertook the duty.

Here sounds another echo from the great world outside. In 1812 Great Britain had, with the Peninsular war, a war with America on her hands. The recruiting sergeant was everywhere, and found access to our boys, of whom he captured several. The governors met in wrath in October, the new Lord Mayor, Bradley King, in the chair, and resolved that recruiting parties had no right to enlist their boys, and would never be permitted to do so on any account. They demanded back those who had joined the ranks, directing the registrar to pay the expenses incurred, and posted notices that any boys enlisting would be expelled in "the most public and ignominious manner," and that none should leave the Hospital save by written permits. And yet some of them might have fared as well in the army as at the trades to which most of them were destined, for the weakness of our School for nearly two hundred years was in the rule which admitted children of eight and nine years, and compelled them inexorably to leave at the end of five years.

Our prestige however had now been restored. In 1810 the Chancellor of the Exchequer, John Foster, became a governor. But in 1813 our Board achieved what we may call its Blue Ribbon in the accession of Charles Lennox, K.G., fourth Duke of Richmond, who came here in 1807 as Lord Lieutenant, with Sir Arthur Wellesley as his Chief Secretary. He came with a mundane *aureole* about him from two famous duels, which were once the topic of the London world. When a young Colonel in the Coldstreams, in 1789, the gossip of the Daubigne Military Club rumoured that he had not acted with sufficient spirit when affronted by somebody. Lennox demanded explanations as to the when, where, and who, of this calumny, and receiving no reply, wrote to Frederick, Duke of York, Commander in Chief, and head of the Club, with the alternative of a challenge in case redress was declined. Frederick was the King's favourite son, but waiving his right as Prince of the Blood, and his quasi ecclesiastical dignity of Bishop of Osnaburgh, he accepted the challenge. He was then living with his brother George, Prince of Wales, who suspected what was afoot; but Frederick, leaving his own hat in the hall to avert suspicion, and taking that of one of the household, met Lennox on Wimbledon Common. When the signal was given, Frederick fired in the air, but Lennox shot point blank, and his ball grazed the Prince's ear, singed the love lock over it, and stirred his hat.[2] The shot would have surely

[2] *Dublin Chronicle*, 27th May, 1889.

been fatal, but that immediately before it was fired, and when the Prince was facing the foe, front to front, his second had peremptorily ordered him to stand sideways. Lennox called out to the Prince, "Your Highness has not fired." " I only came here," was the reply, " to give you satisfaction, and if you are not satisfied you can fire again." On Lennox then demanding a withdrawal of the charge of want of gallantry, Frederick said, "Yes, you have behaved well, better than on the occasion which led to this." The verdict, military and social, in London, was, that Lennox had acted with courage, but not with judgment, and all applauded the calm valour of the Prince. But it didn't end here ; for amongst the public comments was a letter of Theophilus Swift, son of Deane Swift, the great Dean's cousin, which, in eulogizing Frederick, said that Lennox had acted in a cowardly way, and, challenged accordingly, they met in a field by the Uxbridge Road in July.[3] Lennox had chosen pistols, they stood ten paces apart, and Lennox being allotted to fire first, the ball smote Swift in the abdomen and sent him sprawling just as his hand was on the trigger of his own pistol, which went off in vain ; the ball was easily extracted. The name of Swift brought the event nearer to Dublin, where the newspaper's judgment was that the relative " of our immortal Dean " was known for his great eccentricities. But, if a swashbuckler, Lennox was the best of good fellows. When commanding the 35th foot, he played cricket with the rank and file, and made his officers do likewise, a rare mark of condescension then, and the echoes of his social revelries whilst here are still awake in Dublin. In 1813 our governors had resolved to dine together in the Board room on the King's birthday, and the Lord Mayor, Bradley King, of his own impulse, invited the Duke to honour them with his presence. He accepted at once. We have no record of the banquet, but they seem to have had a good night of it, for the governors afterwards specially thanked the Lord Mayor for inviting his Grace, and followed this up by a deputation, asking the Duke to become a governor

[3] *Dublin Chronicle* 4·7, July 1889, in p. 229, 245.

for life, which his Grace also graciously consented to do, with an expression of his wish to render any service in his power to the institution; and he showed his goodwill by promising to provide a place for a boy named Robert Ellward in one of the public offices, when informed by the governors that he was fitted to hold it.[4] But, though elected for life, the Duke was now called away to the great war. He was on the staff of the Duke of Wellington, his former Chief Secretary, at Waterloo, and it was his Duchess who gave the memorable ball in Brussels on the 15th of June, immortalized in "Childe Harold" when "there was a sound of revelry by night," broken by the cannon roar, and the partners, fair women and brave men, parted, many for ever, for many were going to the dance of death next day at Quatre Bras, and three days after at Waterloo. Two of our greatest institutions, the Richmond Hospital and the Richmond Lunatic Asylum, commemorate the lieutenancy of our gallant life governor, which, in the interests of our Hospital, was all too short. Whilst here, his aunt, Lady Sarah Napier, the mother of the three great Napiers, lived at Celbridge; she had been the lovely Sarah Lennox, the first love of young George III., and narrowly escaped being Queen of England.

About this time the Hospital obtained a windfall under circumstances romantic in the history of charities. It may be remembered that Alderman John Preston, one of our founders, had granted the Hospital, with other gifts, £20 a year, and this had been paid for more than one hundred years; it was tabled in the Commissioners' report of 1808 as a simple annuity, but during their inquiry, it transpired that Preston, by deed, had charged this annuity on his estate of Cappoloughlin, in Queen's County, then only yielding £80 a year, with two other charitable devises, to schools in Meath and Queen's County of £35 and £25, thus exhausting exactly the then rental of £80, our annuity of £20 being just one-fourth. Preston had thriven, his descendants owned one of the best estates in Royal Meath, and successively represented Navan or Meath in the Irish

[4] *Minute Book*, 25th November 1813.

Parliament, and in 1800, Mr. John Preston, of Bellinter, was raised to the peerage as Lord Tara, for his rich lands stretched from the Boyne to beneath the Dome of Tara Hill, stronghold of the Irish Kings. It was now found that Preston's deed provided that, if the rents increased, the surplus should go to the three schools as his heirs should direct The Education Commissioners now reported that great abuses had taken place, in the application of the rents of the lands, and that a large proportion remained still unappropriated. We defer the sequel to the time, when, at last, the rights of the Hospital were fully established, noting merely here that in 1812 and 1813 some £400 was paid to our governors, in respect of their claims on the Cappoloughlin rents.

Animated by this, some of our governors now proposed to establish a classical school in the Hospital, with exhibitions in Trinity College.[5] At the same time, our physician, Dr. Harty, who had hitherto gratuitously served with high efficiency, sent in a strong memorial for a salary now, grounded on the late great increase both in the number of boys in his charge and in that of the annual revenue, and those projects might have been carried out, but, that while under consideration, the roseate prospects began to darken. The sinister shadows of the Court of Chancery gathered round them, and the Preston rents, as after told, were dissolving in costs, and unpaid to the Hospital.

Now, too, Chief Justice Downes became unable to attend the Board. He was raised to the peerage in 1822, and dying soon after, his title became extinct, but he has left us a noble memory so long as the Hospital lives. His loss to us may be seen in the fact that in the last five years of George III.'s reign, there were only eighteen board meetings, at three of which no work was done, as against twenty-eight in the five previous years. In 1816 there were only two meetings, and in 1817 there appears to have been none. Lord Downes was succeeded in the King's Bench by the graceful Charles Kendal Bushe.

[5] 17th February, 1814.

For the peace restored after Waterloo did not bring blessings to the Blue Coat. The war rents, as might have been foreseen, fell as swiftly as they had risen. In 1815 the Nodstown £1,400 was unpaid, and the governors were forced to evict poor O'Kearney, and let the lands for six months, pending redemption, for £100, and when, two years after, they succeeded in re-letting, it was at a loss of £400 a year. Similarly our impropriate tithes of Mullingar and Kilcotty, which, of course, depended on the value of farm produce, fell perpetually in like proportion, so that, in 1816, the governors sorrowfully resolved, in view of these losses, that no more boys should be admitted until the debts, " due to the several persons who supply this house with provisions," shall be paid off. But for the strong contingent maintained by the Erasmus Smith Board, the numbers must have fallen disastrously.

As the governors may, at times, have seemed bigoted, we may mention in connection with Nodstown, that at the re-letting in 1810, Rev. James Slattery, the parish priest of Ardmayle, in which the lands lay, petitioned the Board for the site of his chapel, offering any rent they might require, and this request, at a full meeting, was at once granted. It was ordered that this site should be reserved from all projected lettings, and held in trust for the chapel and yard, at a shilling a year. At this meeting, Dr. Brodrick, Archbishop of Cashel, was in the chair. The re-letting in 1816, to Mills, was on the terms asked by the Archbishop, of his giving to the Protestant perpetual curate of Ardmayle ten acres and a house for a glebe, but it was made subject to a rent of four guineas an acre.

The old King died 29 January, 1820. Our last entry in his reign in March, 1819, again reflects history outside. O'Connell was now thundering for Catholic Emancipation, and William Conyngham Plunket, in Parliament, was urging that cause with Ciceronian eloquence. In the *Dublin Evening Post*, their organ just then, appeared a series of paragraphs, asserting that the Protestant petition to Parliament against the proposed concession had been brought to the Hospital, and pressure put on the boys to sign it. A special meeting of governors was thereupon summoned, and a committee of enquiry directed, who duly reported that there was not the slightest foundation for the statements thus made, and the Board resolved unanimously that the publications were false and scandalous, and tending to bring into disrepute this most valuable institution, and to mislead Parliament upon this momentous question, and they ordered this resolution to be published in the *Correspondent*, *The Patriot*, *Saunder's Newsletter*, and *The Hibernian Journal*.

Our Lord Mayor Chairmen from 1801 to the end of George III.'s reign, were :—

1800- 1 Charles Thorpe.	1810-11 Nathaniel Hone.
1- 2 Richard Manders.	11-12 Wm. H. Archer.
2- 3 Jacob Poole	12-13 Abraham B. King
3- 4 Henry Hutton	13-14 John Cash.
4- 5 Meredith Jenkin.	14-15 John Claudius Beres-
5- 6 James Vance.	15-16 Robert Shaw. [ford.
6- 7 Joseph Pemberton.	16-17 Mark Bloxham.
7- 8 Hugh Trevor.	17-18 John Allen.
8- 9 Frederick Darley.	18-19 Sir Thos. McKenny.
9-10 Sir William Stamer, Bart.	19-20 Sir William Stamer, Bart.

CHAPTER XIV.

TEMP. GEORGE THE FOURTH. 1820-1830.

NEW hopes and energies awoke with the advent of a new reign, and our governors now resumed activity. At their first and full meeting in February twenty-eight boys were elected, though the Board had to deal and continue to deal with the depressing tale of claims for abatements in all their rents dependant on the price of agricultural produce; but it was soon understood that the new King would visit Ireland next year, the first royal advent since William III.'s, and as Dublin would take chief place in the welcome, the position of our civic dignitaries became enhanced, and even a seat on the Blue Coat Board an object of ambition. When, in May, 1821, Francis Hamilton was sworn as an alderman, he at once politely wrote enclosing £100 for the Hospital, but his gift horse was looked at in the mouth, and he was curtly reminded that the fine was guineas, not pounds, and requested to send the balance forthwith. Lawyers or doctors similarly treated as to fees could not have done more. Sir William Stamer, Bart., again Lord Mayor, our chairman in the first year of George IV., was now succeeded by Abraham Bradley King, also in his second mayoralty. On him devolved the civic reception of His Majesty. He landed in August, 1821, at Old Dunleary, on the sickle-shaped pier which then formed the port, now only the coal harbour, thenceforth to change the place name from the Fort of Leary, old King of Erin, to the Town of George, King of Great Britain and Ireland. On the 17th he entered the city in state. The Lord Mayor, who received him with all the honours, was already a notable, for, when previously Lord

Mayor in 1813, he had fought for and won for Dublin the privilege, till then enjoyed only by London, of presenting petitions to the House of Commons by the Lord Mayor in person ; and in this year, 1821, he had similarly obtained for the city the right of addressing the Sovereign on the Throne through the mouth of its Chief Magistrate. Thus he now presented the city address to King George at the Castle, and received the then unprecedented distinction of being named a baronet by His Majesty himself. With him was Robert Shaw, who had been our Chairman and Lord Mayor in 1815. He, too, was a notable, Colonel of the Dublin Militia, Member for Dublin in the Imperial Parliament from 1804, a position he held to 1826 ; and he, too, received a baronetcy on this memorable day, in which honour he was followed by his two sons successively, Sir Robert and Sir Frederick Shaw, the brilliant member for the University, and Recorder of Dublin for eight and forty years. On the 23rd the King was entertained at a splendid banquet in the Mansion House, for which the great Rotunda had been specially and rapidly constructed in the gardens of the House, and which is still a striking feature in the city as a centre of the civic hospitality. To complete this tale of honours, Kingston James, our chairman and Lord Mayor in the following year, was knighted by the Marquess Wellesley, and two years after received a baronetcy, giving us four of that dignity on the Blue Coat Board.

But, though keen to take part in symposia themselves, our governors showed little sympathy with the festivities of our boys. In April Alderman Trevor informed the Board he had been told, as if of a scandal, that plays had been performed in the dining hall by the boys, and submitted " the impropriety of such like." It is curious that our chaplain, Allan Morgan, was now attending all the meetings as a governor, and was present then, so that he was presumably cognizant of the practice. But the governors virtuously and unanimously condemned " anything like theatrical performances within the walls as highly improper," and, calling in Dalton, the acting schoolmaster, peremptorily commanded him to suppress the malpractices. They might have done better had they adopted the usage of the great public schools of England, which tends to enlarge the classical taste and elevate the theatrical instinct; where, at the great anniversaries, the boys perform the splendid exemplars of Sophocles, Aeschylus, and Euripides, rehearsed throughout the term, and in the presence of Old Boys, now statesmen and soldiers, and the beautiful mothers and sisters of the lads. But it would seem that at this time the discipline of the School had got somewhat out of hand, probably owing to the mistake of placing the chaplain on the Board. Nominally "Head" of the School, he was the chief and the responsible officer; but it is always a delicate thing, and sometimes impracticable, to treat a colleague as a subordinate, or freely to criticise his action in his presence. Mr. Morgan had been chosen a governor eight years before; he constantly attended the meetings, and this, apparently, was followed by a devolution of the chief duties of Schoolmaster on his subordinate, Mr. Dalton, whom the boys, who are very keen in such matters, well knew was not their real Head. So far back as 1813, just after the chaplain joined the Board, eight boys wrote to Surgeon Leake complaining of Dalton's severe chastisements and injustice. Leake brought the letter before the Board, on which he, too, had a seat. With this letter was read a statement of Dalton's suggesting new regulations. Twenty-six governors were present, including Leake and Morgan. Then the eight complainants were called in and minutely examined, and then the two senior boys were similarly questioned. Finally Mr. Dalton was heard. When these had withdrawn, and after conference, it was proposed "that the Board do approve the conduct of Mr. Dalton, the Master." An amendment was moved to add the words "except in having used an instrument called a Cat, contrary to the directions of the Board." This amendment was voted on and lost, but only on a division, and the original resolution of approval was carried with the same divergence of opinion. It is not stated what the numbers were, but the want of unanimity, we may be sure, became known in the School and that not to the strengthening of Dalton's authority. And so, in 1823, we have a recrudescence of disorder. In July the Lord Mayor, John Smith Fleming, called a special meeting to consider a letter of Mr. Dalton stating that the boys had got into a state of insubordination, and had been guilty of such misconduct lately that he had asked for this meeting with the view of adopting a plan to restore order. The governors took the matter up seriously, and directed a strong committee to sit from day to day and report as to the steps necessary to restore order and " prevent a repetition of such misconduct (as is alleged) in future." The full and able report which followed finds " that a spirit of party and consequent insubordination, originating in the peculiar circumstances now unfortunately connected with the anniversary of the Battle of the Boyne, did exist among the pupils on the 12th, 13th, and 14th July, and that this arose from a partial compliance with the wishes of the pupils, on Mr. Dalton's part, which the committee considers was highly injudicious, as it ought to have been either entire or unreserved or altogether withheld." But it is clear from this report that the root of disorder was in the want of harmony and true cooperation between Mr. Morgan, whom they style chaplain and Head Master, and Dalton, whom they style " the Schoolmaster," and the delegation to the latter of the direct control of the boys, both in school, at meals, and play hours; for they find that the resistance to Mr. Dalton's authority is not, as alleged by him, attributable to the supposed intercourse of the boys with the chaplain's servants, but to the injudicious course taken in respect of the celebration of 12th July, and to other causes affecting the general welfare of the School; and, especially, to the too free intercourse with strangers and with their parents and friends. They find further that Mr. Dalton on the 15th July introduced into the Schools and Infirmary a clerical gentleman unknown to the other officers of the house, who admonished the pupils on the recent occurrences, therein performing a duty which peculiarly belonged to Mr. Morgan. and which he had never neglected, having discharged it on this occasion with the best effects ; and that, in this instance, Mr. Dalton has failed in that respect and deference due to Mr. Morgan, as Chaplain and Head Master of the School. Whilst acknowledging that Mr. Dalton's scholastic duties are efficiently and creditably discharged, they find that he has not sufficiently carried out the conditions of continuously attending at meals, play hours, and dormitories on which his salary had been raised in 1820. As to this, Dalton pleaded that he had fulfilled these conditions in the spirit if not in the letter, but that he would consider himself degraded, and would not be held in respect by the pupils, should he mix with them during play hours. This plea sounds strangely in these times, when one of the first qualifications of a master in a public school is to lead the boys at cricket or football ; but the views of the committee would seem to condemn poor Dalton to an indentured slavery, not only to teach but to attend the boys in all the hours till he saw them safe in bed each night. But there is a further finding, " that, in punishing a boy for presumed disobedience, he struck him violently with his clenched fist, and therein evinced a want of temper and sound discretion, unsuited to his official station and character." A usage of Mr. Dalton's is also condemned, that of allowing the senior boys, who assist him in the school, to leave at 4 o'clock and to take private tuitions in the city until bedtime.

The strange thing which strikes us in this stern report is the absence of any reference to the permission of all that is thus deemed blameworthy by the chiefly responsible officer, the chaplain and headmaster, who, we must presume either had not disapproved or had failed to report to the Board of which he was a member. But then he was at once a colleague and chief salaried official.

This report came before the governors in August. They adopted it, and voted accordingly that all boys above fifteen should provide themselves with situations forthwith. This points to the disorders having been fomented by the senior boys, and to the permission given them to take tuition outside. They recommended that an usher should be appointed to assist the schoolmaster; but, thirdly, they resolved " that, in the opinion of the Board, Mr. Dalton had failed in the discharge of those duties for which he had received the augmentation of his salary, and that he has evinced a temper and disposition, such as will compel the Board to interfere, in a more decisive manner, to remedy the evils, unless Mr. Dalton by his future conduct shall render it unnecessary." This was indeed an application of the Cat to poor Dalton himself; if the reprimand stood it would have enforced his resignation or destroyed his influence with the boys for ever; but gentler counsels prevailed. It was felt that, in supporting the report of their Committee so drastically, the governors had gone too far. At the October meeting the committee were invited to reconsider the subject, with the hope they could make such amicable arrangements as would prevent recurrence of such troubles; and, in November, the Board without dissent resolved that, whilst highly sensible of the meritorious exertions of their committee of inquiry on Mr. Dalton's statements, they felt that, as harmony and discipline were now again restored, and as testimony had been given to the Board that had not been before the committee and which had a favourable bearing towards Mr. Dalton, they directed that the report of the committee and all proceedings had thereon should be rescinded, and rescinded they were accordingly. Richard Smyth, Lord Mayor, presided at this meeting; with him sat the Bishop of Ossory, Dr. Robert Fowler, who had been long on the Board when Archdeacon of Dublin, and several of the governors who had taken part in the reprimand of August.

It were pity indeed had this reprimand stood, for William Dalton had for long years been a devoted servant. In his *History of Dublin*, Whitelaw, who had been one of the Education Commissioners, writing in 1817, speaks of him as the Mathematical Master of most unwearied assiduity, who, himself educated at the School, was thus making the most honourable return to the protectors of his youth. He remarks that Dalton received £20 a year in addition to his salary of £180 from the Guild of Merchants as Mathematical teacher; and recommends the opulent Corporation to furnish him with the scientific instruments of which it is noted the School was then destitute.[1]

This eirenicon was probably promoted by Mr. Sutton, who, as Master of the Trinity Guild, was one of the governors, for he best knew Dalton's work; and he now brought forward an invitation from the Master and Wardens to the boys to attend at their Hall on Wellington Quay on Holy Eve, and partake of cake and wine, they not having had their usual Feast of Cake and Wine on Trinity Eve, and the invitation was gratefully accepted by the Board.

It is noticeable that when the governors rescinded the resolution of reprimand a notice was given by Alderman Archer to move that a letter be written to the Chaplain, Mr. Morgan, and to Dr. Harty, asking their resignation as governors, for the evils of divided authority and the inconvenience of even the best officials being their own employers had now been seen. The motion, however, was not persevered in. It is one thing to unwisely appoint; it is another to undo the unwisdom, without injustice, when a removable has been made irremovable as a rector or a judge.

In 1827 the Catholic Emancipation Bill was becoming a burning question, not merely of Irish, but of imperial politics. The atmosphere was surcharged with its electricity, for the opposition was now boldly militant, led here by the Archbishop of Dublin, Dr. Magee. A great scholar and a great divine, he had been a Fellow of T.C.D.; but he was a statesman too, the intimate of Plunket and the notables of the time; but if a divine, he was not a diviner, for he believed that the reformation was now only beginning in Ireland, thus thinking from the vast growth of the Evangelical revival through the kingdom and the new movement for teaching the Irish in their old language, which was still that of the majority in many counties whence it has long since disappeared. As a preacher it was said he equalled Dean Kirwan as a born orator, with the difference that his sermons,

[1] Whitelaw's *History of Dublin*, by Walsh, p. 572.

when printed, justified their reputation.[2] The Archbishop was now in the field. One of his measures was to assemble the children of all church schools of Dublin in St. Patrick's Cathedral, to which they were to march through the streets on the King's Coronation Day, 19th July. Of these schools the Blue Coat stood first as the school of the Corporation, and the oldest foundation. On the 17th the Archbishop came to the Board of which he was a governor, Samuel Tyndall, Lord Mayor, in the chair, and moved that the boys be permitted to proceed in procession to the cathedral with the children of the other institutions of the city, and this was unanimously agreed to. The report of this design roused to fury the promoters of the Bill, and their press overflowed with denunciations. Sir George Murray, Commander of the Forces in Ireland, recoiled, and refused to allow the Hibernian boys to attend, on the pretext that their school was not a charity; and the Protestant orphans were also held back. But the Archbishop, with all the rest, moved on. Marquess Wellesley, the Lord Lieutenant, rode in the procession, for which, of course, he was duly abused; but the people in the streets, despite the newspapers, took the scene good-humouredly, and the great demonstration went off with *éclat*. Next year the Archbishop repeated the ceremonial, but the cause of the Bill had largely advanced, for O'Connell was returned for Parliament at the Clare Election; so, when the Archbishop came down to our Board in April and renewed his proposal, there was a large attendance of thirty-one governors, and an amendment suggested that the Blue Coat boys, whose orange and blue uniforms made them the most obnoxious to the opponents, should not join the procession but go apart to the cathedral and to a gallery of their own. These more cautious counsels, however, did not prevail, and the Archbishop carried his full project by two to one. The result was similar to that of the preceding year. Next year the Emancipation Act passed, for the Duke of Wellington and Peel had bent before the storm; but the Archbishop did not bend. At a meeting of thirty-two

[2] Dr. Ball's *Reformed Church in Ireland*, 276.

governors in June, Alexander Montgomery, Lord Mayor, in the chair, he carried his motion that the boys should go in procession in manner as in last year, and this time there was no dissent. But this time, too, the opposition was even fiercer than before. The denunciations in their press were so vehement that it was thought they were intended to inflame the mob to attack the children in the streets. The procession, notwithstanding, was organized on even a larger scale than before. On Wednesday, 17th July, five thousand children, including the Blue Coats, marched through the city with flags and banners flying, to the cathedral, where two high thrones were erected, one for the Lord Lieutenant, Hugh Percy, third Duke of Northumberland, the other for the Archbishop himself. Then the five thousand, with full consent, raised their young cheerful voices in the Old Hundreth Psalm. Handel's great Coronation Anthem was sung by the choir, and his Hallelujah Chorus at the close; and all passed off in peace. Despite the press, whose bitterness had been specially aimed at the Blue Coat boys, the populace looked quietly on, for our dear Dublin folk have always had an innate sympathy with pageants, and some even cheered the marching youngsters.

At the same June meeting our governors were called on to elect a new registrar in the room of Mr. Hart, who had just died, and Mr. Addison Hone was chosen. Yet even this within-doors affair was drawn into the political tide outside, for at the preceding City Assembly there was tumult and strife. The Commons renewed the claim made by Charles Lucas eighty years before, and which was supposed to have been set at rest by the Act of 1761, that all members of the Corporation were entitled to be governors of King's Hospital under the charter, and therefore entitled to vote for the new registrar. But the claim again proved futile. Mr. Hone was elected unanimously, and worthily held office for the next thirty years. This office has been remarkable in the long tenures its holders have enjoyed. Mr. Hart, his predecessor, was appointed in June, 1794, and served for thirty-five years. Bartholomew Wybrants for thirty-six; and our present popular registrar, Mr. G. R. Armstrong, who succeeded to the office in June, 1876, is now (1906) in the thirtieth year of his tenure. Robert Hart was at the time deeply regretted, and his services had, as we have seen, been warmly commended by the first Education Commissioners twenty years before, and for a long time he discharged his duties faithfully but it might have been better had this public eulogy not been expressed, for it led to everything being left in his hands, unchecked and unsupervised. It is painful to find that his accounts at his death were in great disorder. The municipal commission of 1835, on whose work the Corporation Act of 1840 was based, reported that in Hart's time the funds of the Hospital were misapplied.[3] This is quoted by the Endowed Schools Commission of 1858 in their summary of the Blue Coat property and the losses sustained by negligence and by permitting the statute of limitations to run. The mode of keeping the accounts from 1818 to 1826 is condemned, when all, as it was said, was left to Hart.

This evil remissness, we may well suppose, was encouraged by the already noticed laxity allowed to Allan Morgan, the chaplain and head master, on whose headship so much depended. A governor himself, he was chaplain to several Lord Lieutenants successively, and took his scholastic duties somewhat lightly. He seems to have been permitted to relinquish them altogether; for, when it was suggested by the Education Commissioners in 1810 that the union of the offices of chaplain and head master should be insisted on, it was said that this should in fairness be deferred to the next vacancy, as Mr. Morgan had so long acted as chaplain only; yet the minute on his original appointment in 1784 is decisive, showing that he was then called in and expressly appointed to the double duty. But, like his father, whom he then succeeded, he had many lofty friends outside the Board. He was the frequent guest of Lord Moira, afterwards Marquess of Hastings, at Moira House, then a chief social centre in Dublin, though now sunk from its high estate to become the Mendicity on Usher's Quay. This social prestige

[a] *Reports*, 185, Vol. I., p. 149.

probably led to the governors making him a colleague and giving him too free a hand. His high friends stood to him to the last. Through the influence of Lord Forbes he was appointed Dean of Killaloe in 1828, whilst still holding our chaplaincy, but died two years after, just when George the Fourth's reign ceased, on the 26th June, 1830. In one respect his career was unique, he was chief officer of the Blue Coat for forty-six years. His connection with King's Hospital is preserved to-day in the person of his great-grand-nephew, our excellent governor, Mr. William C. Stubbs.

Our Lord Mayor chairmen in George the Fourth's reign were :—

1820-21 Sir Abraham Bradley King, Bart.	1824-25 Drury Jones.
21- 2 Sir John Kingston James, Bart.	25- 6 Thomas Abbott.
	26- 7 Samuel W. Tyndall.
	27- 8 Sir Edmund Nugent.
22- 3 John Smyth Fleming	28- 9 Alexander Montgomery
23- 4 Richard Smyth.	29-30 Jacob West.

CHAPTER XV.

TEMP. WILLIAM THE FOURTH AND EARLY VICTORIA.
1830-1841.

THE first act of the Board in the new reign was again to reunite the offices of chaplain and head master in the person of the Rev. James Walker King. He was an able and accomplished man, but he was the son and heir of the late chairman, Sir Abraham Bradley, and he was himself chaplain to the new Lord Lieutenant, Marquess of Anglesea; and the position on the Board of his father, who was a magnate, his own interests outside, and the poor example of Allan Morgan's long headship did not contribute to the zeal and devotion essential in the chief of a public school. In 1834 he married, and this did not attach him more closely to dull routine; he occasionally examined the senior boys, but seems to have left the strain of teaching to Dalton, and matters of discipline mainly to Mr. Hone, the registrar. Then, in 1836, he resigned, and two years after succeeded to his father's baronetcy, and his son is the present baronet, Sir Charles Simeon King, of Corrard, Fermanagh, which his ancestors had possessed from Charles I.'s time; they were kinsmen of the great Archbishop, to whom, as we have seen, our King's Hospital owes so much.

In the early thirties our governors were much occupied in enforcing their claims on Cappoloughlin mentioned above, and the tale unfolds a romance of the mysteries of Chancery beside which Jarndyce *v.* Jarndyce shrinks, acquitting the genius of Dickens of all overstatement of the *cause celebre* by which he wrought reforms which the world had long sought vainly from jurists or judges.

Even old lawyers, not merely of to-day, but those engaged in such causes themselves, could hardly tell how they could last for generations without doing anything, or anything but evil; for they had begun often generations before the counsel or Lord Chancellor of the day had been born. And as in this instance King's Hospital stood defrauded for years and years, and the scandal has not been hitherto disclosed, the scarce credible story must be recorded here.

It has been already told how the Education Commissioners in their report of 1810[1] had included in the Blue Coat endowments an annuity of £20 granted by our old founder John Preston in 1686, and how their inquiry, held on other schools, disclosed that Preston's grant had given his estate of Cappoloughlin, 739 acres in Queen's County, on an educational trust for ever. The rental was then only £80 yearly, for those were the days of the Revolution. Of this £80, £35 was to pay a schoolmaster in Navan, to be named by his heirs; £25, similarly, for one in Ballyroan; and one-fourth, or £20, to the Blue Coat governors; but, if the rental should increase, the surplus was to be divided between these schools as his heirs and trustees should determine. The Commissioners in a second report informed the Lord Lieutenant that Cappoloughlin, with a rental now of £1,400 a year, was in Chancery, and had been the subject of gross mismanagement and abuses. Thereupon, in 1813, a statute (53 Geo. III., c. 107) created a great commission, long known as the Clare Street Commissioners of Education—the Lord Chancellor, the Archbishops, Provost, bishops, and magnates many, armed with the most drastic power over endowed schools; it specially named the Preston foundations, and declared the right of the Blue Coat to one-fourth of the Cappoloughlin surplus.

But it needed a stronger Act to loosen the Chancery clutches. With all their powers the Commissioners must await the final decree in the Attorney-General *v.* Preston, though that might linger to the judgment of all things: and

[1] Chapter XIII.

yet they might hope, for was not Lord Manners the Chancellor and chief in the Commission himself? The suit was indeed then dead, but awaiting resurrection from the limbo of an abatement. So, in 1816, Attorney-General Saurin, on the relation of the Commissioners, filed a Bill of Review which sets forth the shameful and sordid story. It recites Alderman Preston's deed, and how his four trustees and the heirs of their survivors, and his own heir male and heir general for ever were to manage Cappoloughlin and the schools, his heirs to nominate the schoolmasters in Navan and Ballyroan. The trusts were to begin on the death of his widow, and no one knew when that was; but in 1735 the Attorney-General v. Edwards, the original cause, brought estate and trusts into the iron grasp of Chancery, and asked to have the trusts carried out. These were simple enough; if it were to-day, a careful scheme could be at once submitted to the Court and adopted at a moderate expense. But, to follow the sorry sequel, one must recall the noble principles of equity on which this suit was framed. One was the golden rule that everyone, no matter how bare or unsubstantial his interest in the cause, must be a party to it, and that no step, however formal, could ever be taken unless all were present to see equity done. Another was that if any one of all these parties died, the cause in sympathy died with him, and so lay dead till revived by a new bill telling the story all over again. So this Attorney-General v. Edwards made defendants Hugh Edwards and Mrs. Margaret Faviere and her husband John, representing the co-heiresses of David Cairns, the last of John Preston's four trustees of 1686, and Mrs. Mary Ludlow and her husband Peter, for she was Preston's heiress at law, and the golden theory required that husbands must be present to protect the rights of their ladies, though these were nil; and with these were John Preston of Bellinter, now heir male, who, with his tenant defendant, Fysher, were enjoying Cappoloughlin in breach of the trusts. In 1737 Lord Wyndham made his seemingly simple decree to carry out the trusts, and directing that the heirs and trustees should lay a scheme before the master, and that Mr. Preston should give an account of the estate since old Mr. Preston's death. But we are now naively told that "before anything was done under the decree Mr. Edwards died and with him the cause, though this descendant of a long dead trustee, who had never acted, had, perhaps, never even heard of Cappoloughlin till dragged into a suit he had no concern in. Equity had then, as now, the power to appoint trustees of its own when the legal trustees were not available, but another golden rule forbade that this should be done till, at any cost, the heirs of the last trustee should be found, though he might, when found, prove to be a pauper, a fool, or a felon. So the suit was revived, and a full new decree was made against Hugh Edwards' heirs, three little girl minors, Olivia, Jane, and Elizabeth, who were gravely commanded to carry out the trusts. Thus time sped over, and other defendants died, and again we are naively told that many new bills of revivor were filed "as deaths of the parties required." Pending these, nothing was done, save that Cappoloughlin was "administered" by the Court, every new letting being attended by all the parties to see justice done, all being allowed their costs.

Thus we come to 1758, when the suit was only twenty-three years old, and a new Attorney-General revived it, asking that Mr. Preston and his tenant should be ordered to give up Cappoloughlin, whither they had retired in the years of suspended animation; but new heirs were now indispensable parties, for Olivia Edwards had grown up and was now Lady Rosse, and, with her husband, Earl Richard, and Faviere's son, were now the heirs of the old dead trustee Cairns. Mrs. Ludlow, John Preston's heir when the suit began, was now represented by her son, Lord Ludlow. But this new suit lingered and broke down, the Evil One knows why. Lord and Lady Rosse and her maiden sisters, Jane and Elizabeth, now renounced any share in the fraudful game, and it was only in 1773 the cause was again fully heard, when the Chancellor, Lord Lifford, solemnly decreed that Lady Rosse and her sisters should be discharged, and that all the remaining heirs and trustees should be at liberty to lay a scheme before the Master in Chancery exactly as had been ordered in vain by Lord Wyndham only thirty-five years before.

The case then was with Master Walker for two years, and, on his reports, emerged before the Chancellor in 1776 for another perfect decree, which ordered Lady Rosse and her sisters to convey Cappoloughlin to a body of trustees well chosen by the Master, including, with the remaining heirs, three bishops, a Fellow of Trinity College, and Lord Dawson of Portarlington. It directed £345 a year to be allocated to the schoolmasters of Navan and Ballyroan *when these should be appointed*, but reserved further action till the heirs should decide whether they wished to exercise their powers of appointing the schoolmasters, though all of them were then before the Court. This order, however, looked too much like business; so it was found when the ladies came to assign the estate to the new trustees, that though prepared at great cost, the name of Lord Dawson, now become Lord Carlow, who had nothing to do with Cappoloughlin, had been omitted. A new decree must be obtained from the Chancellor to remedy this fatal defect; and as it now transpired that there were no school buildings or homes for the masters either in Navan or Ballyroan, this last decree again ordered a scheme to be proposed for these and laid before the Court.

It would seem that, after this, upon the next death, the dead suit was allowed to lie dead. Possibly when Lord Clare was Chancellor the ring of delinquents dared not let the case come before one who would have stamped out the iniquity instanter. For here a deeper dark settles on the lurid drama, which the discoveries of the Clare Street Commissioners in 1816 only partially dispel. Attorney-General Saurin's reviving bill, however, tells such unbelieveable things as that the conveyance of Cappoloughlin to the new trustees ordered by Lord Lifford in 1777 had never been even executed, and no schoolhouses had yet been built; and that meanwhile two receivers, who as officers of the Court had the estate in hands, had successively put the rents into their pockets, the loot of

Mr. John Jones reaching £2,000, followed by that of Mr. Mark M'Causland, being £1,500 more. The Court, which, like a silly pedigreeist, had been spending years and hundreds in hunting after the heirs of the dead, who had never the slightest interest in the case, never seems to have made inquiry after these brigands or the sureties answerable for their defaults. Further it was found that Preston's heir-at-law, who had become Lord Tara, had somehow been paid out of Court for years, the salaries allocated to the two schoolmasters, amounting to £175 yearly, and in 1794 had nominated his brother, the Rev. Joseph Preston, as schoolmaster, both in Navan and Ballyroan, the latter being forty miles from his reverence's home. This gentleman, it was averred, had only been in the schools some seven times in as many years, and, whilst appropriating the salaries, had named poor ushers as deputies at starving wages. Meanwhile Cappoloughlin, re-let in 1807 at the war rents, yielded nearly £6,000 in four years, of which more than half was devoured in costs and expenses. The Commissioners further told that in 1813 they had, under the powers of their Act, turned out the Reverend Joseph from the mastership of Cavan, there being then only two children in the school of the High Court of Chancery. He had voluntarily resigned Ballyroan six years before, when the old Commission was on the trail, but his brother, Lord Tara, appointed one Hamilton deputy instead, and he, too, never entered the walls. The Commissioners then resolved on a large effective mercantile school, but here Lord Tara again stepped in and, as Chancery nominator, named Rev. Alex. Frankin, who, being required by the Commissioners to discharge the duties, admitting his disability, resigned ; and one M'Loughlin, named by Lord Tara instead, at the new salary of £150, was found to be one of the old ushers at £15 a year, and was disallowed by the Commissioners as wholly unfitted.

It is refreshing to read that one at least of these hereditary trustees now refused to act further with the Chancery gang. The reverend defendant, Joseph Faviere, one of the heirs of Cairns, the last trustee, did so because he wished the trusts to be left wholly to the Commissioners, who, winding up with the statement that both schools are in ruins, pray the Lord Chancellor to discharge Tara as nominator, to vest Cappoloughlin in themselves, and allow them to execute their statutory duties.

But that would have stopped the cause, and the pleasant little parties in the Master's office whenever the smallest game was afoot, and where everyone was allowed his costs, though nothing at all was done, since everyone must be there according to the golden rule, and if anyone was absent, though by negligence, there must be a further little party; for by another, and what we may call a brazen rule, the Master could not disallow the costs, though he knew the absence to have been negligent. This amazing impotence was only remedied by statute in the fourth year of George IV., the partial reform being perhaps partly due to the scandals of this very case.

So answers were filed by Lord Tara and others, five-barred gates and wire entanglements to prevent the capture of the Fortress of Fraud. Tara pleaded his sacred rights as Alderman Preston's heir male, and that his co-defendant, Earl Ludlow, heir general, had always joined in his nominations of the schoolmasters, which, he says, *had always been sanctioned by the Court.* Ludlow lived in England and probably didn't even know where Ballyroan was, but he also aided his kinsmen, putting in a similar answer. As to the abuses charged they were discreetly silent. Then there were replications and rejoinders, and the suit trailed on like a slimy boa-constrictor till, nearly four years after the Commissioners had intervened, it came before Lord Manners for what was now hoped would be the final hearing.

In January, 1820, His Lordship did indeed decree that the estates should be conveyed to the Commissioners, but, with the appalling facts all before him, the prayer to displace Tara and Ludlow as nominators was dismissed with costs; all parties were to have their costs out of Cappoloughlin, and the cause was to stand over—for what ?—to ascertain who were the heirs of David Cairns, the last trustee of the deed of one hundred and thirty years before, and who himself had never lived to act. But next year, again before anything was done, Lord Tara died, and with him the cause; but his brother, the Reverend Joseph, was now his heir and heir male of Alderman Preston, and so the boa-constrictor, scotched, not killed, must be galvanised, and the suit recommenced against that exemplary clergyman.

But the barbed wires and five-barred gates were again erected by him. His answer reads as a delightful sample of subtle irony. As to the ruined school buildings, the incompetent masters, the paucity of scholars, without admitting the facts, he pleads that, if these be true, they were all the work of the Court itself, with whom lay the administration of all, and if enough money was not allowed, surely the Court and not he or his brother was to blame. As to the several abortive decrees of successive Chancellors, he had no information, but would refer His Lordship to the files of his own Court, where he could find it all himself. Did the Lord Chancellor wince at this? Surely Charles Dickens could scarce have beaten it! But as to the future nominations, he relies on his rights as heir of the Founder, which he is quite prepared, he says, to exercise.

So after a modest delay of three more years the case came again before Lord Manners in June, 1824. Surely now there must be an end. The decree is indeed a mighty one. It fills thirty-two immense folio pages in our Record Office, closely written, and would, if spun out like the cause itself, have reached a furlong. In the first thirty-one pages it rehearses all that we have hitherto told; the last half page contains His Lordship's wise decision on it all.

One would like to ask all the judges to guess what this long sought judgment was. They couldn't. It sublimely directs an inquiry—In whom the right of nomination of masters to Navan and Ballyroan rests, and who are the heirs of David Cairns, the last trustee of 1686!

The scandal is enhanced when we reflect how, whilst a century was passed in hunting for the phantoms of a phantom, the heirs of an old trustee, on the golden rule that all interests must be represented, nobody, of all the Chancellors, Masters, Attorney-Generals, or solicitors, ever thought it right to give notice to the Blue Coat governors of their interest in the estate, in their ignorance of which they accepted for two generations the yearly pittance of £20, whilst the surplus rents, of which they should have had a full fourth, were lavished on a futile litigation.

The mountain was in labour; this ridiculous mouse emerged. Reading the reams of recital one might think the Chancellor had tired before he came to his judgment, like the little Dutchman who, wanting to win momentum to jump a fence, took a mile to run at it, but, just as he reached it, lay down fatigued before he could rise to spring. The inquiries he directed had been made and answered to his predecessor eighty-seven years before, the pedigree of heirship had been represented ever since, and the then heirs were there before him; but certainty must be more certain, for was not the golden rule that the wish of the pious founder that his trustees for ever should manage his bounty far more sacred than that his bounty itself should go according to his wish for the training of the children upon his estate? So the ghost of David Cairns must again be captured. It is hard to forbear surmise that the Chancellor was jealous of the statute that gave commissioners the control of trusts that were vested in himself, and shrank from the just condemnation of their discharge by his Court; and yet he was himself, as has been said, one of the leading Commissioners, and thus doubly a trustee of the very first magnitude.

So the boa-constrictor trailed on once more; three years elapsed before Master Ellis reported what everyone knew; after telling all about Hugh Edwards and Lady Rosse and her infant sisters, he declared the Reverend Joseph the true nominator of schoolmasters, and Rev. Joseph Faviere to be the heir or ghost of David Cairns.

And thus it might have trailed to the crack of doom. During all this sordid lapse the Commissioners, annually reporting to the Lord Lieutenant, told how they were hopefully awaiting a final decree, or that it scarcely can be much longer deferred. Through all the dreary time the Blue Coat had been basely defrauded. The governors seem never to have seen John Preston's grant, until they learned from the old Commission of their right to the surplus of Cappoloughlin. When this was declared by the statute of 1813, their fourth share was found to be £362 yearly, and that was actually paid them by the Clare Street Commission for 1812 and 1813, but after Attorney-General *v.* Lord Tara the payments became intermittent and scant, the apology being always "the cause and the costs." But in 1831 our board grew angry. John Claudius Beresford, who was still one of our governors, and possessed the grit of his gallant race, attacked the Clare Street Commissioners themselves, boldly suggesting that they were baffling us. And, indeed, here again it is hard to avoid surmising that their lawyers had entered the vicious circle in Chancery which was grinding the estate to costly powder without moving it an inch towards the door. They pleaded to the demand of a settlement, that the receivers' last account must first be passed, and that the final decree was expected daily. But Beresford declining to submit to any further delay, a King's Counsel was appointed arbitrator, and he awarded in 1833, £1,460 due to the Hospital after all deductions, though but for the costs our arrears were then nearly £5,000.

How the boa-constrictor actually died is somewhat misty. We cannot find a final decree in the Record Office, but we know that the Clare Street Commissioners reported to Government in 1834, that the great cause was at last ended, adding as their pathetic requiem—"after exactly NINETY-NINE YEARS."

Ninety-nine years doing nothing but mischief; debasing the great court, whose proud boast is to be the King's royal guardian of charities and trusts, into an instrument of chicane, rifling the charity with breaches of trust of the grossest. Fraudulent trustees now earn penal servitude for far less rapine than this, our Jarndyce *v.* Jarndyce, discloses. To those who ask how these things could be the answer is "The system and routine." The judge only decided on what was laid before him at long intervals on the Masters' reports. The Master only decided what the parties brought before him from time to time, and the lawyers worked on from term to term, changing often, and nobody ever looking back on the past. And yet the result was as bad as though all concerned, Chancellors, Masters, parties, lawyers, had been banded together as Sicilian brigands.

The Clare Street Commissioners have long since merged in the Land Commission, and it is our comfort to know that old John Preston's annuity still yields us some £140 yearly, and to take such solace for our losses as we may from the humorous side of this comico-tragedy. John Claudius Beresford, who forced the falling of the curtain, was not a man to be trifled with safely. Strong himself, he was a son of one of the strongest and perhaps then the most influential potentate in Ireland—the Right Hon. John Beresford, President of the Revenue Board, of whom Lord Fitzwilliam complained that he had far more power than the Lord Lieutenant himself. John Claudius was himself also a member of the Privy Council, but he was a city magnate too, and had been chairman of our Board when Lord Mayor in 1814.

Under the somewhat *laissez faire* regime of Mr. King, discipline had gone a little out of hand. The boys had been allowed to go home or through the city too much as they pleased, with the sure consequence when such laxity exists, but the governors now had an invaluable addition in Dr. Charles Elrington, the regius professor of Divinity in the University. He came as treasurer of the Erasmus Smith board, to follow in the steps of his great predecessors, Archbishop King and Lord Chief Justice Downes. In paying this tribute, it is a pleasure to know that he is still represented in the Blue Coat, for his grandson, Frank Elrington Ball, the late Lord Chancellor's son, is one of our worthiest governors to-day. In 1835 Dr. Elrington carried a scheme of new rules; these restored the controlling power over all in the Chaplain and Headmaster, with the sole and specific charge of the religious instruction; they carefully guarded the system of *exeats*, which must be given in writing by the Headmaster or Registrar. The classes were all remodelled, and provision made for an usher to assist Dalton; they defined the hours of roll call, when the boys rose, and at curfew, and they strictly required that under no circumstances or at any time should the boys be left without the presence of some master—" as controlling power over their actions." Had Mr. King remained to carry out these excellent reforms all might have been well, but he probably found them too irksome a task, for next year he left us; and before they were given time to operate, the Reverend Fielding Ould was elected to the united office.

This appointment was most unfortunate, for he proved to be deficient in all the qualities requisite in the head of a large public school. He failed as a teacher, whilst he was absolutely devoid of the disciplinary faculties so essential to his position. He was a chronic invalid, and was continually asking leave of absence, and the most that could be said for him, was that he was a blameless clergyman. Though now headmaster, he interpreted his duties as such in the light of his predecessors, Morgan and King, by confining his tuition to the religious teaching, only occasionally taking a secular class, but devolving all the routine instruction on Dalton, the second master, and Courtney, the usher, and all disciplinary powers on these and Mr. Hone, the Registrar. The result was that in the next five years a spirit of anarchy was evoked which took years to allay, and which made the last lustrum under our old constitution domestically the most troubled of any in our annals. The recurrent friction might well be forgotten, but that it developed a saving element of humour which, we may hope, gave some solace to the governors who had to deal with the troubles, and which preserves for it a niche in this modest narrative now.

Had Dalton and Courtney been other than they were, harmony might still have endured, but though poor Dalton was a devoted officer, and had profited by the reprimand of a few years before, we have seen that he was somewhat lacking in tact; he had become, however, popular with the boys. But Courtney, the usher, who now styled himself junior master, shewed one title to the name, in that he claimed, not only to be master over the boys, but to be master of Dalton, whose subordinate he was. Dr. Elrington's rules giving them a dual control over the pupils through all the long day, gave an occasion for strained relations which had not been foreseen. During King's headmastership peace was preserved, but when enough time was given to allow Mr. Ould's incapacity to transpire, the war broke out.

In December, 1837, Dalton sent to the governors a moderate statement, which, without any incriminating complaint, asked for some more clear definition of the relative duties of the usher and himself, as there was now some friction between them. Before any action was taken, Courtney became aware of this proceeding of Dalton's, and thereupon the strain stretched to breaking point.

In calling the roll in the school-room at seven in the morning, as ordered by the Elrington rules, Dalton's usage was to call it twice, and any boy coming in afterwards was asked by him to account for his absence. After roll the boys passed to their classes under Courtney. One December morning a boy came in after second call, and Dalton directed him to come over and account; but, as the school hour had just rung, Courtney had arrived to take up the class to which the belated boy belonged, and, seeing this, Dalton told him he might go, but this did not satisfy the usher; in presence of the school, he ordered the boy not to obey his superior in office. This was too much, Dalton now commanded the boy to come forward, but Courtney cried : " I will not let him," and on Dalton approaching the lad the usher interposed, and grasped Dalton in a personal encounter, amid cries of " shame " from the assembled school. Dalton having, as he afterwards said—" no alternative but to repel force by force or to submit to the usher's domination," chose the latter, merely observing, "Your conduct, sir, is exceedingly improper."

One might have supposed that this was a case for the arbitrament of the Head Master, but no one seems to have even thought of appealing to Mr. Ould. Dalton wrote to the Lord Mayor, Samuel Warren. "as head governor and authorized to act in cases of emergency." But the governors seem to have only desired to hush the affair. Courtney had been appointed by them under the new rules, and would appear to have had some powerful influence amongst them, for they took his excuse that he was acting under their orders in taking his class, and they kindly suggested to Dalton that as he had now been in office thirty-three years it might be better for him to retire on a pension. His reply in writing is modest and dignified; expressing his desire to meet the Board's wishes, he suggests that on the precedent in Beasley's case his pension of two-thirds of salary and value of his rooms would amount to £250 yearly. This caused the Board to shrink, so they allowed things to go on for the present, merely counselling peace.

They should have known, if they were wise, that things could not end there. The boys had now espoused Dalton's cause, and openly rebelled against Courtney. The latter had, moreover, taken on himself the right of inflicting corporal punishment, and used this freely, and friction recurred in January; but in February the boys, finding that Courtney's cane had become keener since they had cried out "shame," refused to go up to his night roll in the dormitories, and, locking themselves in the dining room, barred Courtney out. He did apply then to Ould, who at first vainly begged the boys to open the door; but, on being asked why they rebelled, there arose a shout, "the usher, the usher." But Dalton now came on the scene, and then the rebels quietly slipped out by the further door, and the authorities entering found the dining room empty and the boys gone to bed. The usher could not complain of Dalton in this *emeute*, for he had warned the rebels in the usher's presence that they must be punished for disobedience. So Courtney, thinking there might be danger in again directly appealing to the Board, wrote a fierce indictment of the boys to Mr. Hone, giving the names of nine ringleaders whose conduct was such as no corporal punishment could adequately meet, " as they not only seem still to exult in their misconduct, but to be under the impression that no further notice will be taken of it, and that the singing boys only seem to be under the displeasure of the governors." This allusion to the choir referred to a well-founded complaint that on practising night an unmentionable thing had been placed in the usher's seat in the chapel, which must have been perpetrated with the knowledge of all. This extreme measure of the contempt in which the usher was held made it impossible to allow things to continue as before. The inaction of the governors on the usher's insubordination towards his superior naturally had reacted in the boys' insubordination to the usher himself. So Courtney was relieved of his office with an apparently handsome testimonial; but, as this class of literature is read by the wise rather for what is omitted than for what is said, we note that this one, whilst highly lauding Mr. Courtney's literary endowments, his zeal, and his moral character, is silent as to his temper or discretion or his qualification for the management of schoolboys; but the practice of accelerating the departure of undesirable subordinates by high encomium to facilitate their employment elsewhere is not quite unknown even in these days.

The Board elected to the vacant places Mr. Fenby as second master and Mr. Hanly as usher, but unfortunately leaving Mr. Ould his nominal headship. For Fenby proved so far worse than Courtney that he was now chief teacher, and thus had colour for his treatment of Hanly, *his* subordinate, whom he proceeded to discredit *coram pueris*. Mr. Ould he treated with undisguised contempt. He took from the usher the Scripture classes, which the chaplain himself had placed in Hanly's charge, prohibited his taking any part in the teaching of the seniors; and, when, in his own necessary absence, Hanly had taken up an algebra class, by a message through one of the boys he obliged him to desist.

It seems that the poor usher was the son of a shoemaker who had supplied the School, so, in the presence of the boys, Mr. Fenby produces some newly mended shoes and directs the poor usher to inspect them, adding "I am no judge of such things; the last shoemaker was too poor to afford wax," and then joined in the laugh his refined pleasantry evoked; boys are, alas, too ready to rejoice when any of their masters are put to the torture. Thus the usher's authority was for the time wholly undermined; the rebellious spirit, of course, re-awoke, and Fenby, too, had to face it. In December, 1838, he joined with Hanly in a charge of sedition against a boy, Hautainville, who had been one of the ringleaders against Mr. Courtney some months before. The Committee who heard the charge included Dr. Elrington; they ordered that Hautainville should be removed from the institution, and that Mr. Ould should read the sentence next day in the full schoolroom. But the chaplain himself now came in, and in what the Committee records as a long and interesting conversation told them the School as at present constituted could not succeed in its objects; he was directed to send a written report to the next Board meeting. He, however, had scarce withdrawn when Fenby, asking an interview, lodged the following counterblast. It is given in full as a specimen of the nadir which anarchy had now reached :—

FIRST—that no gentleman coming into a large public school for only one hour a day, and who is entirely unacquainted with the various branches of science taught in the schools, and who is likewise without any knowledge of the late improvements adopted in the government and discipline of large schools, can with any propriety, be considered as fully competent to be the head-master without serious injury and impediment to the school. Second.—That it is altogether impossible that the second master can, with any degree of consistency, take on himself to arrange the school on a new plan, and change its mode of discipline, being at the same time interfered with by the head-master, a gentleman, who from his age, temper and want of practical experience in the tuition and management of boys, is altogether unfit for so important, difficult and arduous an undertaking. Third.—That the assistant might be placed under the control of the master, otherwise not being responsible for the state and order of the school he has it in his power, should he feel himself offended by the master, instead of being a useful auxiliary, to be an annoyance and destroyer of the discipline of the school.

This striking model of discipline the Committee simply ordered to stand to the ensuing meeting.

Next day, when the school assembled to witness the sentence of expulsion of Hautainville, Mr. Fenby, who had joined in the complaint against him, walked out of the room, presumably to leave the odium of the execution on the chaplain and usher, for he was now courting the favour of the boys, as a despot often stirs Acheron, in view of the pending inquiries. Thereupon a general hiss broke out from the boys, who, on the following Sunday, armed with stones, flung them at Hanly, and crying out they would have him out of that, followed him to his room, and, assailing the door, filled the lock with stones and sand. This fracas occupied the next Committee to the exclusion of the larger pending cases. The examination disclosed that the ringleaders were chiefly those who had been denounced as such by Courtney the year before. They admitted throwing stones, but pleaded it was not at Hanly but *after* him. One little fellow, Charles Bilton, was caught with a stone in his pocket, so, unable to deny his missile, he explained that it was not there for throwing, and, as it was not flung in fact, it might be that it was only a stone in his sleeve to be used in the general melee as occasion might require. The Committee adjourned all the cases till after the Christmas holidays, so of course the anarchy ceased not. Before the meeting in January, 1839, Mr. Ould had a further charge against Fenby that he had refused to give him a copy of the new rules—rather strange that the Head Master should not have a copy himself.

At the meeting the Committee, having before them all the cases, Fenby *v.* Ould and *vice versa*, and Hanly *v.* Fenby, came to the astounding conclusion that it did not appear necessary to adopt any proceedings on the above complaints, all of which were left in damning record on the minute books. It is noticeable that Dr. Elrington was not present at any of the last preceding committees.

So of course there was soon a recrudescence. One of the Elrington reforms directed that the boys should be periodically inspected by examiners from outside, a salutary measure, acted on ever since until the Intermediate system made it unnecessary. The first examination was fixed for May. Preparing for it in April, Mr. Ould took up one day Mr. Fenby's history class, and, finding it utterly ignorant, observed to the boys " I don't blame you." " To whom do you refer ? " said Fenby, who was present. Ould replied " To you, as their teacher." This scene had a sequel

A Mr. Irvine and another examined all the School during two days in May. His report on each class was fairly favourable, but contained two ominous passages. After praising the neatness of the boys, than whom he had seldom seen a more interesting set, he adds that " When the respective duties of each individual is properly defined, and so limited as to prevent the duties coming in collision, then may those interested in the well-being of the institution hope for prosperity ; " and he thus concludes, " These are circumstances on which I am not aware it is my duty to remark, but as they seem to mar the advancement of the School I cannot refrain from saying that they are worthy of the investigation of the governors, in which I would be happy to give any explanation as far as these things have come within my knowledge." This calm verdict of an outsider, which in truth was a severe reflection on the apathy of the governors, at last compelled a decisive inquiry.

This was forthwith held, and occupied two days ; Ould and Fenby were present, and a charge was made that, immediately before the examinations, the latter had bid the boys not to answer in Scripture, which would thus secure condemnation of the chaplain, whose special subject of teaching it was, and so prepare for a breakdown in his own subjects, wherein Ould had found his class so deficient. A boy, M'Donald, alleged that Mr. Fenby told him if the boys tripped or broke down in Scripture he, Fenby, would be all right, otherwise he would lose his situation ; and asked him, as he could not himself interfere directly, to pass the word through the senior boys and all would be right. Another boy, Clarke, stated he had heard the word go round generally, but could not tell where it originated. A third boy, Colgan, heard the words "Don't answer" go round, and passed it himself to three others: he explained, however, his real reason was only to cover his own bad answering. As Colgan was one of the rioters of the year before and one of the Hanly stone throwers, his ingenuous plea was highly likely. *Per contra* Master Nathaniel Joint said he had himself answered as well as he could, but advised the other boys not to answer. This, however, he naively explained, was to secure the premium himself. The Committee, failing to see any humour in this, made poor Joint their first victim, and sentenced him to be turned out of the School. M'Donald, recalled, was severely cross examined by Fenby, but without effect, and solemnly asked to reconsider his evidence, said he would swear to it if necessary. The cup was full. The Committee reported to the Board their unanimous opinion that they should dispense with the services of Mr. Fenby; and this at last they did.

In his place was chosen one of the very best officers the Blue Coat has ever possessed, Mr. Louis Le Pan, of one of the Dublin French refugee families. He had all the characteristic faculties essential for a true head master. In this position he was now placed, and retained it with the commendation of all for more than a generation. He was not now in orders, so he could not be made chaplain too. Mr. Ould was retained in that latter office, but was relieved of all his other scholastic duties. Even as chaplain he was a melancholy failure. He was cautioned, however, not to interfere with the Master's headship. Mr. Hanly, too, was retained with a caution, and a new official, Shirley, was appointed as Superintendent to aid in the care and discipline of the boys out of school hours. And peace was at length restored in the schoolrooms.

But it would have been too much to hope that the heated atmosphere, so long surcharged, should not have reached the basement storey, where the feminine staff, which included five nurses, were under the housekeeper, Mrs. Sherwin. As this lady had £80 a year, with her maintenance and rooms, she might have been thought the proper person to select the kitchen chief, but the Board, who had taken charge of domestic routine themselves, elected Miss Georgina Crawford, with the common result when men take on them women's functions. Miss Crawford's personality is so unique as to merit a portrait ;—if the qualifications for a cook had been literary, her selection was good, for she could quote Shakespeare, and Miss Edgeworth might have envied her writing. She began by spurning Mrs. Sherwin's authority, on the ground that, having been appointed by the Board, they alone were her masters. Then she brought in her father, who, an absolute intruder, took upon him, in Mr. Le Pan's absence, to order the boys into the dining hall before the prescribed hour. As Le Pan had never even seen this man, he naturally asked an explanation. Thereupon the gentle Georgina gave a double knock at his door ; and, as he was just then not in, she made her way to the sittingroom, where a member of his family sat, with an outburst of vituperation. This, on Mr. Le Pan's return, she re-poured upon himself in language so violent and insulting that it would be difficult, he says, to convey an idea of it, and ended by saying her father would have a Board called and have him turned out for insulting her father (whom he had never personally seen), as also the housekeeper, who apparently had suggested that this queen of the kitchen had been drinking. Mr. Le Pan, calling in Mrs. Sherwin, as the supposed regulator of things downstairs, the invectives were only repeated with further force. All the above was very moderately reported to the governors by Le Pan at their own request. Mrs. Sherwin told the Committee that Miss Georgina's language was such that, had she been her own servant, she must have been discharged at once. The Committee sat to four o'clock waiting for Georgina, who only appeared when they had risen, and, taking advantage of this absence, they postponed the inquiry for a more convenient season, thus weakly adjourning it *sine die* ; but Georgina was no ordinary person, they had chosen her themselves and they could trust to the magnanimity of Mr. Le Pan ; they were so far right, for she did not collide with him again.

But of course it did not end here. Within three months the Committee sat on a protocol of Miss Crawford's, which is indeed unique and beyond even the fancy of Swift in his studies of the Servants' hall. The penmanship looks really like that of a lady, and there is little doubt that both in this and the style not one of the governors, save Dr. Elrington perhaps, could have distantly approached it. In form it can only be likened to the King's Speech ; there are six stately paragraphs, each commencing " My Lords and Gentlemen," but, unlike those gracious yet cautious pronouncements this is an impeachment of the whole staff, high and low, as engaged in a vile conspiracy against her. " My Lords and Gentlemen," one paragraph runs, " you cannot but too plainly see that a conspiracy exists against me because I am conscientiously and faithfully endeavouring to protect the property of the institution and doing justice to the boys, this, my Lords and Gentlemen, is the head and front of my offending, and a few weeks will but too plainly prove the truth of my economy in every branch under my care." ; and she concludes, " I am very fond of my situation, and I take a delight in performing its duties, and it is my determination to continue to render justice to all parties. My Lords and Gentlemen, I only ask in return your kind protection and support to enable me to fulfil the duties of my situation with satisfaction to your institution and credit to myself."

Her specific complaints are against the nurses and housekeeper, and, with one exception, refer to small domestic details ; but even these are couched in Johnsonian clauses ; but she directly charges that on Sunday, 25th October, Nurse 5 wilfully threw a gallon of scalding broth on her hands and arms as she leaned over the boiler, which caused her " excruciating pain," and obliged her to discharge her duties for a week in torture ; and her evidence of conspiracy is that the whole staff, whom she names, from Mr. Le Pan down, showed an utter want of sympathy, Mr. Hone, the registrar, refusing her demand to summon a Board, as her complaints were too trifling for such a step. The refusal was natural, for all who were present at the scalding had informed him that her charge against Nurse Johnston was wholly baseless, that they had seen how she herself when filling the vessel had accidentally tilted it into the boiler, and Nurse Johnston solemnly declared in the presence of God that she had never touched either gallon or pail, whilst all five nurses sent in a statement that Miss Crawford, ever since she came, had kept them in complete confusion, and had told them she would drain the last drop of her veins to be revenged on them all.

Her clause aiming at Shirley, the superintendent, can scarcely be passed by—"He, during the Fair week of Donnybrook," she says, "was absent on three several occasions, having taken with him the key of the hall. Did Mrs. Sherwin, or Mr. Le Pan, or Mr. Hanly," she asks, "report his absence to Mr. Hone, and, if so, has Mr. Hone reported such negligence to the Board?" This would have done credit to a cross-examining counsel, though, perhaps, the famous fair green would have been the most fitting scene for the exercise of her impartial warfare. Yet, in the face of all this, the facile governors retained Miss Georgina with a gentle reprimand, accompanied by another on Mrs. Sherwin for not exercising greater firmness, and they added a comic postscript which points to an oral hint from Georgina. It orders that Mrs. Matthews, *alias* Baily, the infirmary nurse, do exhibit her marriage certificate to the registrar, and, in default, be immediately dismissed.

They were perhaps influenced by Georgina's apparent zeal for economy. If so, their wisdom was tested when, two years later, it was found that the charges for bread far exceeded the estimated expense. The police were set to watch the gates, and forthwith arrested an under-servant, burdened with a large fresh loaf. Taken to the station, she now deposed that she was habitually thus sent out by Miss Crawford to sell the loaf for sixpence and bring back the proceeds in the form of whiskey. A special committee of inquiry then disclosed a long prevalent system of abuses under which the rations given out to the under-staff were regularly sold to purchasers who came to the Hospital weekly as to a market. The housekeeper successfully pleaded that as the governors had confirmed Miss Crawford's claim to be the officer of the Board, independent of her, she could exercise no control, and had already felt the results of interference. The scandals had now gone before the public through the Magistrates' Court. Forensic skill could no longer screen even the gentle Georgina, who, at last dismissed, henceforth disappears in oblivion. Mrs. Sherwin was pensioned off, and her successor was duly charged with the selection of the new kitchen queen.

But, meanwhile, the radical change in our constitution had come. In August, 1840, the Municipal Corporations Act (3 & 4 Vic., cap. 108) was passed, by which the Blue Coat ceased to be the city school. Section 113 provides that the existing sixty-one governors, the majority of whom were members of the Corporation, should continue as individuals, but no longer as representing the city. They were now incorporated in accordance with King Charles's original charter, but when they had become reduced to fifty, at which number the Board should thenceforth stand, vacancies should be filled up by the Lord Primate, the Lord Chancellor, the Archbishop of Dublin, and the Bishop of Meath, except the treasurer and three governors of the Erasmus Smith Board, who are always to be four of the fifty as delegated by themselves, they also to have the co-option of four Blue Coat governors for their own board, as provided by Archbishop King's statute of George I. But the old power, once so salutary, of co-opting eminent members, is taken away from the newly constituted Board.[1]

For the present, however, there was little change, and under Mr. Le Pan efficiency reappeared on all sides, save in the chaplain's classes. Dr. Harty, appointed in 1811, only retired in 1854, having served with the utmost satisfaction not only as physician, but as one of the most active members of the Board, for the long term of forty-three years. His

[1] See Appendix C.

colleague, Dr. Read, appointed surgeon in 1823, so continued up to 1861; on Harty's retirement he took upon him the twofold medical duties, for each of which £40 a year had been assigned, at a salary of £50. He in turn retired after good service of thirty-eight years. The medical officers certainly took care of themselves. Hanly, relieved of such overlordship as Mr. Fenby's, remained second master up to 1876, thus earning his pension after also having served just thirty-eight years. These long terms may be deemed a tribute to the peacefully effective rule of the responsible Head master.

But the chaplain Ould still remained for nine long years an incubus, indeed an Old Man of the Sea; in every year he is found defective. By a thoughtful order the governors had directed "that his discources from the pulpit shall be, both in substance and duration, such as are calculated for the moral instruction and religious information of the boys entrusted to his care." For failure in this he is censured next year. Then in the successive annual examinations his classes are always reported as deficient in Scripture and Catechism, and he is each time summoned to explain. His excuses are failing health and leaves of absence, or that he has sent a sufficient substitute. But though the governors sanctioned an assistant clergyman approved by Archbishop Whateley and Dr. Elrington, the same unsatisfactory results recurred. At last the governors resolved that in default of amendment they must exercise their power of dismissal under the charter. Thereupon the chaplain went alone to the Archbishop. Now Dr. Whateley, like many strong and masterful men, had the weakness of being open to flattery, or what is coarsely called to be earwigged, and he very incautiously wrote Mr. Ould a letter angrily condemning the governors for presuming to suggest the dismissal of the chaplain without resorting to him, our Diocesan, and intimating that he would not approve a successor under the charter. This letter Ould had printed and sent to the governors. In a dignified missive to the Archbishop they asked whether this treatment of his letter had been sanctioned by his grace, and whether he was aware of the facts on which they had acted. Then Dr. Whateley perceived the mistake he had made. Satisfied presumably with Dr. Elrington as a due representative of the Church, he had not personally taken part as a working governor. He now explained that though he had not forbidden publication, he had intended his letter as a private one, and would certainly not think of acting officially until he had heard both sides. The chaplain was thereupon summoned by the Board and asked to defend his recent action, and on his wholly failing to do so, the former resolution of conditional dismissal was unanimously passed in his presence. He shortly after disappeared. Le Pan had now graduated in divinity in the University, and was immediately sanctioned by the Archbishop as chaplain; he obtained his Doctor's degree, and as chaplain and head master ruled till his superannuation in 1876, after a splendid record of thirty-seven years.

The drastic quality of the new statute does not seem to have been realized at first, for the majority of the governors were still, in fact, members of the Corporation. They might have seen what was coming from such a sign of the times as the election of Daniel O'Connell to the mayoralty in immediate succession to Sir John Kingston James, our last chairman under the old Protestant regime, O'Connell being the first Lord Mayor of his communion since the days of Sir Thomas Hacket and Tyrconnel, a century and a half before. But in 1842 the government auditor under the Act sent to the Board from London requiring a full statement of the revenue from all sources, which led to the exhaustive report of Mr. O'Brien, which has been already referred to, and he warns the governors of the serious loss entailed by the cessation of the Corporation grants; he sympathetically suggested that the new nominators should be asked to enforce a gift of £100 from each governor nominated in future. The Board thereupon resolved on an address to Government setting forth that in the last twenty years they had received from the city on the election of 22 aldermen £2,210, and in respect of the 40 sheriffs in the same period £4,200, the interest of which maintained fifteen pupils, and they asked for an amending bill providing that all future Protestant sheriffs and all future governors should contribute one hundred guineas to the Hospital. This, of course, proved abortive, their civic power had gone for ever. Dr. Whateley, asked by them to arrange that the nominators should require from each nominee a contribution as above, as was usual in Christ's Hospital in London, declined, believing that the selection being thus limited to the wealthy few, would prevent that of useful governors who would not or could not afford such a payment. This loss was deeply felt. When the Act had passed there were 123 boys in the School, but the numbers fell to 60 in twelve years, and twenty years ago they only attained to 80.

But apart from this, all went well. Our Board in 1840 comprise the Primate, Lord J. G. Beresford, Archbishop Whateley of Dublin, the Right Hon. Frederick Shaw, the Recorder, then M.P. for the University, and Dr. Elrington, who for many years after, as treasurer of the Erasmus Smith Board, gave his high services and continued to send the additional seven boys, representing his treasurer's personal fees; he continued to superintend the religious training and the annual examinations which he had instituted, and which have been continued up to our time. After the old Corporate governors had declined to fifty, and as the lives of these continued to drop, the eminent prelates and the Lord Chancellor, appointed by the statute as nominators, have ever and anon sent to our Board some of the best representatives of the social, official and commercial life of Dublin, and the system up to now has always worked well. The great changes by which in the last half century vast sums from public resources have been expended on Elementary Education have gradually and necessarily raised the Hospital, which has no share in Parliamentary grants or in rates, to the distinct status of a Public School.

We have now reached the years of living memory, and our task is done; but in so far closing our annals it is very grateful to know that never in its past has this historic place attained such a position as it now holds under the auspices of its present chaplain and head master, Mr. Richards. Under him improvement has been signal in all departments. The numbers have been gradually raised from seventy-eight to one hundred and thirty pupils, and at all recent Intermediate examinations, and in many of those for the Dublin and the Royal Universities, the boys have made successful marks. The playground, the old Bowling Green of Dublin, which a few years since was in winter a swamp, has by Mr. Richard's ingenuity been raised some three feet without any felt expense, so that now the King's Hospital stands high in the annual records of cricket and football; whilst in the late examinations in Christian Knowledge, including the Greek Testaments, held under the sanction of the General Synod of the Church of Ireland, King's Hospital stood amongst the highest places.

Thus the torch that was lighted two hundred and thirty-seven years ago has been handed on and down through all the generations. May we trust that the principles of truth and justice, religion and piety, on which our royal charter was originally founded, are quickening to-day the life of this School, to make it fragrant with the spirit of Christian charity, and so may we conclude with the fervent hope that, as in the coming time the successive tides of boyhood go forth each year from its walls to the world, its best traditions may be living powers to animate and sweeten their lives and the lives of those that may gather around them. *Et nati natorum et qui nascuntur ab illis.*

Our Chairmen and Lord Mayors in William IV., and to 1840 were:

1830-31	Sir R. W. Harty, Bart.
1831-32	Sir Thos. Whelan
1832-33	Charles F. Archer
1833-34	Sir George Whiteford
1834-35	Arthur Perrin
1835-36	Arthur Morrison
1836-37	William Hodges
1837-38	Samuel Warren
1838-39	George Hoyte
1839-40	Sir R. W. Brady
1840-41	Sir John Kingston James, Bart.

CHARLES II.
KING of ENGLAND, SCOTLAND, FRANCE & IRELAND,
Defender of the Faith &c.

From a Picture in Bridewell Hall, London, the Original painted by Sr. Peter Lely kt.   Geo Vertue Sculp. 1736.

[To face page 293

APPENDIX A.

THE ROYAL CHARTER, Etc.

CHARLES THE SECOND, by the Grace of God, of *England*, *Scotland*, *France* and *Ireland*, King, Defender of the Faith, &c. To ALL to whom these Presents shall come Greeting. WHEREAS the Mayor, Sheriffs, Commons and Citizens of our City of *Dublin*, in our Kingdom of *Ireland*, have humbly petitioned Us, thereby setting forth, That several of our Subjects in that our City and Kingdom, being charitably affected towards such as through Age, Sickness, or other Accidents, are reduced to Poverty, or disabled to gain their Living by their own Labour; and piously considering also the great Benefit of the good Education and Instruction of Youth; have proposed the Erection, building and establishing of an Hospital and Free School, within the Liberties of our City of *Dublin*, and have shewed great Willingness to contribute to so good a Work, which they hope to accomplish, in Case they may, by our Royal Authority, be enabled and capacitated to purchase Lands, Tenements and Hereditaments for the erecting and maintaining of such an Hospital and Free School, and to make good, wholesome and necessary Laws for the Rule and Government thereof. KNOW Ye therefore, that We of our princely Disposition, for the Furtherance and Accomplishment of so good and charitable a Work, of our especial Grace, certain Knowledge and mere Motion, by and with the Advice and Consent of our right trusty and well beloved Counsellor, *John*, Lord *Berkeley*, our Lieutenant General and General Governour of our said Realm of *Ireland*, and according to the Tenour and Effect of our Letters, bearing Date of our Court at *Whitehall*, the four and twentieth Day of *October*, in the three and twentieth Year of our Reign, and now enrolled in the Rolls in our High Court of *Chancery* in our said Realm of *Ireland*, Have given, granted, released and confirmed, And by these Presents for Us, our Heirs and Successors, Do give, grant, release and confirm unto the said Mayor, Sheriffs, Commons, and Citizens of Our City of *Dublin*, and their successors for ever, ALL that Piece or Parcel of Ground on *Oxmantown Green*, near

Our said City of *Dublin*, on which the intended Hospital and Free School is already begun to be built. AND all and singular the Edifices and Buildings thereon, and all Yards, Backsides, Lands, Tenements, Ways, Waters, Water-courses, Easements, Liberties, Privileges, Profits, Commodities, Advantages, Appurtenances, and Hereditaments whatsoever, to the same belonging or appertaining, of what Quantity, Quality, Nature, Kind, or Sort soever they be, and by whatsoever Name or Names the same are called or known, or reputed, accepted or taken, together with their and every of their Rights, Members and Appurtenances whatsoever; and also the Reversion and Reversions, Remainder and Remainders of all and singular the Premises, and every Part and Parcel thereof, and also all the Estate, Right, Title, Interest, Claim, Property, Challenge and Demand whatsoever which We Our Heirs or Successors have, or at any Time hereafter may, can, might or ought to have of, in, or unto the Premises, or unto any Part or Parcel thereof. TO HAVE AND TO HOLD all and singular the Premises before, in and by these Presents given, granted, released and confirmed, or herein or hereby meant, mentioned, or intended to be given, granted, released and confirmed, and every Part, Parcel and Member thereof, together with their and every of their Rights, Members and Appurtenances whatsoever, unto them the said Mayor, Sheriffs, Commons, and Citizens of Our City of *Dublin*, and their Successors for ever; to be held and enjoyed by the said Mayor, Sheriffs, Commons, and Citizens of Our said City of *Dublin*, and their Successors for ever; to the only Use, Ends, Intents and Purposes hereafter in these Presents mentioned and expressed; that is to say, Upon the especial Trust and Confidence, and to the End, Intent and Purpose, that the said Piece of Ground on *Oxmantown Green* aforesaid, hereby granted, or meant, mentioned, and intended to be granted, and the building thereon erected, and to be erected, Shall for ever more hereafter be, remain and continue a Mansion House, and Place of Abode for the Sustentation and Relief of poor Children, aged and impotent People; to be holden of Us our Heirs and Successors, as of our Castle of *Dublin*, in Free and Common Soccage, without any Rent or other Payment to be rendered or paid unto Us, Our Heirs and Successors for the same. AND FURTHER of Our more abundant Grace, certain Knowledge, and Mere Motion, and princely Disposition for the Furtherance and Accomplishment of so good and charitable a Work, by and with the Advice and Consent aforesaid, and in Pursuance of our said Letters, We have given and granted, and by these Presents for Us, Our Heirs and Successors, We do give and grant unto the said Mayor, Sheriffs, Commons, and Citizens of Our said City of *Dublin*, and their Successors for ever, full Power and Authority, at their Will and Pleasures, from Time to Time, and at all Times, to place therein such Master or Masters of the said Hospital, and such Numbers of Poor People and Children, and such Officers or Ministers of the said Hospital and Free School, as likewise an able, learned, pious and orthodox Minister, to be approved of from Time to Time by the Archbishop of *Dublin*, for the time being; the said Minister to read Divine Service, and preach and teach the Word of God to such as shall reside within the same, and catechize such Children as shall be in the said Hospital or Free School, as to the said Mayor, Sheriffs, Commons, and Citizens, and their Successors, or such as shall be appointed as aforesaid, shall seem convenient; and from Time to Time, as they shall see Occasion, to remove, displace, and amove such Masters, Minister, Poor, poor Children, People, or any other Officers or Ministers to the said Hospital or Free School belonging, and put some other or others in his or their Place or Stead, and to apportion, appoint, and allow, from Time to Time such Fees, Salaries, and Wages, and such Allowances for Maintenance, Relief and Sustentation of the said Preacher, Master or Masters, other Officers or Ministers, and the said poor People and Children, as to them the said Mayor, Sheriffs, Commons and Citizens, and their Successors, shall seem meet; And that it shall and may be lawful to and for the said Mayor, Sheriffs, Commons and Citizens, and their Successors, from Time to Time, and at all Times hereafter, when and as often as it shall seem expedient, or Necessity shall require, to make, constitute and appoint all or any such apt, wholesome and honest Ordinances, Statutes, Rules and Orders for or in Relation to the well governing of the said Hospital and Free School, or either of them, or the Master, Minister, Poor, poor Children, or any other Officers or Ministers to the said Hospital, or Free School, belonging or to be belonging, as to them the said Mayor, Sheriffs, Commons and Citizens, and their Successors, shall seem meet, convenient, or necessary, giving and hereby granting unto them the said Mayor, Sheriffs, Commons and Citizens and their Successors, full and absolute Power and Authority to perform and execute all Act or Acts, Thing or Things whatsoever, that shall be requisite and necessary to be done for the putting in Execution or compelling a Performance of all such Ordinances, Statutes, Rules and Orders that shall, by Vertue of these Presents, be made, constituted or appointed, without Interruption of Us, our Heirs, or Successors, or any of the Justices, Escheators, Sheriffs, Ministers, Servants, or other Subjects whatsoever, of Us, Our Heirs, or Successors, any Statute, Act, Law, or Direction heretofore done or made, or hereafter to be done or made to the contrary notwithstanding; so that such Statutes, Ordinances, Rules, or Orders so to be made, constituted, or appointed by Vertue of these Presents, be not contrary or disagreeing to the Laws and Statutes of Our Kingdom of *England* or *Ireland*, or Our Royal Authority, and such Rules, Ordinances and Statutes to disanul and make void as shall by the said Mayors, Sheriffs, Commons and Citizens be found from Time to Time prejudicial and hurtful to the Government of the said Hospital and Free School. AND further of Our more abundant Grace, certain Knowledge, meer Motion, and princely Disposition, for the Furtherance and Accomplishment of so good and charitable a Work, by and with the Advice and Consent aforesaid, and in Pursuance of Our said Letters, We have also given and granted, and by these Presents for Us, Our Heirs and Successors, do give and grant unto the said Mayor, Sheriffs, Commons and Citizens of our said City of *Dublin*, and their Successors for ever, That the said Hospital and Free School shall be named, Incorporated, and called THE HOSPITAL AND FREE-SCHOOL OF KING CHARLES THE SECOND, *Dublin*, and by that Name shall be and is hereby erected, founded, established and confirmed, and to have Maintenance and Continuance for ever, and that the Mayors, Sheriffs, Commons and Citizens of Our said City of *Dublin*, and their Successors, shall be from Time to Time Governors of the said Hospital and Free School, and of the Lands and Tenements, Possessions, Revenues and Goods, unto the same belonging, or to be belonging, and shall be called and known by the Name of the Governors of the Hospital and Free School of King *Charles* the Second, *Dublin*, and that the said Governors shall be and for ever continue by the Name of the Governors of the Hospital and Free School of King *Charles* the Second, *Dublin*, a Body Politic and Corporate, to have Successors for ever, and by that Name shall be and continue, and shall be able and capable in Law from Time to Time, and at all Times, to sue or be sued in any of Our Courts Spiritual and Temporal, within Our Kingdom of *Ireland*, or other Our Kingdoms and Dominions, in Relation to the said Hospital and Free School, or any of the Lands, Tenements or Possessions, Revenues or Goods unto the same belonging, or to be belonging, or for any Transgressions, Offences, Matters, Causes, or Things made, committed, or done, or to be done, in or upon the Premises, or any Part thereof, or any Thing in these Presents specified, and to purchase, take, hold, receive and enjoy to them and their Successors for ever, to the Ends aforesaid, as well Goods and Chattles, as also any Manors, Lands, Tenements, Rents, Reversions, Annuities, and Hereditaments whatsoever, as well from Us, our Heirs, and Successors, as of any other Person or Persons whatsoever, not exceeding the yearly Value of Six Thousand Pounds Sterling, the Statutes of Mortmain or any other Statutes to the contrary notwithstanding: And further of Our more abundant Grace, certain Knowledge, meer Motion, and princely Disposition, for the Furtherance and Accomplishment of so good and charitable a Work, by and with the Advice and Consent aforesaid, and in Pursuance of Our said Letters, We have also given and granted, and by these Presents for Us,

Our Heirs, and Successors, do give and grant free Liberty and License, that the said Governors, and their Successors, may have and enjoy a Common Seal for the sealing of any Instrument, or Instruments, Deeds, or Writings, touching and concerning the Lands, Tenements and Hereditaments, Businesses, or Affairs of the said Hospital and Free School; nevertheless Our Royal Pleasure, Intent, and Meaning is, that the said Governors, or their Successors, shall not do, or suffer to be done, at any Time hereafter, any Act or Thing whereby any of the Lands, Tenements, or Hereditaments, or the Estate which shall belong to the said Corporation, shall be conveyed, alienated, or transferred, to any other Use whatsoever than to the Use of the said Hospital or Free School, and that the said Governors, for the Time being, shall not make any other Lease or Leases of any of the Lands, Tenements, Possessions, or Hereditaments, which shall belong to the said Corporation than for the Term of Forty-one Years, of Houses, or Buildings, or Ground to be built on, and of Twenty-one Years of Lands, Tythes, or other Hereditaments, and these to be made either in Possession, or not above Two Years before the Expiration of the State in Possession, and that without Fine or Income, at the best yearly Rent that *bona fide* from good and solvent Tenants may be had, and that no Lease be made to any of the aforesaid Governors, or to any other Person or persons to the Use, or for in Trust for any of the said Governors: AND further of our more abundant Grace, certain Knowledge, and meer Motion, by and with the Advice and Consent aforesaid, and in Pursuance of our said Letters, We have given and granted, and by these Presents for Us, Our Heirs, and Successors, do give, and grant unto the said Mayor, Sheriffs, Commons and Citizens of Our City of *Dublin*, and their Successors, that these Our Letters Patents, or the Inrolment thereof, and every Clause, Article, Matter, and Thing whatsoever, herein contained, shall be in, by and through all Things firm, good, valid, sufficient, and effectual in the Law unto them the said Mayor, Sheriffs, Commons and Citizens, and their Successors, against Us, Our Heirs, and Successors, as well in all Our Courts within our said Realm of *Ireland* as elsewhere wheresoever, notwithstanding the not finding, or not returning, or ill finding, or ill returning of any Office, or Inquisition, of the Parcel of Ground and Premises in and by these Letters Our Patents, meant, mentioned, and intended to be given and granted for the Ends and Purposes aforesaid, whereby our Title should have been found of, in, and unto the said Premises and every Part and Parcel thereof, before the making of these Presents, and notwithstanding the not naming or not rightly naming of the Premises, or any Part or Parcel thereof, or the Parish, Ward, Liberty, Freedom, or Place, in which the Premises, or any Part or Parcel thereof, is, are, or do lie, and notwithstanding the not naming, or not rightly naming, the Quantity, Quality, Nature, Kind, or Sort of the Premises, or any Part or Parcel thereof, and notwithstanding that of the true annual Value, Rate, Survey, Quantity, or Quality, of the Premises, there be no true, certain, or no mention made in these presents, and notwithstanding the not naming, or not reciting, or ill naming, or ill reciting, of any Grant or Grants, Lease or Leases, heretofore made of the Premises, or any Part or Parcel thereof, to any Person or Persons whatsoever for Term of Life, Lives, or Years, in Fee Simple, or Fee Tail, or otherwise howsoever, remaining of Record, or not of Record, and notwithstanding that of the rent heretofore reserved upon any former Demise or Demises, Lease or Leases, heretofore made of the Premises, or any Part or Parcel thereof, there be no full, true, certain, or no mention at all made in these Presents, and notwithstanding a certain Statute made in the Parliament held at *Westminster*, in Our said Kingdom of *England*, in the Eighteenth Year of the Reign of King *Henry* the Sixth, late King of *England*, Our Predecessor and notwithstanding a certain statute made in the Parliament held at *Limerick*, in our said Kingdom of *Ireland*, in the Thirtieth Year of the Reign of King *Henry* the Eighth, late King of *England*, Our Predecessor, the Title of which Act is, An Act for Lands given by the King, and notwithstanding any other Statute or Act made in Our said Kingdom of *Ireland*, in any of the Years of the Reign of the said King *Henry* the Eighth, and notwithstanding a certain statute made in Our Said Kingdom of Ireland, the Second Year of the Reign of Queen *Elizabeth*, late Queen of *England*, Our Predecessor; and notwithstanding any other Statute or Act, Statutes or Acts, made in our said Kingdom of *Ireland*, in the said Second Year of the Reign of Queen *Elizabeth*, or any other Year of the Reign of the said Queen *Elizabeth*, or of any other the Kings or Queens of *England*; and notwithstanding any Act, Clause, Provision, or Ordinance made in the Parliament begun at *Dublin* in the Fifteenth Year of the Reign of our late Royal Father, of ever glorious Memory, deceased; and notwithstanding any other Statute, Act, Ordinance, Provision, or Restriction, or any other Cause, Matter, or Thing whatsoever, to the Evacuation or Annihilation of these Our Letters Patents; and notwithstanding a Writ of *ad quod damnum* hath not issued to enquire concerning the Premises. AND Our further Will and Pleasure is, and We do by these Presents for Us, our Heirs and Successors, give and grant unto the said Mayor, Sheriffs, Commons and Citizens of our said City of *Dublin*, and their Successors, That they the said Mayor, Sheriffs, Commons and Citizens of Our said City of *Dublin*, shall have these Our Letters Patents under Our Great Seal of *Ireland* without Fine, great or small, to be therefore paid to Our Use in Our *Hanaper*, in Our said Kingdom of *Ireland*, Although Express Mention is not made of the clear yearly Value, or of the

Certainty of the Premises, or that any Gift or Grant heretofore made by Us, or Our Progenitors, to the said Mayor, Sheriffs, Commons and Citizens of Our said City of *Dublin* of the Premises, any Statute, Act, Ordinance, or Provision, or any other Cause or Matter whatsoever to the contrary notwithstanding ; Provided always that these Our Letters Patents be inrolled in the Rolls of Our High Court of *Chancery* in Our said Kingdom of *Ireland*, within the Space of Six Months next ensuing the Date of these Presents. In Witness whereof We have caused these Our Letters to be made Patents. Witness Our aforesaid Lieutenant General and General Governor of Our said Kingdom of *Ireland* at *Dublin*, the Fifth Day of *December*, in the Three and Twentieth Year of our Reign.

                DOMVILE.

Irrotulat in Rot. Paten. Cancellar. Hibnie Vicessimo Sexto Die Januarii Anno Regni Regis Caroli Secundi Vicessimo Tertio, et examinat per me

          Ra. Wallis, *Cleric. in Offico Mri. Rotolor.*

APPENDIX B.

See p. 156.

SECTIONS AFFECTING KING'S HOSPITAL IN AN ACT, 10th, GEO. I, ENTITLED, "AN ACT FOR FURTHER APPLICATION OF THE RENTS AND PROFITS OF THE LANDS AND TENEMENTS," FORMERLY GIVEN BY ERASMUS SMITH, ESQ., DECEASED, TO CHARITABLE PURPOSES.

AND whereas the Governors of the said Schools have come to an agreement with the Governors of the Hospital and Free School of King Charles the Second, Dublin, commonly called the Blue Coat Hospital, in the City of Dublin, on the terms hereinafter mentioned, viz. : that the Governors of the Schools shall give, to the Governors of the Blue Coat Hospital, three hundred pounds sterling, towards building an Infirmary for the said Hospital, for the reception of forty boys : that in consideration of the said sum of three hundred pounds, the Governors of the said Hospital shall find convenient reception in the said Hospital for any number of boys to be named and placed therein by the Governors of the Schools, not exceeding twenty, to have the same reception, maintenance and clothing, and be, every way, under the same regulation as the other boys in the said Hospital are : that the Governors of the Schools shall find bedding and the usual furniture for each room, for such boys as shall be placed by them in the said Hospital at their first entrance therein, until such time as provision shall be made for the number of twenty boys, agreed upon, to be placed in the said Hospital, after which the repairing and keeping the said bedding and furniture are to be charged in the annual expense, for the maintenance of the said boys, according to the usage and custom of the said Hospital : that the Governors of the said Schools shall pay, to the Governors of the Blue Coat Hospital, for the maintenance of each and every boy placed by them in the said Hospital, the same rate that the other boys in the said Hospital are maintained at, and that such sums as are found necessary for maintenance of each and every boy placed in the said Hospital, as aforesaid, shall be paid quarterly, and the accounts shall be made once every year : that the Governors of the said Schools shall pay five pounds per annum, to the Schoolmaster of the said Hospital, for teaching the boys which shall be placed in the said Hospital by the Governors : that the Governors of the said Schools shall pay the same rate that is paid for the other boys, who are taught the mathematics in the said Hospital, if the Governors of the Schools desire that any of the boys placed by them in the said Hospital be taught the same : that the Governors of the Schools shall and will, at their own expense, bind out each and every boy that shall be nominated and placed by them in the said Hospital, as soon as he and they shall be fit to be put out apprentice, to such Master as the Governors of the Schools shall approve of, and shall give such fee as the Governors of the Hospital give with the other boys to be put out apprentice by them ; that the Lord Mayor, Recorder, and two Aldermen, by the Governors of the Hospital to be chosen, shall be standing *Governors of the Schools founded by Erasmus Smith, esquire :* that four of the Governors of the Schools, by them to be chosen, shall be standing Governors of the said Hospital : that the Governors of the Schools shall and will, at their own expense, next sessions of Parliament, endeavour to get an act of Parliament passed in this kingdom, to make the foregoing agreement effectual.

THEREFORE, for rendering the said agreement effectual, and for the encouragement of so good and charitable a work, be it enacted, that the said agreement be, and is hereby ratified and confirmed, and be it therefore enacted, by the authority aforesaid, that the Treasurer of the Governors of the said Schools shall, out of the cash now in, or which shall hereafter come to his hands, with all convenient speed, pay, to the Governors of the said Hospital and Free School of King Charles the Second, Dublin, commonly called the Blue Coat Hospital, the said sum of three hundred pounds, sterling, towards building an Infirmary as aforesaid ; and also find and provide bedding and other usual furniture for each room for such boys as shall be by them placed in the said Blue Coat Hospital, the keeping and repairing of which bedding and furniture is thereafter to be charged in the annual expense for maintenance of the said boys, according to the usage and custom of the said Hospital : and to the end the boys, hereby designed to be placed by the Governors of the Schools in the said Hospital, may be maintained, clothed and educated, in the same manner as the other boys in the said Hospital, be it enacted, that the Governors of the said Schools, for the time being, shall, yearly, for ever hereafter, pay, out of the surplus rents of the lands vested in them, to the Governors of the said Blue Coat Hospital, such yearly sum and sums of money, for the maintenance of such boys, as shall, by the Governors of the said

Schools, pursuant to the aforesaid agreement, be placed in the said Hospital, as the Governors of the said Hospital shall, from time to time, *bona fide*, yearly lay out and expend for the maintenance of the like number of other boys in the said Hospital, and all and every sum and sums of money hereby appointed to be paid for the maintenance of the said boys to be placed in the said Hospital, shall be paid by the Governors of the Schools, quarterly, to the Treasurer or Agent of the said Hospital, for the time being, and the accounts of such money shall be made up, stated and settled, by the Governors of the said Schools and the Governors of the said Hospital, once in every year, for ever hereafter; and also that the Governors of the said Schools shall, for ever hereafter, out of the said rents, pay the yearly sum of five pounds per annum to the Schoolmaster of the said Hospital, for teaching the said boys to read, write and cast accounts, as the other boys in the said Hospital are taught and instructed, the same to be paid half-yearly, by equal payments, to such Master; provided, always, that if the Governors of the said Schools shall, at any time, appoint any of the said boys by them placed in the said Hospital, as aforesaid, to be instructed in the mathematics, the said Governors, over and above the payments herein before appointed to be made, shall pay and allow unto the Governors of the said Hospital such sum and sums of money, and after the same rate for instructing and teaching such boys in the mathematics as are paid for instructing other boys in the mathematics in the said Hospital, any thing herein contained to the contrary notwithstanding.

AND be it further enacted, by the authority aforesaid, that the Governors of the said Schools, for the time being, shall, from time to time, at their own expense, put and place out apprentice, to such trades and employments as they shall think fit, all such boys as shall be by them, from time to time, sent to be maintained and educated in the said Hospital, as soon as such boys shall, respectively, be qualified for that purpose, and shall also, out of the yearly surplus rents of the said lands, give such apprentice fees with the said boys, respectively, as the Governors of the said Hospital usually give with other boys of the said Hospital, by them put out apprentice to the like trades or employments, it being the design and meaning of this Act, that all the boys who shall be placed in the said Hospital by the Governors of the said Schools, shall be by them maintained, educated and provided for, in such and the same manner, and be subject and liable to the same rules and regulations as all other boys in the said Hospital are or shall be liable unto.

AND be it further enacted, by the authority aforesaid, that the Lord Mayor and Recorder of the city of Dublin, now, and for the time being, and two of the Aldermen of the said city, such as the Governors of the said Hospital shall, from time to time, elect and appoint, shall, for ever hereafter, be standing Governors of the Schools founded by the said Erasmus Smith, and added to the thirty-two Governors in the said letters patent mentioned; and also that the Treasurer and three other of the Governors of the said Schools, now, and for the time being, such as the said Governors of the said Schools, shall, from time to time choose and appoint, shall be and are hereby declared to be standing Governors, and added to the Governors of the said Hospital and Free School of King Charles the Second, Dublin, commonly called the Blue Coat Hospital.

PROVIDED, always, and be it further enacted, by the authority aforesaid, that all annual and other payments hereby mentioned, intended, or appointed to be made to or for the use of the said College of Dublin, or any Fellow, Lecturer, Member or Scholar thereof, shall at all times, hereafter, be made to the Bursar of the said College, for the time being, and that all annual and other payments hereinbefore mentioned, or intended to be made to or for the use of the said Hospital, or any boys to be placed therein, shall, at all times hereafter, be made to the Agent or Treasurer of the said Hospital, for the time being, and that the receipt and receipts of the Bursar of the said College, and also that the receipt and receipts of the Treasurer or Agent of the said Hospital, respectively, for the time being, shall be a sufficient discharge to the Governors of the said Schools, and their successors for the same.

AND whereas the Governors of the Hospital and Free School of King Charles the Second, Dublin, are seized and possessed of several waste plots of ground, in the city of Dublin, and suburbs thereof, which, by reason the said Governors are restrained from making leases for a sufficient term, to encourage building thereon, lie waste and unimproved, to the great loss and prejudice of the said Hospital and Free School; be it therefore enacted, by the authority aforesaid, that it shall and may be lawful to and for the Governors of the said Hospital and Free School to make lease of said waste plots, or any of them, whereof they are seized of an estate of inheritance, and of which no lease shall be in being at the time of making thereof, for any term or number of years, not exceeding the term of ninety-nine years, at the best and highest rent that can be got for the same, without fine or other income, in order that the said premises may be built and improved upon, for the benefit of the said Hospital and Free School.

AND, be it further enacted, by the authority aforesaid, that if, at any time or times hereafter, the rents, revenues or profits of the said lands, and tenements so set apart by the said Erasmus Smith, shall happen to increase, or be raised to better or greater yearly value than they now yield, or if any part of the present yearly rents of the said lands shall be and remain in the hands of the Treasurer or the Governors of the said Schools, over and above the annual payments, charges and expenses heretofore, or by this Act appointed to be made, out of the said lands, that then, and in such cases, it shall and may be lawful to and for the Governors of the said Schools, for the time being, from time to time, for ever hereafter, to apply and dispose of the residue and overplus of the said yearly rents for and towards some public work or use in the said College or Hospital, in putting out poor children to school, or apprentices, or in setting up and founding one or more English School or Schools in any place or places in this Kingdom, as the Governors of the said Schools, for the time being, shall think most proper and convenient; and, in like manner, that if, at any time or times hereafter, the yearly rents, revenues and profits of the said lands and tenements so set apart by the said Erasmus Smith, shall decrease or grow less, that then, and in such cases, it shall and may be lawful to and for the Governors of the said Schools, for the time being, and they are hereby empowered, from time to time, and at all times hereafter, either to lessen the number of the Pensioners or Exhibitioners of the said College, or to make such deduction and abatement out of all or any the pensions, exhibitions, salaries, or other yearly sum or sums of money hereby appointed, or continued to be paid by them, as they shall think fit.

PROVIDED, nevertheless, that no deduction or abatement whatsoever shall be made out of the sums mentioned to be payable to the said Mayor and Commonalty and Citizens of the City of London, Governors of the possessions, revenues and goods of the Hospitals of Edward, King of England, the Sixth, of Christ Bridewell, and St. Thomas the Apostle, or the salaries hereinbefore appointed to be paid to the three junior Fellows herein before mentioned, or out of any provision of this Act intended for the boys, to be, by the Governors of the said Schools, placed in the said Blue Coat Hospital, or to the Master for teaching of the said boys, but that all the last-mentioned sums shall continue and remain payable, anything hereinbefore contained to the contrary notwithstanding.

AND be it further enacted, by the authority aforesaid, that the Governors of the said Schools shall pay and be allowed the charges of obtaining and passing this present Act; provided that nothing herein contained shall extend, or be construed to extend, to defeat or prejudice the payment of the said sum of one hundred pounds per annum, payable to the said Mayor and Commonalty and Citizens of the City of London, Governors of the possessions, revenues and goods of the Hospitals of Edward King of England, the Sixth, of Christ Bridewell, and St. Thomas the Apostle, but that the same shall continue to be paid and payable, without any deductions or abatement whatsoever, as if this Act had not been made.

Saving, nevertheless, to the King's Most Excellent Majesty, his heirs and successors, and to all and every other person and persons, bodies politic and corporate, their heirs, executors, administrators, successors and assigns, (other than and except the said *Governors of the Schools founded by Erasmus Smith, esquire;* the Provost, Fellows and Scholars of the College of the Holy and Undivided Trinity, of Queen Elizabeth, near Dublin, the Governors of the Hospital and Free School of King Charles the Second, Dublin, commonly called the Blue Coat Hospital, in the City of Dublin, and the said Mayor and Commonalty and Citizens of the City of London—Governors of the possessions, revenues and goods of the Hospitals, of Edward King of England the Sixth, of Christ Bridewell, and Saint Thomas the Apostle) all such estate, right, title and interest, trust, claim, and demand whatsoever, as they, or any of them, have or hath, or can or may have, or claim of, in or to all or any of the said lands, tenements, hereditaments and premises, as if this Act had not been made any thing herein contained to the contrary notwithstanding.

CARLETON P. HOLLES.
NEWCASTLE.
ROXBURGH.
CADOGAN.

APPENDIX C.

See p. 287.

———❖———

THE CLAUSES OF THE MUNICIPAL CORPORATIONS OF IRELAND ACT, 1840 (304 VIC. C. 108), RECONSTITUTING THE KING'S HOSPITAL.

And whereas by Letters Patent of King *Charles* the Second, bearing Date the Fifth Day of *December* in the Twenty-third Year of His Reign, the Lord Mayor, Sheriffs, Commons, and Citizens of the City of *Dublin*, and their Successors, are constituted a Body Politic and Corporate, by the name of " The Governors of the Hospital and Free School of King *Charles* the Second, *Dublin* :" And whereas the Government, Management, and Direction of the said Hospital and Free School are now exercised by Sixty-one standing Governors (whereof Four are the Treasurers for the Time being and Three other Governors of the Schools founded by *Erasmus Smith* Esquire, appointed by the Governors of the said last-mentioned Schools, in pursuance of an Act of the Parliament of *Ireland*, made in the Tenth Year of the Reign of King *George* the First): Be it enacted, That from and immediately after this Act shall come into operation in the said City of *Dublin* the Persons who at that Time shall be the Governors of the said Hospital, and the Survivors of them, and their Successors, to be appointed in manner, herein-after mentioned, shall be and they are hereby constituted a Body Politic and Corporate, by the aforesaid Name of " The Governors of the Hospital and Free School of King *Charles* the Second, *Dublin*," in the Place and Stead of the said Lord Mayor, Sheriffs, Commons, and Citizens of the said City of *Dublin*, who shall no longer be such body Politic and Corporate, in like manner, to all Intents and Purposes, as if the said Sixty-one Persons, and the Survivors of them, and their Successors, had been the Persons appointed by virtue of the said Letters Patent, instead of the said Lord Mayor, Sheriffs, Commons, and Citizens, and all and singular the Hereditaments, Sums of Money, Chattels, Securities for Money, and other Personal Estate of the said Body Corporate, constituted by the said Letters Patent, and all the Estate, Right, Interest, and Title, and all the Rights, Powers, Privileges, and Immunities of such Body Corporate, and all Rights of Action and Suit vested in such Body Corporate, shall be and are hereby vested in the Body Corporate, hereby constituted in the Place and Stead thereof and the Body Corporate thereby constituted shall be subject to the same Liabilities, and governed according to the same Regulations, as the Body Corporate appointed by the said Letters Patent shall be subject to and governed by; Provided always, that the Treasurer for the Time being, and Three other Governors of the Schools founded by the said *Erasmus Smith*, such as the Governors of the said Schools, shall from Time to Time choose and appoint, shall and they are hereby declared to be standing Governors of the said Hospital, in like Manner as by the said Act of the Tenth Year of the Reign of King *George* the First they were made Governors of the said Hospital : Provided also, that the Governors of the said Hospital hereby constituted shall never consist of less than Fifty, and that when and so often as any of the Governors hereby appointed, or to be appointed as hereinafter is mentioned, (other than the said Treasurer and Three other Governors of the said Schools founded by the said *Erasmus Smith*), shall depart this Life, then it shall be lawful for the Lord Archbishop of *Armagh*, the Lord Chancellor of *Ireland*, the Lord Archbishop of *Dublin*, and the Lord Bishop of *Meath*, for the Time being, or the Major Part of them, and they are hereby empowered, by Writing under their Hands and Seals, to appoint One or more Persons or Person in the Place or Places and as a Successor or Successors of the deceased Governor or Governors, or any of them, so as to make up, with the surviving Governors, the Number at the least of Fifty Governors, including the said Treasurer and Three other Governors of the said Schools founded by the said *Erasmus Smith ;* and every person so appointed a Governor shall be a Governor jointly with the surviving Governors for the Time being, and shall have the same Powers and Authorities as if he had been appointed a Governor by this Act.

And be it enacted, That from and immediately after this Act shall come into operation in the said City of *Dublin* so much of the said Act of Parliament passed in the Tenth Year of the Reign of King *George* the First as provides that the Lord Mayor and Recorder of the City of *Dublin*, then and for the Time being, and Two of the Aldermen of the said City, such as the Governors of the Schools founded by *Erasmus Smith* Esquire, should from Time to Time select and appoint, should for ever thereafter be standing Governors of the said Schools, shall be and the same is hereby repealed ; and that four of the Governors for the Time being of the said Hospital and Free School of King *Charles* the Second, *Dublin*, such as the Governors of the said Schools founded by *Erasmus Smith* shall from Time to Time select and appoint, shall for ever thereafter be standing Governors of the said Schools founded by the said *Erasmus Smith*.

INDEX.

In this Index Gov. means Governor of B. C. and B. C. means Blue Coat School.

A.

ABERCORN, Earl of, Gov., 160.
Addison, Rt. Hon. Joseph, 135.
Aldermen, All Govs., 65; Constitution of, 189; Fines on, given to B. C., 128, 254, 289.
Allen, Sir Joshua, Gov., 48, 58, 65, 109.
Allen, Lords, 58.
Anne, Queen, 125, 142, 172.
Anne's, St., Guild Wardens of Govs., 122.
Annesley, Sir A., Earl Anglesea, 2.
Arlington, Earl of, 34, 68.
Aston's Quay, 237.

B.

BALL, Benj., Gov., 211.
Ball, F. Elrington, 208, 211, 275.
Ballast Office, Grant to B. C., 131, 163.
Beasley, Ed., Gov. and Steward B. C., 227, 247.
Benefactors, Original List of, 48.
Beresford, Lord John G., Primate, Gov., 290.
Beresford, Rt. Hon. J. Claudius, Gov., 274.
Berkeley, Lord, of Stratton, L. L., 49, 65; His Corporation Rules, 52.
Berkeley, George, Bp. of Cloyne, 184.
Bishops, Consecration Fees to B. C., 86, 184.
Blackhall, Sir Thos., Gov., 203, 207, 210.
Blackhall Street and Place, 211.
Blackpool of Dublin, 6.
Blue Coat School—
 First Hospital, 69.
 Second Hospital, 214.
 Charter of, 63; App. A.
 Original Pupils, 71.
 Boys expelled by Tyrconnell, 110.

Blue Coat School—
 Boys sent to Christchurch, 116.
 Numbers of, 1675—60; 1692—32; 1702—82; 1714—127; 1725—188; 1731—162; 1737—138; 1771—170; 1800—110; 1808—130; 1840—123; See above years.
 Chaplains and Headmasters of, see C.
 Alliance of B. C. with E. Smith Board, 155, 244, 290 and App. B. and C.
 B.C. attacked by Lucas, Chap. IX.
 Parliament in, Chap. VIII.
 Unruly Boys, 101, 170, 182, 224, 280.
 Theatricals in, 255.
Boulton, Primate, Gov., 162, 183.
Boyle, Archbp., Chancellor and Primate, 54, 69, 92, 125.
Brabazon, Lord, 79.
Bradogue-Riveret, 27.
Bradstreet, Sir Saml., Rec. and Gov., 193, 213, 218.
Brewers, Tax on for B. C., 76.
Brewery in B. C., 130.
Brodrick, Chas., Archbp. Cashel, Gov., 241, 252.
Bysse, Sir John, Rec. and C. Baron, Gov., 55, 65, 120.

C

CABAL Ministry, 49, 83.
Cage for Corner Boys, 18.
Cappoloughlin, Endowment of B. C., 57, 250, 266.
Carlisle Bridge, 237.
Carr, Bishop of Killaloe, Chaplain B. C., 120, 131, 153.
Carter, M. Rolls, 197.
Carteret, Lord, L. L., 167, 170.
Cassels, Architect, 232, 233.
Chairs, Old, in B. C., 226.

Chaplains and Headmasters of B. C.,
Rev. E. Wettenhall, desig., 1673.
— — Lewis Prythirch, 1675.
— — Benj. Colquit, 1681.
— — Nich. Knight, 1685.
— — Thos. King, 1687.
— — Thos. Hemsworth, 1692.
— — Chas. Carr, 1700.
— — Rich. Gibbons, 1716.
— — Ralph Grattan, 1732.
— Hamilton Morgan. 1763.
— — Allan Morgan, 1785.
— — Jas. Walker King, 1830.
— — Fielding Ould, 1836.
— — Louis Le Pan, Head Master, 1839; Chaplain, 1848.
See under above years.
Charlemont, Viscount, Gov., 127.
Charlemont, Earl of, 209, 235, 236.
Charles, II., Petition from B. C., 66; Holds Council thereon, 66; gift to Lord Mayor of Collar of S.S., 83.
Christchurch, Manor and Barns of, 22; Litigation with Archbp. King, 131.
Churchill, Sir Winston, 38.
Claims, Court of, 33.
Clarendon, Earl of, L. L., 104.
Coaches and Chairs, Tax on, to B. C., 154.
Coghill, Sir Marmaduke, Gov., 161, 170.
Colquit, Chaplain, B.C., order appointing, 88.
Connolly, Rt. Hon. Sir. W., Speaker, Gov., 165, 187.
Constantine, Ald. Robert, Gov., see Three Years War.
Conyngsby, Lord, 112.
Cooke, Sir Saml, L.M., Gov., 140, 144.
Cooke, Sir Saml. (2), 202.
Cooley, Thomas, Architect, 232, 239.
Corporation, Dublin. Riding Franchises, 22; Constitution of, 55, 189, 191. Attacked by Lucas, Chap. IX.
Courtney, Master, in B. C., 276, 277.
Craddock, Dean of S. Patrick's, 221.
Crawford, The Gentle Georgina, 284 et seq.
Cupola, 219, 245, 246.

D.

DALTON, Master in B. C., 247, 256 et seq., 276 et seq.
Damas Gate, 6, 11, 233.
Dame Street, 234, 238.
Danes in Dublin, see Oxmantown.
Davys, Sir Wm, Rec. and Ch. Justice, 47, 52, 63.
Desmynieres, Louis, Gov., 49, 57.

Domville, Sir William, 64.
Donellan, Sir Nehemiah, Rec., Ch. Justice, Gov., 115.
Dongan, Lord, Limerick, Gov., 108.
Dopping, Bishop Anthony, 88.
Downes, Lord Ch. Justice, Gov., 244; Reform in B. C, 244-247; sends more boys from E. Smith, 245, 251.
Drelincourt, Dean of Armagh, Benefactor of B. C., Gov., 133, 134.
Drogheda, The Lords, 21.
Drogheda Street, 21, 233, 237.
Dublin—
Aspect of, at Restoration, Chap. I.
Ancient Gates, Towers and Walls, 11, 15, 16, 99.
Ballast Office, 129.
Blackpool of, 6.
Boundaries, Old, 21.
Churches at Restoration, 16.
City Music, 17.
Drink in, 15.
Evolution of, 98, 124, 129, 163, and Chap. XII.
Free School of, 36 et seq.
Recorders of, see R.
Regiments, 18, 57.
Social state of, at Restoration, 29 et seq.
Workhouse, 109.
Dudley, Lord, L. L., 173, 246.

E.

EDUCATION Commission, 1806—242, 251; (1812) (Clare St.), 266, 275; (1854), 225, 243, 263.
Ellis, Bp. Welbore, 132, 134.
Elrington, Rev Dr. Charles, Reforms in B. C., 275, 290.
Encroachments, Fines for, to B. C., 75
Essex, Arthur, Earl of, L. L., 55, 91; His New Rules, 55, 105, 141, 189.
Essex Bridge, 90 et seq.
Eustace, L. C., 7, 81.
Evelyn, John, Diary, 51, 120
Evolution of Dublin, see D.
Expulsion of Founders, 49.

F.

FALKINER, Daniel, Gov., 143, 151, 183.
Faulkner, Ald. George, Gov., 205.
Fenby, Master in B. C., 279 et seq.
Fielding, Sir Chas., 127.
Forster, John, Rec., Ch. Justice, Gov., 122, 139, 142, 147, 149.

INDEX

Foster, Rt. Hon. John, Speaker, Gov., 215, 223, 241, 248.
Fownes, Sir Wm., L. M., Gov., 135, 144.
Free School, Chap II.
French, Humfrey, L.M., Gov., 173.
Fullerton, Sir James, 37. See Free School.

G.

GALWAY, Earl of (Ruvigny), 153.
Gandon, James, Architect, 237, 238, 239.
Gardiner, Rt. Hon. Luke, 183.
George I., 135.
George II., 200; Statue, 201, 232.
George III., Recommends Lucas to favour, 199; Statue by Van Nost, 234.
George IV., Visits Dublin, 254.
George, Denis, Rec. and Baron, Gov. 218, 247.
Gibbons, Grinling, Sculptor, 120.
Gibbons, Rev. Rich., Chaplain B. C., 171, 175.
Gore, Sir Ralph, Speaker, Gov., 162, 166.
Grangegorman in Sylvis, 25, 26.
Grattan, James, Rec. and Gov., 198.
Grattan, Rev. Ralph, Chaplain, 176, 182.
Grattans, The, and B. C., 176, et seq.
Gressingham, Ald.; Silver Cup, 56.

H.

HACKETT, Sir Thos., L. M. Gov., 107, 109.
Hamilton, James, Lord Clandeboy, 39.
Hanly, Master in B. C., 279, 288.
Harcourt, Earl, Simon, L. L., 205.
Hardwick, Earl of, L. L., 241.
Harrington, Earl of, L. L., 194.
Hart, Robert, Agent of B. C., 229, 243, 263.
Harty, Dr., Gov., 247, 287.
Harvey, Dr., Phys. to B. C., Gov., 123.
Hemming, Capt., Benefactor, 225.
Hoadley, Archbp., Gov., 166, 184.
Hoggen Green, 7.
Hone, Addison, Reg. B. C., 262.
Hutchinson, Ald. Daniel, Gov., 49, 65.

I.

ISOULT, La Belle, Tower, 13; Fountain, 22; Tristram and, 99 note.
Ivory, James, Architect of B. C.; His Plans in Brit. Museum, 208, also 235.

J.

JAMES, Duke of York, 35, 54.
James II., Chap. V.
Jarndyce v. Jarndyce, of B. C., 265 et seq.
Jervis, Sir Humphrey, 90 et seq.
Jocelyn, Lord Newport, L.C., Gov., 183.
Johnston, Francis, Architect, 245.
Jones, Bp. Henry, 8, 32.
Jones, Sir Theoph., 21, 32.

K.

KANE, Sir Nathaniel, L. M. Gov., 179, attacked by Lucas, 195.
Kavanagh, George, Benefactor B. C., 223.
Kilcotty, Tithes of, granted B. C., 223.
Kildare, Marquess of, Benefactor B. C., 203.
King, Rev. Thomas, Chaplain B. C., 110, 112, 127.
King, Sir Abraham Bradley, L. M., Gov., 159, 249, 254.
King, Archbishop, Bishop Derry, 112; Archbp. Dublin, 127; Conflict with Christ Church, 131; Letter to Swift, 139; Great Gov. of B. C., 154 et seq.; Forms alliance with E. Smith's Board, 153; Memorial in St. Patrick's, 158.
King, Rev., Sir James W. King, Bart., Chaplain of B. C., 159, 265.
Knight, Rev. N., Chaplain in B. C., presentation to Archbishop, 101.
Kirwan, Dean of Killala, Charity Sermon for B. C., 222.

L.

LAND Values of Endowments, 223, 251.
Latin in B. C., 89.
Latouche, James Digges, 189, 194.
Latouche, Rt. Hon. David, Gov., 216, 240.
Leake, Surgeon, B. C., 227, 256.
Leasing, Powers of, B. C., 156; and App. B.
Leighton, Sir Ellis, Recorder, 49, 51.
Leinster, William, 2nd Duke, 207, 236.
Le Pan, Rev. Louis, Chaplain, B. C., 283, 287, 289.
Linen Trade and B. C., 186.
Loftus, Dr. Dudley, 55, 113.

Lord Mayor, Chairmen of B. C., 74; List of, 98, 123, 152, 130, 164, 202, 230, 253, 264, 291; Laws of Election, 55, 137 189, 198, 202; Fines to B. C. in lieu of Feasts, 165.
Lucas, Dr. Cha., 42, chap. IX., statue by Ed. Smyth, 199, 234.

M.

MACAULAY, Lord, on Oath of supremacy, 105.
McDermot, Terence, L. M. Gov., 111
Madden, Dr. John, Gov., 123.
Magee, Archbishop, Gov., 260.
Martyn, Gyles, Donor of Nodstown, 84.
Malone, Prime Sergeant, 193, 196.
Manners, Lord Chan., 267, 271, 272.
Marlborough, Duke of, at Free School, 38.
Mary's, St., Abbey., 21.
Mathematical School in B. C., 127.
Mead, James, Master, in B. C., 75.
Merchant Seamen's Act, Fines to B. C., 171.
Michan's, St., Parish and Church, 20, 22, 132, 238.
Midleton, Lady, Legacy to B. C., 158.
Morgan, Rev. Allan, Dean of Killaloe. Chaplain B. C., 219, 255, 257, 263.
Morgan, Rev. Hamilton, Chaplain B. C., 219.
Molyneux, Sir Thos., Gov., 123.
Molyneux, William, Gov., 122.
Mullingar, Tithes of, 87, 110, 223.
Municipal Corporation Act, 1840, 287, and App. C.
Mynchin Fields, 7, 232.

N.

NICOLINI, Cavaliere, sings in B. C., 128.
Nodstown Endowments, 81, 242, 252.
Normanton, Earl, of, Archbishop, Cashel and of Dublin, Gov., 216, 240, see Somerton.

O.

OATH of Allegiance, 55, 97; of Non-Resistance, 62; of Supremacy, 55 104.
Ormonde, James, Duke of, 35, 66, 78, 80, 82, 86, 204.
Ormonde Bridge, 93.
Osborne, Henry, Benefactor of B. C., 117.

Ossory, Earl of, Chap. III.: His Letter to Corporation, 45, 66.
Ostmen in Dublin, 18.
Ould, Rev. Fielding, Chaplain, B. C., 276, 280, 288.
Oxmantown, 19 et seq.; Allotments of, 42.

P.

PARLIAMENT. in B. C., Chap. VIII., 165 et seq.
Patrick's, St., Cathedral, Memorial of Dr. King, 158; B. C. Boys march to, 261
Paul's. St., Church and Parish, 126.
Penal Laws, 159.
Pepy's Diary, 49.
Philpot, Ald., Silver Cups, 56.
Phipps, Constantine, Lord Chan., 132, 148, 149.
Physicians, K. and Q. College of, connection with B. C., 123, 129 153, 166, 227, 247; Presidents of, Physicians of B. C., 123.
Percy, Sir Anthony, L. M. Gov., 120.
Pooley, Bp. Raphoe, Benefactor B. C., 136
Preston, Alderman John, Benefactor of B. C., Gov., 57, 250.
Preston, John, Lord Tara, 57, 251, 270, 272.
Preston, Rev. Joseph, 270, 272.

Q.

QUINN, Ald. Mark, 46, 49, 59.
Quin, James, 60, 62.

R.

RAM, Sir Abel, L. M. Gov., Expelled by Tyrconnell, 107.
Read, Dr., Phys. to B. C., 288.
Reader, Enoch, Evicted Gov., 49.
Recorders Govrs.—
  Sir John Bysse, Ch. Baron, 1660.
  Sir Wm. Davys, C. J. King's B., 1660, 1680.
  Sir Richard Ryves, 1680; Evicted by Tyrconnell, 1688; Lord Commr. Great Seal, 1690.
  Sir John Barnwell, 1688; Baron Exch., 1689.
  Gerald Dillon, 1689; Evicted by William III., 1690.
  Thos. Coote, 1690; Justice K. B., 1693.

INDEX

Recorders Govrs.—
  Nehemiah Donnellan, 1693; Baron Exch., 1695; Ch. Baron, 1703.
  Sir William Handcock, 1695.
  John Foster, 1701; Ch. J. Com. Pleas, 1714.
  John Rogerson, 1704; Ch. Justice, K. B., 1727.
  Francis Stoyte, 1727.
  Eaton Stannard, Swift's Rec., 1733.
  Thomas Morgan, 1749.
  James Grattan, 1756.
  Sir Samuel Bradstreet, Bart., 1766; Justice K. B., 1784.
  Dudley Hussey, 1785.
  Denis George, 1785; Baron Exch., 1795.
  William Walker, 1795.
  Sir Jonas Greene, 1822.
  Sir Frederick Shaw, Bart., 1828.
  See under above years.
Religious Education in B. C., 88, 101, 120, 157, 175, 176, 275, 279, and see Charter.
Richards, Rev. T. P., 76, 291.
Richmond, Duke of, L. L., Gov., 248.
Rice, Chief Baron, 107.
Rogerson, Sir John, L. M. Gov., 114, 163
Rogerson, John, Rec. and L. C. J., 162.
Rokeby, Lord Primate, Gov., 118.
Royal Arms in B. C., 115.
Rutland, Duke of, L. L., 220.

S.

SACKVILLE Street, 233, 237.
Scaldbrother's Hole, 23, 210.
Shannon, Lord, Henry Boyle, 196.
Shaw, Sir Robt., 255.
Shaw, Sir Frederick, 289.
Sheriffs, High, Fines to B. C., 207, 226, 241, 289.
Shiel, Rt. Hon. R. Lalor, 85.
Smith, Erasmus Board, 155, 240, 244.
Smith, William, Gov., Whittington of Dublin, 76 et seq.
Smyth, Edward, Sculptor, 199.
Social State of Dublin, 1660, 29 et seq.
Somerton, Viscount, 240, see Normanton.
Somerville, Sir James, Gov., 181.
Stanley, Sir John, 25.
Stannard, Eaton, Rec., Gov., 192.
Stephens, St., Green, allotted, 43.
Steyne Riveret, 2; Pillar, 5.
Stone, Primate, 196.
Strafford, Lord, Open Spaces order, 8.
Sutton, Alderman, Gov., 225, 260.

Swift, Dean—
  On Mark Quinn, 59; On Three Years War, 140; Swift and Lord Abercorn, 159; The Grattans, 176; Gov. of B. C., 159, 161, 162, 186; Influence on Lord Carteret and Parlt., 169, 226; Three Unpublished Letters, 184.

T.

TANDY, J. Napper, Gov., 216.
Temple, Sir John, M. R., 7, 65.
Temple, Sir John, Sol-Gen., 86.
Thingmount, Danish, 8, et seq.
Thorkill, 20.
Thorne, Steward of B. C., 171, 178.
Three Years War, 137 et seq.
Tichborne, Sir H., Benefactor, 48.
Tickell, Irish Secretary, 171.
Tighe, Ald. R., Gov., 49, 57.
Toll Corn Annuity to B. C., 136, 221, 240, 242.
Tottie, L. M, Gov., 52.
Trench, Thos. F. Cooke, 151.
Trinity College Buildings, 231, 233, 235
Trinity, Guild of Merchants, Annuity, to B. C., 121; Mathematical School in B. C., 127; Wardens, Govs., 122.
Tristram and Isoult, 99; Note.
Tyrconnell, Duke of, Chap. V.

U.

USHER, Sir William, 3, 29.
Usher, Primate, 37, 158.

V.

VAN HOMRIGH, Bartholomew, Gov., 108, 116.
Van Nost, Statue of Geo. II., 201, of George III., 234.
Vaughan, George, and B. C., 185.
Vierpyl, Simon, Statuary, 199, 209.

W.

WARE, Sir James, 20.
Wellesley, Marquess, 261.
Wellington, Duke of, 165.
Wesley, Lord Mornington, Gov., 165.
Wettenhall, Ed., Chaplin B. C.; Bishop of Cork, 41, 87.
Whateley, Archbishop, 288, 290.
Whitelaw, Rev. James, 243, 259.

Y

Whiteway, John, Surgeon B. C., 226.
Whitshed, Ch. Justice, 60, 62.
Wide Street Commissioners, 235, 237.
Williamson, Rev. W., 131.
William III., King, 111; gives Collar SS. to Lord Mayor, 112; Statue by S. Gibbons, 118.
Wilson, John, Architect and Regr. B. C., 211, 227.

Wybrants, Barth., Regr. B. C., 116; Tragedy in Family, 174.
Wyndham, Lord Chan., 166, 171, 267.

Y.

York, Frederick, Duke of, Duel with Richmond, 248